CUMBRIA

CUMBRIA
LAKE DISTRICT LIFE

A Celebration of 40 Years

Edited by

HILARY GRAY

PELHAM BOOKS

PELHAM BOOKS

Published by the Penguin Group
27 Wrights Lane, London W8 5TZ, England
Viking Penguin, a division of Penguin Books USA Inc
375 Hudson Street, New York, NY 10014, USA
Penguin Books Australia Ltd, Ringwood, Victoria, Australia
Penguin Books Canada Ltd, 2801 John Street, Markham, Ontario, Canada L3R 1B4
Penguin Books (NZ) Ltd, 182–190 Wairau Road, Auckland 10, New Zealand

Penguin Books Ltd, Registered Offices: Harmondsworth, Middlesex, England

First published 1991
1 3 5 7 9 10 8 6 4 2

Typeset in 11/12pt Baskerville to 16ems by Cambrian Typesetters, Frimley, Surrey
Printed and bound in Great Britain by Butler & Tanner Ltd, Frome, Somerset

ISBN 0 7207 1956 9

A CIP catalogue record for this book
is available from the British Library.

CONTENTS

CONTENTS

INTRODUCTION

OUR FIRST FORTY YEARS

Hilary Gray

'HAVE YOU heard of a little magazine called *Cumbria*?' I am told that was often the opening gambit over the years whenever a good story presented itself.

Now, as our monthly magazine celebrates its fortieth anniversary, there can be few people in the county who are not familiar with its pages. *Cumbria* sells to a loyal readership of 16,000 and is estimated to be read by at least five times that number.

A reader recently wrote concerning a topic which had been featured six months previously in our letters page. 'I'm sorry it's taken me so long to write,' she apologised, 'but my sister reads it first, then swops it for her daughter's copy of *Dalesman*' . . .

Dalesman, our highly respected sister magazine, concentrates on life in neighbouring Yorkshire and both magazines are produced in the village of Clapham in the Yorkshire Dales, only 25 miles from the heart of the Lake District. The office premises is a converted vicarage coach house and estate workshops and, instead of the screech of traffic and cries of 'Hold the front page!', there is the bleating of sheep in the lane and the cry of the curlew.

After one Christmas break, we returned to the office to find a note which warned 'Don't touch the sugar, there may be glass in it. A white pheasant flew through the window during the holidays.' I would wager that never happened in Fleet Street's heyday.

I remember when I first arrived at the Clapham office in the spring of 1987, looking for freelance work. Finding a fellow wrapping parcels in the storeroom, I asked him where I might expect to find the editor, W. R. Mitchell. 'You've found him!' was the reply.

I was introduced to David Joy who was responsible for the extensive Dalesman Books programme and the outcome was that I would become a full time member of staff just prior to the retirement of W. R. 'Bill' Mitchell. I was unknowingly maintaining a long tradition, as no journalistic post on *Dalesman* or *Cumbria* has ever been advertised.

David Joy succeeded Bill Mitchell in April 1988 as editorial manager and editor of *Dalesman*. As an editorial team of two, we continue to produce twenty-four magazines and about two dozen books a year. David is indeed a joy to work for – I have never seen his good humour desert him and I can always count on his support and encouragement.

Our editorial secretary, Helen Price, helps us keep track of the enormous volume of manuscripts, letters, artwork and photography submitted by contributors and we are extremely grateful to her for keeping us on the straight and narrow!

Dennis Bullock, who joined the firm in 1961 and is now our general manager, recalls the days when the sorting of the mail was a rather more informal affair. Before acquiring our present premises the publishing company was run from Fellside, the cottage home of Harry J. Scott who was founder of *Dalesman* and who took over *Cumbria* in 1951, a bi-monthly magazine at that time produced by the Youth Hostels Association. 'It was really quite amusing – at Fellside, all the letters were opened among the toast and marmalade during breakfast!'

Today there are fourteen members of staff, covering worldwide subscriptions, distribution and advertising ranging from Lakeland accommodation to cars and furniture.

Tony Jefferies, our sales manager, has covered the area for over a quarter of a century and many of his regular clients have become good friends and staunch supporters of the magazine.

I knew Bill, with his extensive knowledge of the area, would be a hard act to follow, but my ignorance turned out to be to my advantage. Cumbrians bent over backwards to introduce me to people they felt would 'make a story' and to keep me informed generally. I am now beginning my fourth volume of the magazine and I am well aware that I haven't yet begun to scratch the surface of Cumbrian topics. When the number of pages was increased at the beginning of Volume 39 things were made a lot easier from an editorial point of view. It has never been a problem wondering what to put IN *Cumbria*, but it can mean considerable agonising trying to decide what to leave OUT!

Assuming the role of photographer/reporter I would turn up at various events wearing the appropriate 'hat' –

I've helped with lambing, talked with artists at exhibitions, sat chatting in front of roaring firesides in farmhouses and cottages while the wind raged outside, sailed on the Lakes, met a horse called William Wordsworth, enjoyed personal guided tours of stately homes and gardens, talked to a lady who marketed perfume for dogs and walked the fells in the mist listening to a description of the view I would have seen, had the mist cleared.

One contributor who has also become a dear friend is 'Polly Thwaite', who pens our monthly feature 'From a Lakeland Cottage'. One reader wrote to me 'We love Polly Thwaite's column. That lady even manages to make a central heating boiler sound interesting.'

Readers write to us on all sorts of topics – I have been asked train times for the Settle–Carlisle railway, the correct length for a walking stick and the best place to buy a replacement for a beloved 'Herdwick' cap which had worn out after twenty years of faithful service!

When Bill Mitchell did an interview with the Rev. Bramwell Evans, better known as 'Romany' of broadcasting fame, readers continued to submit their own recollections for the next two years!

We have never attempted to be political, controversial or even topical in our approach – reading through the past forty volumes, the majority of articles have stood the test of time and would still be of interest today.

In our very first issue, Harry Scott wrote of the magazine 'Its objects are quite simple. They are to reflect through illustration and the printed word the life, industry, crafts, sports and characters of the district. It will seek to portray to visitor and resident alike something of that richness which is inherent in the Lake counties. It will attempt at once to heighten and to deepen the appreciation of all that is signified in the words "the English Lake District".' Our editorial policy continues with these aims in mind.

This book in no way attempts to cover every aspect of Cumbrian life – after nearly five hundred issues of the magazine, there is still plenty of scope! I would take this opportunity to thank all our authors, artists and photographers who have contributed to *Cumbria*'s success. The following articles are a small nostalgic reflection of life in our county, which I hope you will enjoy sharing.

W. R. MITCHELL'S YEARS WITH *CUMBRIA*

FOR ALMOST forty years I edited two magazines simultaneously, my area of concern extending from Solway to Humber and from the Tees to the Hodder in Bowland. Feeling it was vital to keep my finger on the pulse of the vast area, I spent as much time as possible 'in the field', at times leaving the office with no clear idea of where I might go.

This meant that on reaching the main road I had to decide either to turn left (for Yorkshire, which was *Dalesman* country) or right (for the Lake Counties, served by our magazine *Cumbria*). My pulse as well as the car engine began to race when I headed towards the Cumbrian Hills, especially in snow-time when they could be clearly seen from local hills. It looked as though someone had pitched a group of bell tents on the northern horizon.

Both magazines were edited, with true northern thrift, using one desk, one chair, one telephone – but two files! Year after year, two streams of editorial material flowed across that desk and, amazingly, not once did an item intended for *Cumbria* find its way into *The Dalesman*, and vice versa.

Cumbria had been founded by a small dedicated group of members of the Lakeland Region of the Youth Hostels' Association. The editor, Leslie Hewkin, worked for the Freshwater Biological Association at Ferry House, overlooking Windermere. In his leisure time, he liked nothing better than to write about Lakeland. Leslie and some of his committee felt that *Cumbria* would benefit from a more professional approach, a notion which flattered us at *The Dalesman*. We were unsophisticated scribes-turned-publishers who regarded amateurism as a virtue to be cultivated.

The Youth Hostellers made an appointment to visit Clapham and after pleasantries and cups of tea they explained their proposal, which was immediately accepted by Harry J. Scott, whose small publishing company this was. No directors' meeting was called, for the simple reason there were no directors. I cannot recall the exchange of solicitors' letters stating terms. *Cumbria* was offered to us and we accepted it, issuing Vol. 1, No. 1 (New Series) with faith and a minimum of fuss.

When we took over *Cumbria*, one snag was that no car was available – and the bicycle was unreliable. Harry J. Scott, sitting in state at a large desk in a small room, and supervising affairs between naps and cups of tea, turned me into an expert with railway timetables. In those days, all the little branch lines were operating. It was a heaven-sent oppor-

MONTHLY

NINEPENCE

CUMBRIA

LAKELAND LIFE AND LITERATURE

DERWENTWATER FROM ASHNESS WOODS. Photograph by Christopher Stringer

VOL. 1 (New Series)   APRIL, 1951   NO. 1

MY LAKELAND FARM.

MEGALITHS ON MOUNTAINS.

SPORT AMONG THE FELLS.

LAKELAND HUMOUR.

A CUMBRIAN LETTER-BOX, Etc.

tunity to get around cheaply. I began to know the rail journey to Barrow and on up the Cumbrian coast to Ravenglass, where the sea smacks its lips against sand and every other person I met was a local person – and a character!

I wrote an article about every village along the Settle–Carlisle line; I ventured up to Coniston and along the Penrith-Keswick-Bassenthwaite Lake route, photographing the latter station simply because my fancy had been taken by the length of the station sign. At other times, the company funds – always stretched – extended to hiring a taxi for the day. Dear old Mr Carr, the father of the Newby taxi proprietor, took me to his childhood haunts around Lupton, and John 'Holme, from Austwick, was my chauffeur into the midst of Lakeland.

One day we made what then was the awesome journey over Honister to interview the quarryman. He told me of the fickle winds and especially when the wind was 'in the crack', two streams of air meeting noisily on the face of the crags.

The homely prose of Harry J. Scott is detectable in the first editorial. 'It has made many friends and has established a bond of affection between itself and its readers . . . It is issued in the faith that the many thousands who have a deep and lasting affection for the Lakeland area will find in the magazine at least the outlines, which we hope to fill in later, of a magazine worthy of this part of England.' It was, for some years, the only monthly magazine covering Lakeland.

Cumbria? Whenever I mentioned the name while introducing myself to the folk of the area, most people were bemused. Those were the days when Cumbria was

OPPOSITE
The cover of the very first 'New Series' issue.

divided administratively into three wedges. Let Harry J. Scott's prose provide an explanation: 'The very title, *Cumbria*, denotes the scope of the journal, for it covers no one specific county but the whole of the old Kingdom of Cumbria, made up of Westmorland, Cumberland and North West Lancashire.'

As the years went by, most residents of the three counties became familiar with the ancient name Cumbria, so that when the boundaries were re-organised in 1974, and Cumbria became the official title, few explanations were necessary.

The quirks in the county boundaries were mentioned in many articles we used, including a series I wrote for some years. It was called 'Cumbrian Days'. My commission (received from myself, as Editor) was to wander where the spirit moved me and to chat with whosoever I would. An early 'victim' was an octagenarian at Coniston. 'How old are you?' I asked. 'Eighty-five.' 'You don't look eighty-five.' The old man snapped back: 'Can't help that!' It was clear that characters remained in the Lakeland countryside. A man at Penruddock described his state of health as being poor. 'I've yan foot in t'grave and anudder on a banana skin, ready for slipping in . . .'

Cumbria shared the same printing press as *The Dalesman*. For some years, I made a monthly pilgrimage to Messrs Dixon and Stell, at Cross Hills, in Yorkshire, to 'put the magazine to bed'. Then, with a change of printer and over a spell of many years, I travelled northwards, to Kendal, where Harry Firth presided over the Works department of the *Westmorland Gazette*. Not wishing to confuse the *Gazette* and *Cumbria*, nor to give the impression that the two magazines were in the same 'stable', we resurrected the name of an old printing firm the company had absorbed. We were now printed by Atkinson and Pollitt.

Kendal was the home of two men who had been reared in urban Lancashire and who in due course settled here to find their greatest satisfaction in recording the landforms of Lakeland. I refer to Joseph Hardman and Alfred Wainwright.

Joseph was a photographer. He and his wife worked as a perfect team. They used a taxi and often had the company of attractive nurses from Kendal hospital who, in return for their days out in Lakeland, posed (demurely, of course) in various places, such as at the Surprise View above Derwentwater. Each August, a batch of photographs from 'J. Hardman' contained some snow pictures with pretty young ladies holding sprigs of holly!

The photographs, which are among the best ever taken in the Lake District, and now (happily) have a good home at the Museum of Lakeland Life at Kendal, were made from plates, not film. I recall seeing the photographer at work, with his heavy camera on a substantial tripod and his wife attending to the plates, receiving those he had exposed and handing him others with unexposed plates. The weight must have been considerable.

In the first issue of *Cumbria* (New Series) appeared Mr Hardman's 'Spring Pastoral, Langdale', taken against the light, with the fells in various dark shades, some light-rimmed cattle and a halo-ed wall in the foreground, and a thorn – heavy with blossom – to the left. It was the first of many hundreds of his pictures that appeared in our pages.

The other Lancastrian is, of course, Alfred Wainwright – AW to his friends – whose lasting contribution to Lakeland life is that astonishingly fine and detailed series of guides to the fells. When I saw the first to be published, it was still in

manuscript, and I marvelled that anyone should have the skill and patience to work in such intricate detail.

Soon afterwards, I met AW himself. He was still working as borough treasurer in one of the offices of the Town Hall. I gathered that Harry Firth had agreed to print the book in the confidence they would sell. If they had not sold, AW would have expended about £900 he did not possess.

F. S. Sanderson's artistry with scraper-boards was never less than inspired, yet he instructed in his will that on his death, the remaining drawings should be scrapped. This certainly did not apply to the watercolours of Edward Jeffrey which adorned the cover of *Cumbria* for a considerable period of time; the originals were snapped up, at £3 a time, by members of the staff. Meanwhile, Mr Jeffrey had a steady sale for the large watercolours he exhibited at Grasmere and elsewhere.

He had settled in Ravenstonedale and had high hopes for a cartoon character he had devised and called Toby Twirl. In the event, it was not successful enough to keep him without further work. His versatility impressed. Having started out as a commercial artist, he was capable of working in every medium, from simple line to oils. I had a feeling that if I had said that I had thought of a wonderful new way of producing a picture, using soot, white-wash, red ink and dolly blue, he would have heard me out and then said, a little wearily: 'I last used that method 20 years ago!'

Another well-loved artist was Sydney Buckley, of Cartmel. One of my most anxious moments came when, having decided to interview members of the local art group standing beside their pictures in the hall at Grange, I discovered that

Mr Buckley was 'off-colour'. He was more than 'off-colour' and was, indeed, in bed, quite ill. He agreed to be photographed and was dressed and rushed to and from the hall at great speed. Happily, he did not suffer any further distress.

An unassuming, gentle artist who adorned our covers on many occasions was Basil Rowbotham, who had settled in Cartmel. I gulped when he sent me a study of Cartmel Priory, not only in time of snow but at night, with a full moon and a deep blue sky full of stars. I had not seen anything quite like this before. It was used, of course, and an astonishingly large number of readers were to mention it with appreciation in successive weeks.

Among the photographers we used was W. A. Poucher, who did not inquire further when no payment was made. My own favourite picture was his study of Sphinx Rock, Great Gable, the view including Wastwater and the patterned fields of Wasdale. Colin Denwood, of Cockermouth and later Penrith, turned in many hundreds of first rate black-and-white photographs which by themselves form a worthy social history of the area.

Frank Haley, who was manager of a well-known pharmacy at Keswick, indulged his passion for writing and provided *Cumbria* with some of its most vivid prose. He had a feel for the real Lakeland life, such as when he described the Blencathra Tatie Pot – the 'boisterous, crowded, good-naturedly boastful uproar of that Tatie Pot lunch which celebrates the first day's hunting by the Blencathra Pack in the second week of October.'

In the early days, Mary Fair of Eskdale sent a monthly letter elaborating points made in the current number and pointing out the various mistakes. Her letters were as well-read and appreciated as, much later, were the gossipy notes of Clara

Boyle of Ambleside and the monthly 'Cottage on the Fell', by Anne J. Utting (a series of monthly notes continued to the present day by a well-known writer who uses the pen-name Polly Thwaite).

Clara was an off-comer in the sense that she was born and reared in Poland; she had married into the well-known and respected Lakeland family of Boyle and wrote so candidly that now and again there were protests by some readers who knew her and felt she was 'near the bone'.

Anne Utting, from her cottage near Caldbeck, wrote notes that had a strong appeal because they were so wonderfully down-to-earth and she was not too proud to mention disasters as well as triumphs. Every year she planted up her garden; and in most years the plants were shredded by high winds or nipped in the bud by frost. If anything could go wrong in the house, it did. The readers loved it. She had an enormous fan mail.

Women were the best writers. They achieved style without striving too hard for it. Doreen Wallace, the novelist, wrote of her Exile and Return to Lakeland:

We moved back to Lorton eventually, to the house called Kirkfell, fairly well up on Whinlatter Pass. Here we had some views. And if there is a more rewarding walk or ride than that from Cockermouth (where you do your shopping), back to Lorton, I don't know it. There is a point on that road [which goes] forward to an ever-narrowing valley choked with mountains; and if the sun shines, the mountains are so rocky that they flash and gleam like cut jewels.

Up in Eskdale lived Dudley Hoys, writer of Lakeland short stories, many of which were published in *John Bull*, which then was one of Britain's most famous journals. The illustrations to the tales were reproduced in colour. I remember Dudley lamenting that the work was given to

[7]

Southern artists, who had their Lakeland farmers striding nonchalantly across the fells with hands in the pockets of flannels and with stylish shirts and jumpers! After about seven years as President of the Cumbrian Literary Group, he told me he had managed to get himself 'demoted to vice president'.

A letter in *Cumbria* belittling John Peel, the famous huntsman, brought a letter in which Peel was defended. 'Let us give honour where honour is due; and if anyone does not know the facts at first hand, then the least they can do is to say nothing, instead of making harmful and irresponsible statements.' The letter was signed by – John Peel. He was the great great grandson of the huntsman. In following years, I often chatted with him at his home overlooking Lowther Park, near Penrith, and he gave me first-hand accounts of the lifestyle of Lord Lonsdale, the 'Yellow Earl'.

Verse was a regular feature of *Cumbria*. It ranged from 'passable' to 'good', with a sufficient number in the excellent category. One of my favourites, *Rocks*, by G. D. Ragland Phillips, starts with the exclamation of a boy on a London bus:

Look, mum – lovely rocks – there in that garden!
Are they real rocks, mum, like on mountains?

The poet invited the boy to visit the mountains of Lakeland:

Come, feel the granite grip the steel,
Stretch your knee, spring your heel.
Hear the wind yell in the heart of the fell
Booming around Helvellyn's bowl . . .

For some years, Lakeland was a cosy, homely little area, full of characterful natives, with a few off-comers and rather more summer visitors. I remember going to see Mr Gunning at Grange Town Hall about this business of publicising Lakeland, a topic which was then being spoken about. Yet who wanted publicity? said some of the councillors. Surely, if anyone was interested in the Lake District, they could find their own way there!

The Lakeland of today has affinities with that of 40 years ago, as for example in the lofty forms of the fells and the still (mercifully) uncluttered shorelines of lakes and tarns. The National Trust owns a quarter of the area and sees that it is not exploited in unseemly ways. The Friends of the Lake District continue to act as a ginger group, monitoring the proposed changes and vigorously but sensibly objecting to them if they feel the spirit of Lakeland is being affronted. The National Park Authority is careful about granting planning permissions.

Yet change is part of the nature of things. Change is evident everywhere. The magazine *Cumbria* has changed and, happily, has endured.

FROM A LAKELAND COTTAGE

Polly Thwaite

MY FIRST flirtation with *Cumbria* magazine ended in a lover's tiff. The chosen and the rejected. Knowing nothing of the goings-on, the co-habitation or should I say holy wedlock at the Dalesman Publishing office, I submitted an article. It was addressed to the editor of *Cumbria* and received acceptance from the editor of *The Dalesman*. Was it not good enough for *Cumbria*? The reply to my complaining letter asked what I was fretting about as *The Dalesman* had a bigger circulation. To be fair, it was a general article, but it proved a valuable lesson in making sure I was writing for a specific market.

The editor at that faraway time was not Mr Mitchell who has been a good friend to many of us since I importuned him to address the members of the Cumbrian Literary Group on his requirements for *Cumbria*. We ran a competition which he kindly judged, selecting and criticising material. What a chore for a busy editor who was also writing books.

What did he want? What he didn't want was too many adverbs and adjectives. The material was a roving brief as there is always something not previously covered about Cumbria and the lives of Cumbrians. Accuracy must be paramount. Since then I'm anxious about 'Indignant' Tunbridge Wells' letters and I've received two, one right and one wrong criticism. Checking facts leads to discoveries which I don't necessarily use but which are rewarding in themselves. When researching the history of Char dishes I spent a happy day in Liverpool's Walker Art Gallery, which has a splendid collection of the dishes and helpful leaflets.

At intervals I would submit an article, then one day Mr Mitchell telephoned to say Anne J. Utting who wrote the delightful 'Cottage on the Fell' articles, was moving south and would I like to write 'From a Lakeland Cottage' to fill her slot? Always the first to refuse a challenge, I declined. With soft-voiced persuasion – what a loss to the Diplomatic Service – he said: 'Give it a try and if it doesn't work

we can discontinue the series'. So off went my first Lakeland Cottage, then another and another. That was seven years ago.

The question arose of using my own name or a pseudonym. Remembering when I told my mother I'd sold an article to *The Guardian* and she said: 'Not under your own name, I hope!' in shocked tones, as if I'd robbed Woolworths, it made me wary. The arrival of the cheque staunched my wounds but the scar of uncertainty remained, so a pseudonym was devised.

When I don my Polly Thwaite hat a different facet of myself emerges. Not the world-weary cynic I fear I am, but an uncomplicated country innocent with an injection of fresh mountain air into my approach to life. It has also heightened my powers of observation about the heavenly countryside around me and the lucky natives, fur, feathers, two paws or four. The first letter addressed to Polly Thwaite arrived and I wondered who was coming to stay with that odd name. A friend pointed out that 'thwaite' meant a clearing and was hardly suitable considering the state of my back kitchen.

It was a blow when Mr Mitchell retired. Thinking the new editor would want to stamp his own impression on the magazine, I made my gesture of renunciation to save him the embarrassment of having to ditch me.

Behold, within a day, I opened my cottage door to find a most prepossessing young lady announcing that she – it was not a 'he' – was the new editor and would I stay on. Hilary Gray with her wit (I save all her amusing letters), charm and enviable vitality had entered our lives.

I was grateful and glad to continue. It is a discipline for idle me to work to a deadline, and more important, I relish the new friends I've made and the letters I receive. My farthest flung reader comes from Oregon and this year she is touring around England and would like to call. Shall I recognise her? One could guess at the face of someone likely to take *The Financial Times*, but is there a *Cumbria* reader's face? I think not. I asked an assistant at W. H. Smith's what kind of person bought *Cumbria*. She said it was impossible to say as the range was so wide.

Not only the letters, but when I wrote about longing for a white geranium, a reader from 40 miles away brought one for me. Such kindness. Perhaps one day I'll mention my yearning for a diamond tiara and see what happens.

So, for these and all thy mercies, thank you *Cumbria* for the hospitality of your pages this long time. Congratulations on achieving your 40th birthday and best wishes for forty years on.

TEN YEARS AGO . . .

Ron Sands held the post of Public Relations Officer at Brockhole, the National Park Centre at Windermere, for many years and has been a great friend to Cumbria. *He remembers the last occasion we celebrated a special anniversary . . .*

CONTEMPLATING THE prospect of *Cumbria*'s 40th anniversary immediately brings to my mind the thought of bacon sandwiches. Can any other readers of our much-loved monthly explain the association? I doubt it – unless, that is, you either have deductive powers of truly Holmesian proportions, or you were one of the select band who ten years back attended the celebrations of Cumbria's 30th anniversary at Brockhole.

It was an occasion I shall never forget; the limited number of tickets were available to readers on a first come, first served basis – although there was an 'overflow' celebration later the same afternoon for those who were disappointed at not obtaining tickets for the main tea party.

We had decided months before that the most appropriate fare would be home-made Cumbrian cakes and pastries –

certainly not bacon sandwiches – and the mouthwatering spread in Brockhole's gleaming cafeteria would have weakened the resolve of the most determined weight watcher. Editor Bill Mitchell described the feast as one to make even Billy Bunter's eyes pop.

Before we could get 'fell in' to the food, we assembled in the lecture theatre to hear some brief but heartfelt tributes to the first three decades of the magazine's life. John Nettleton, then Director of Brockhole (and a Cumbrian born and bred), presided in his genial way over the proceedings and introduced the guest speaker – the lecturer and historian Dr William Rollinson, whose now classic book *Life and Tradition in the Lake District* had been recently published in paperback form by *Dalesman*.

I had to slip quietly away to attend to some matter at the information centre downstairs; when I returned to the lecture theatre (via a side door) my nostrils were assailed by the unmistakable odour of bacon sandwiches and I found a rapt audience sitting in darkness – save for a flickering, spluttering naked flame which hovered about and around Dr Rollinson's head.

Our eminent speaker, anxious to bring alive the sight, sound and smell of the past, had lit a rush-light. This he had made by dipping a single rush into bacon fat, attaching the rush to a special metal holder which secured it at some critical angle, and then setting light to one end.

Thus it is that I shall ever associate *Cumbrian* anniversaries with bacon sandwiches, try as I might to elevate my thoughts to more seemly topics.

Now, ten years on, we celebrate the 40th anniversary – and still the magazine brings joy and enlightenment every month of the year. Varied, entertaining, lively and wonderfully readable we rejoice in the magazine's continued success and look forward to the *next* forty years. Whatever beverage we might choose to celebrate this fourth decade, it will certainly not be Phyllosan . . .

2

WHAT MAKES CUMBRIA SPECIAL?

THE LAKE DISTRICT AT ITS BEST

THE OTHER morning our postman brought me a letter from one who had just returned to his home and work in London after a holiday with us in Lakeland. Here is a portion of it:

'If you want to appreciate the Lake District at its best, I will tell you how to do it. You must work for at least eleven months of the year amid the rush and fumes and noise of London; you must almost at the eleventh month be afraid that you will not after all be able to get away; you must hurry to the station at the last minute, probably with an incipient head-ache; and then you must arrive at your host's house late at night, weary and drooping from exhaustion.

'The next morning you wake early and look out upon the Lakeland scene in the glory of early morning sunlight, you look on green fields and smell the fragrance of hawthorn, and your eyes catch the glint of a lake and rise to the foothills of the mountains and so to the tops themselves. That is when you most appreciate your lovely country.'

That is not a letter from a woolly sentimentalist; the writer is a mountaineer of some repute who knows Lakeland in its grim moods as well as in its sunlight.

I realised when I read that letter that we who live in this district can never enjoy Lakeland quite like that. We, as 'natives', are apt at times to look down upon the holiday-maker, the week-ender, and the tripper. We feel that the visitor can never really appreciate Lakeland as we do. But is that quite true? May it not be that the holiday folk often have a fuller appreciation of our hills and dales than we who live in them?

Folkdancing festival at Grasmere, May 1951. (*A. Stephens*)

I know that we have that very precious thing – a stake in the countryside. It is our home, and we belong. But do we not always value it as highly as the person who has paid for it all by long months of dusty effort in a world of fog and smoke and grit?

(July 1956)

CUMBRIAN SIGHTS AND SENSATIONS

In 1971, a competition was held inviting readers to submit their favourite Lakeland experiences of sight, hearing, smell, taste and touch. The winning entries were:

SIGHT: Sunrise from Great Gable at the dawn of a new day.

HEARING: The 'scream' of a hawk circling majestically over the crags of Upper Ennerdale.

SMELL: The mingled scents of valley freshness after rain.

TASTE: Packed lunch eaten en route for the mountains.

TOUCH: The firm rock of a summit cairn which gives a sense of achievement.

(Mrs) A. B. MacDonald, Blackburn.

SIGHT: Daffodils nodding in the breeze at Easter in Grasmere churchyard.

HEARING: *D'ye Ken John Peel?* sung in a Lakeland inn by the followers of the Ullswater Hounds.

SMELL: Woodsmoke from cottage chimneys when taking an evening stroll around Hawkshead village.

TASTE: Kendal mint cake eaten at the top of Helvellyn.

TOUCH: The springy feel of sphagnum moss underfoot when fell walking.

(Mrs) M. Kilner, Huddersfield.

SIGHT: September mists hanging low over still lakes.

HEARING: Rich Cumbrian dialect, like a foreign language to me.

SMELL: At the Grasmere gingerbread shop.

TASTE: Rum butter.

TOUCH: The icy coldness of water rushing under Ashness Bridge.

(Mrs) K. Mathias, Luton.

SIGHT: Birds on the Kent Estuary, seen from the train.

HEARING: The Duddon on a starry night.

SMELL: The wind amid the pines of Duddon woods.

TASTE: A juniper berry.

TOUCH: The fleece of a Herdwick sheep.

Dorothy G. Crocken, London E.3.

SIGHT: Shepherd with his collie dogs gathering sheep from the hills near Keskadale at the top of Newlands Hause.

HEARING: The call of the curlew across Skiddaw Forest.

SMELL: The scent of the bog myrtle on the way to Watendlath.

TASTE: Freshly-baked scones with rum butter after a walk on the hills.

TOUCH: The satin-smooth bark of young silver birch trees in Tilberthwaite Ghyll.

(Miss) H. M. Moses, Carlisle.

To see the white lambs gambolling in
    Duddon's intake fields,
To taste the hot rum-buttered scones the
    farmhouse kitchen yields,
To touch the turf of Skiddaw's flank,
To hear the Esk Fells silence, blank.
To smell the scent of Rydal's flowers—
Sensations all of Cumbria, relived in
    'memory hours'.

(Mrs) J. C. Symonds, Liverpool.

SIGHT: The red glow of the sunset behind the fells.

HEARING: The ring of ice skates on frozen Derwentwater.

SMELL: New-baked bread in a farm kitchen.

TASTE: Cumberland ham and eggs in a village inn.

TOUCH: Ice-cold water in a mountain stream.

(Mrs) Bacon, Keswick.

SIGHT: Watendlath Tarn viewed from the fells above.

HEARING: The bleating of lambs in the early morning in the Borrowdale valley.

SMELL: The faintly pungent aroma of fern and heather after rain.

TASTE: The sharp, sweet flavour of bilberry tart.

TOUCH: The old dry-stone walls, warm in the sun.

(Mrs) N. B. Rayner, Kent.

STORM AND SUNSHINE

A Lakeland Weather Miscellany

The weather has made the scenery and people of Lakeland what they are, and while it would not be true to state that the Weather Clerk is always friendly towards us, our weather is not 99 per cent rain, as some people would suggest. It is unpredictable, and so are the views expressed about it, as this miscellany shows. . .

W. Heaton Cooper, the well-known Lakeland artist, has no harsh feelings against the weather:

You've got to accept the weather as part of the countryside. I never say it's a bad day. It's either a wet day or a dry day. There is nothing you can do about the weather, and without rain you would not have the lakes, rivers and mists. I wouldn't have any other weather in the district at all.

Percy Withers, in his book entitled 'In a Cumberland Dale' (1914) was not quite so happy:

Rain, and wind, and cloud! Our dieties, like the Witches in *Macbeth*, take their ingredients and mix and stir them in their mighty cauldron of hills, for ever chanting the words of the refrain backwards and forwards. Cloud, wind, rain! – there is not a month of the twelve on which we can count on anything different.

Wordsworth did not mind bad weather:

Insensible must he be who would not congratulate himself upon the bold bursts of sunshine, the descending vapours, wandering lights and shadows, and the invigorated torrents and waterfalls, with which broken weather, in a mountainous region, is accompanied. At such a time there is no cause to complain, either of the monotony of midsummer colouring, or of the glaring atmosphere of long, cloudless, and hot days.

Arthur Gardner, in 'Britain's Mountain Heritage' (1942) was optimistic:

Some holidaymakers are deterred from visiting the Lakes by tales of its bad weather. It is true that several times as much rain falls there as in southern England, but the sunshine records do not compare so unfavourably. When it rains among the hills it usually rains hard, and so cuts less into the finer intervals than the figures suggest. It may rain much harder in one valley than in the next, and it is possible sometimes to escape from a rain-soaked valley into broader spaces where the weather is better. It is said that the rainfall at Keswick is only half that of the other end of Derwentwater.

Crabb Robinson despaired. He wrote to Wordsworth:

Did I once see a bright sun in Cumberland or Westmorland? I very much doubt it!

Sometimes the weather-wise have been stirred to jot down comments in verse:

> If it rains with the ebb
> You can go to bed.
> If it rains with the flow
> You can go to plough.

When is the best time of the year to visit the Lakes? Canon Rawnsley wondered:

When will people understand that the times of the year to visit our English Lakes are spring and autumn? When will they remember that our hills are never so full of expression as when powdered with the first October snow, and that our dales are never so sweet with colour of copse and leafage as in the merry month of May?

Baddeley, in his famous 'Guide', suggested:

June is, on an average, the finest month of all, and during the first half of it nothing can surpass the freshness and variety of the immediate environs of the Lakes.

When you are on the hills, move cautiously when mist descends. In 1914, Nancy Price chatted to a Lakeland woman and reported in 'A Vagabond's Way' what she said:

'Leuk at mist drivin' – thoo mun be careful o' 'im – aye, indeed. Ah've learnt t' fear 'im, 'e can drive t' sun oot o' tha life as easy as off t' fellside. Ah lost ma boy through 'im yance, an' 'e tuk ma man eears agone. Aye, 'e near oalas forgits ta send 'em back.'

Then comes the snow, inconveniencing the isolated farmsteads and hamlets but, for all that, adorning the Lakeland scene very attractively. John Richardson wrote in 1876:

> It com doon as whisht an' as deftly as
>   death,
> O' soond, nut a murmur, o' air nut a
>   breath;
> Flake reacin' wi' flake. Oh! 'twas bonny
>   to see
> Hoo it cuvver't up moontain, an' valley,
>   an' tree.
> Doon, doon it com floatin', sa' white an'
>   sa' clear,
> Ivvery twig, ivvery leaf, hed its burden
>   to bear;
> Ivvery dyke, ivvery hoose, ivvery rough
>   cobble wo',
> Hed its blossom its reuf, or its copin' o'
>   snow.

M. R. FitzGibbon told us:

There is rarely any ice before New Year. Tarn Hows, near Coniston, and Tewfit Tarn, near Keswick, are two of the first tarns to freeze. Esthwaite Water is a glorious place to skate, and Rydal bears quite soon on the northern side of the island. If snow is to come, the heaviest snowfall may be from the end of January to March, when we get out our skis and climb the Helvellyn and Skiddaw ranges, which give the best ski-ing slopes. And there is a charm about these still winter days when the leafless trees are seen in all their beauty of outline.

(August 1955)

LAKELAND IS the result of carving of a most delicate and intricate nature, for many processes have gone into the making of it. That is why it is one of the most fascinating and, in some peculiar way, enriching country-sides in the world. Each valley, each mile, every few yards are full of character and variety. Each mountain can look quite different according to the angle at which we see it. Added to this, the fells stand close to a western seaboard and the prevailing wind is from the west. The land reacts quicker to cold and heat than does the ocean, and this affects the moisture-laden winds according to the time of year, creating an ever-changing atmosphere, sometimes quite subtle, and at others sudden and violent.

W. HEATON COOPER.
(1954)

Middlefell Place. Dungeon Ghyll. (*D. Dakeyne*)

Comments on Scenery

I WAS TRAVELLING through Lakeland with my father and another friend. Neither father nor his companion had ever been in Lakeland before, so as we motored along I kept telling them in advance to look left or right for a grand view.

My friend could hardly find words to express his admiration, but father sat silent until he suddenly exclaimed, 'Ah doon't kna what's come ower ye two feauls, talkin' sike rubbish.'

'Nay, we are not talking rubbish, John, neither you nor I have ever seen such scenery in our lives.'

'Whar's ther' any scenery? I see nowt t' mak a song aboot.'

'Just look across the lake. Did you you ever see anything like it?'

'No, nor I don't want either,' says father.

'What's wrong with it?'

'What's reet we' it? Ther's nowt b't rocks an' bracken, and oat grund 'at should be good land is covered i' watter. Ah waddn't be fun deead i' sike a wilderness.'

I've often thought of this dialogue, though the Lakes are more dear to me as the years go by.

T. C. CALVERT,
HAWES.
(1963)

HOMES WITH A DIFFERENCE

Some thoughts on Cumbrian buildings in European Architectural Heritage Year, 1975.

THE TYPICAL stone-built houses of Lakeland are worth more than a passing glance. You notice, of course, the doorways and windows framed in whitewash as a reflector of light. Some of you may even have wondered why so many farms and cottages face away from the view. These are two very small points in the fascinating story of the development, background and siting of these mountain homes.

One of the main characteristic features is the thickness of the walls – 30 inches in old buildings and from 21 inches to 24 inches in the more modern ones. The reason was to make them weatherproof. When it rains in the hills, it often does so on a grand scale – for days on end. In the old days of extreme poverty, bricks were too expensive to use. As local stone was to be had for the picking up, a way was devised of building farms and cottages that defeated the driving rain.

An outer and inner wall was erected, and the cavity filled with rubble, but the whole art in building lay in placing each separate stone at a slight angle – sloping down and outwards, so that capillary action would have no effect.

As no mortar was employed, flat bedding would have been useless, and the only fault of such a method of building (called 'building to a water-shot') was that rooms were inclined to be draughty if the plaster cracked. Wooden panelling was not a means of decoration, but a method of keeping down draughts. It was also more durable than plaster – and often cheaper.

Nowadays, lime mortar is used for stone building – provided the owner is lucky enough to be able to employ one of the few remaining men capable of building in local stone. This mortar binding is kept back about an inch or more from the outside face of the wall to give the impression of true dry-stone building.

This recessing also serves the purpose of preventing the rain washing the mortar down the wall and spoiling its appearance. Such an additional weatherproofing obviates the necessity for extremely thick walling.

Oddly enough, Lakeland stone is not truly stone at all, but coarse-grain slate, unsuitable for splitting, and therefore discarded by the quarries. They call it slate metal.

We often read of amateur builders putting up their own homes. That can be done with brick, but not with slate stone. If you miss sloping a single stone, you might as well pull the whole wall down because the rain is sure to get in! You could roughcast, of course, but in that case, why not use bricks?

Houses in the Lake District are mostly individual. The rows of cottages of one type are so rare as to be noticeable, and were mostly built by quarry companies to house workmen and their families.

Round chimneys are peculiar to most of the district and, in northern areas, stepped gables – as a protection against storms – are quite a feature. On the whole, Lake country architecture has no great amount of beauty, but it has a style of its own and one that blends with the scenery.

Sites in the old days were chosen with both eyes on protection against the elements. The view was not considered at all. Anywhere that gave freedom from snowdrifts, shelter from the prevailing wind, and proximity to water, was a good site.

It is unfortunate that only too often these houses are without sun for three or four months in the year, besides which, the prevalence of building against a hillside has meant that one wall at least, is below some level of the ground. Sufferers from rheumatism could never be happy in such a place.

Practically 100 per cent of Lakeland houses are roofed with local slate. Once of a day it was cheap, but now an average small bungalow roof would cost not much less than £1,600 to cover – in material only. One of the expensive items is roof timbering, which has to be extra strong to carry the heavy weight of slates compared to tiles.

On the other hand, a slate roof (green slates, not thin blue or purple ones) will last 300 or 400 years with a minimum of attention.

There may be moss, lichens and even yellow stonecrop on a roof. It is all very pretty, but as this 'roof garden' draws water, it means damp living. Then there is the local way of covering a chimney stack by setting up two slates to lean against each other. These certainly make a more charming picture than tall, red pots, but they have a tendency to make a chimney smoke!

I do not know of any 16th century cottages in the Lake District, and there are precious few 17th century ones. It was 100 years later that the great building urge spread over the district. It was then, also, that so many yews were planted around the farms. We even have the name – Yewdale, near Coniston.

From time to time, one hears of people who are tired of the universal colour scheme in the Lakes – green paint, green stone, and white roughcasting (with a few exceptions in pink or pale green).

Colour does brighten up any scene. The argument that the Swiss Alps have not been spoiled though the chalets are brightly coloured, may be perfectly sound.

However, we may as well be different in England. Lake District houses are, without doubt, houses with a difference.

T. Smithies

LAKELAND COTTAGES

THE TOWNSMAN goes to Lakeland exploring mountain and torrent; the connoisseur finds history, local custom and handicraft; the exile looks for a home.

Some Englishmen live and work abroad, spend their home leave wherever friends, hotels or clubs will permit them, and

A Cumbrian kitchen, circa 1850.

finally retire disconsolately to boredom wherever it is warm enough. Others, wiser, maintain or develop a dual life at home and abroad and, like good generals, make a firm base in a chosen home.

From the moment of our arrival in England, above all the works of nature and devices of man, we admired the beauty of English homes. The cottages of England are beautiful everywhere, but nowhere does situation so enhance their beauty as in Lakeland. Simple architecture in a complex natural scene.

The discovery of cottages is an endless delight, and the mind's collection of them is a treasure store. Neither pen, paint nor camera can show the harmony of old stone, gable and chimney with old stone, woodland and stream. Among our favourite, with respect to the happy owners, are two on the threshold of the Sanctuary of Great Langdale, one under Lingmoor, in Little Langdale, one not far from Skelwith, one wee neuk in Dunnerdale, two by the Rothay under Loughrigg, and one at the 'Water Gate'.

D. A. Fyfe, Malaya (Letterbox, October 1954)

PORTRAIT OF WATENDLATH

BORROWDALE IS an old fairy story, but it is new to me. It was once a chain of magic-sounding names strung out on a brown map. Now it is a gallery of pictures in my memory – Derwentwater at sunset from above the Lodore falls; an island of twisted oaks among the reeds at the head of the lake, grey cottages and grey bridges and the ever-present hills; and Watendlath.

Whenever you climb a hill there comes a time when, as the valley opens out before you, so everything falls into perspective and the mind is at once stimulated and strangely stilled. The path rose steep and stony out of Crosthwaite and the sun was hot on the side of the hill. Suddenly there was a fresh cold wind from the other side of the fells, and on one side of the path a wood of larches.

I climbed higher among the boulders to the left of the larches, leaving the path which now plunged sharply down beside its scree, as if it could hardly wait to get there.

Ashness Bridge, Watendlath. (*J. J. Thomlinson*)

Immediately below me lay Watendlath. Beauty is like all mysteries, incommunicable. And yet the urge remains to describe it. There was the tarn, very dark and yet so shining, darker at the centre like the heart of a jewel; round the edges the wind made waves and ripples of light and there were brown and golden reeds.

To the left of the tarn was a huddle of cottages, grey like the boulders, except for one set higher than the rest, and newly white-washed. Their smoke rose like a blue gossamer over the tawny backcloth of the hill-side. There was the lacquered green of the tiny valley cut out by the Watendlath beck, and the bluey-green of a plot of potatoes no bigger than a pocket handkerchief. Above the white cottage a line of washing was blowing very white and merry in the stiff breeze.

And far above this, on the fellside, the last rowan flamed beside its gully. Here and there Scots pines stood singly or in twos and threes, like an artist's master stroke to a picture that one would have said was already perfect.

At this height there was a frame for the picture, too – a grey, uneven frame of mountain after mountain, growing greyer and dimmer until the last and grandest became the outline of a dream. But you cannot paint a dream, neither with words nor colours. You can only remember and be glad.

M. Dickinson (January 1956)

TIMELESS TROUTBECK

TROUTBECK IS still a charming and timeless village. A sense of history is strong there and a fund of tales, both amusing and sinister, are told by some of the older inhabitants.

In the drought last year an old lady told me: 'It'll not rain while t'wind is blowing from Blue Ghyll.'

'Oh?' I questioned.

'An old parson once said it,' she told me, 'and it's mostly proved true. Those parsons were farmers, too, you know, so they reckoned to be good weathermen.'

They must also have been artful dodgers, for the next tale concerned a parson-cum shepherd. He was driving his sheep along the main Kirkstone road when a fine carriage pulled up beside him. It was the Bishop from Carlisle on a quick trip round his ecclesiastical flock.

'Could you direct me to the Parsonage?' he wanted to know.

Fortunately there was a long and a short way round the village. After directing the Bishop the long way, the parson took his sheep up the short, steep slope to his house, arriving in good time to don his robes and greet his superior in proper fashion.

I went to look at a cottage which was reputed to have a tree running through its middle. It had been a typical rough slate farmhouse once, but sometime around 1867 had been divided into two. Perched with its back to the hill, and facing the deep valley, it looked as permanent as the rocky outcrop on which it stood.

At the base of the rounded chimney were the letters G.B. with the date between, 1626. That was George Browne, I thought, the builder of Townend, and famous for that.

He must have been an ingenious man. All those years before tractors and bull-dozers, when faced with an immovable object, he had elected to incorporate it into the building. It supported the spiral staircase, a long-dead tree, black with age and with a patina induced by the polish of many hands.

The solid oak treads might well have been made from its branches, winding about the trunk as once they did in life. The richly carved spice cupboard and panelled wall of what might have been the hallan, were also of the same black oak.

'He was a well-thought-of man in these parts,' said my friend, as though she were speaking of a man who lived yesterday.

'Do you think he built Gallow Howe?' I asked. That area of the village has a grim history.

It's hard to imagine anything so sinister in Troutbeck, but high on that windy ridge there once stood a gallows tree, dating back no doubt to those years before the union of the Crowns when Scottish reivers might, at any time, drift down through the mists of Kirkstone to steal and rob and kill without warning.

Did they get short shrift from the villagers, if caught red-handed? Were they hoisted aloft without benefit of judge or jury? Three hundred years is a long time, and skeletons unearthed near the site after so many years tell no tales, except that these were felons, and could not lie in the churchyard.

Did G.B. pull down the gallows and build a house with that name, and do those uneasy ghosts forever flit about there, unable to find their way back by the High or the Low road to their own Scotland?

E. M. Campbell (August 1977)

TATIE POT

A RECENT reference in your pages to tatie pot reminds me how sadly this once-famous dish has fallen from grace, even in the North-West of England. At one time tatie pot was to the Cumbrian what Yorkshire pudding is to the Yorkshireman, haggis to the Scotsman and pigs' trotters to the Lancashireman. Now I am told there are Cumbrians who do not even know its smell, let alone its taste.

And what a smell, and what a taste, and what a wonderful dish! In the way I have always known it made, the neck and loin chops of mutton, neatly trimmed, were placed in wide shallow roasting tins and partly cooked in the oven. Then the meat was covered with a good layer of peeled potatoes and chopped onions, roasting being continued until the top potatoes were well browned.

There were those who insisted that tatie pot had to be made in a special deep earthenware jar, and others who declared that it was not complete without a black pudding. But those were the finer flights of fancy. The tatie pot itself was the thing. And only a Cumbrian housewife could really make it as, I am told, only a Yorkshire woman can make Yorkshire pudding.

Geoff. Ramsden (November 1952)

3

CUMBRIAN CHARACTERISTICS

THE CUMBRIAN

AS A CUMBRIAN I was amused when some years ago I read this summing up of the typical Cumbrian by the then Bishop of Carlisle, Dr Herbert Williams, after he had been seventeen years in the diocese:

He is stubborn but intensely loyal. He has tenacity and resolution. He has a great gift of silence. There is nobody who dislikes criticism so much. He is conservative in his habits. He is by no means sentimental, but you can go to him with your troubles. He does not express his amazing affection for those who live in his vicinity until he is quite certain that they are safely dead.

Richard Yeomans (June 1952)

SOME CUMBRIAN ATTITUDES

A NEW MASTER at my old Cumbrian school once caned the whole class for what he called 'cursing and swearing' in the playground. Our headmaster explained to the irate teacher that we had not been cursing or swearing; we had only spoken and shouted in our own dialect! As a matter of fact, the headmaster had been with us at playtime, smoking his pipe, and no one dared to use strong language within his hearing!

Mention of the headmaster's pipe reminds me of the day when I first tried to smoke some cheap tobacco. A local wit shouted: 'Ez thoo got a licence for that thing?'

Aye, they're very witty, these Cumbrians, but it sometimes turns to sarcasm. Cumbrians have their own method of dealing with persons who make sarcastic remarks. They retort with a remark that is twice as nasty.

The proud father of a bouncing baby boy was teased with the traditional witty remark: 'Thoo hesn't proved theesel' a man yit!' Mystified, the young dad asked what that comment meant. He was told: 'Well, lads is two a penny in this Coonty, where males far ootnumbers females. Any feul can be fadder of a boy, but it teks a real man to be fadder of a lass. Aye, birth of a lass is summat special. Lads is ower commonplace.'

There again, we have the time-worn idea that, to be tough, one must speak coarse Cumbrian. Many of us have tried to better ourselves by speaking standard English, but have been accused of effeminacy or of 'putting it on'. Even though we don't overdo it with such terms as 'barth', 'parth' or 'carstle' (castle), we can sense some hostility when speaking proper English in the presence of those who knew us in our early days.

The dislike of 'fancy southern ways' seems to persist mainly among Cumbria's old folk. One old lady refused the help of W.V.S. personnel because she couldn't stand what she termed 'their modern, lah-de-dah methods'. An old woman complained to me about having to take regular baths at a retirement home. Another elderly soul groused about her relatives finding fault with her boiling eggs in the kettle and using the same water for brewing tea. 'Saves watter, fuel an' time,' she wailed.

Many older Cumbrians still follow old wives' tales and customs, so I wasn't at all surprised to find a grannie giving her grandchild some cinder tea to ease wind pains, nor was I amazed to hear that the liquid from a boiled mouse was still considered a cure for bed-wetting. Even cow dung poultice is regarded as good for chest complaints.

Strangers sometimes wonder why many Cumbrians stare at nothing. I've seen them staring at nothing in pubs and on the streets, just like old horses in a field. Dickens wrote about it in his *Sketches from Boz*. He mentioned looking out of the window at the *King's Arms*, Wigton. He saw drizzle, and loafers standing at the pump, looking at nothing. One of the loafers spat in the gutter, then looked at nothing again.

That tradition exists in Wigton to this very day. The late Gerald Findler told me the custom stemmed from olden times, when Wigton was only a few scattered hamlets. After each day's work was done, men would meet on the central green to gossip – and look at nothing. I once timed a man looking at nothing on Melmerby Green. He stood in one position for nearly an hour, staring at nowt.

An officer at Kirkbride aerodrome once asked me why Cumbrians seldom or never said 'sir'. I explained that they were a proud people who considered themselves as good as anyone else. They were not given to fawning on superiors, neither would they lower their dignity (as they thought) by uttering that despised word 'sir'.

Which reminds me that our Cumbrian hero, Earl Boethar, once declared: 'Never shall my people address a Norman as Lord.' So Cumbrians are unconsciously perpetuating their Lakeland ancestors' proud independence and defiance of those who rule our benighted land.

To sum up, we have a tough, sturdy population in Cumbria, whose rough dialect matches their native hardiness. Most of the working men prefer rugged masculinity to finer, more elegant manners, hence their prowess in gruelling sports and hard graft.

In war, they proved themselves valiant fighters. In times of depression and want, they bore the strain with courage and fortitude. In view of such qualities, one can overlook the apparent deficiencies.

Tom Jackson (January 1977)

A YOUNG couple who were on holiday in the Lake District heard that a local farmer had some terrier puppies for sale.

They went along to inquire about them, and were told: 'Nay, we've nobbut yan left.'

The dog was always called 'Yan'.

(1965)

A Patterdale farmer at home. (*W. R. Mitchell*)

YOU ONLY HAVE TO KNOW THE LANGUAGE

The Cumbrian dialect is Homeric in scale; it had to be because its greatest contributors were the Norsemen who were ever people with tales to tell.

LEEDS UNIVERSITY students conducting a nationwide survey of local dialects came to the conclusion that we Cumbrians swear too much! There is, they pronounced from the depths of their wide knowledge of the twin counties and their dialects, far too much 'cussin' ' going on.

Perhaps they got themselves somewhat muddled between the native tongue of the West coast collier or ironworker (with a large mixture of Geordie, Yorkshire and Lancashire blood, imported during the district's own industrial revolution) and the native, ten-generations-and-more Cumbrian whose utterances in dialect would sound like swearing to anybody unused to it.

However, the charge, for a charge it indeed is, cannot go unanswered.

The defence rests on one irrefutable fact: the Cumbrian dialect does not need 'cuss' words. It is colourful enough without having to resort to such foreign, Anglo-Saxon words. Colourful indeed as befits a language developed to tell of stirring deeds; better equipped perhaps than Homer was when he committed the *Odyssey* and the *Iliad* to writing.

I have always felt that the Cumbrian dialect is not a sympathetic sound at all. It is in fact a violent language with a large vocabulary of violence available for those who told tales of deeds of derring-do against the Scots raiders or stories of the latest rumble with the neighbours about grazing rights.

The 109 words for beating or bashing are proof, says Dickinson in his *Glossary*, 'of the combative proclivities of our ancestors.' They range from bang, bash and bat to whezzle, wipe, yark and yedder, and in between are such beauties as benzal, which means a severe thrashing, clapper-clowe (to beat and scratch), to giving somebody a cloot or a corkin, a dander ower t'head or a lambastin' (not in Dickinson's *Glossary*). These all come within the bounds of assault and battery but when somebody is massacred it is obviously in the class of grievous bodily harm. Man's inhumanity to man was carried on within the family when a mother skelped her children and grown-ups welted one another. And, contrary as Cumbrians are inclined to be (a characteristic which accounts in part for such an extensive vocabulary of fighting), the Cumbrian's 'punch' was, in many districts, a kick with the foot.

The Cumbrian might have called a spade a speadde but he had sixty-seven varieties of fool or weak-minded person and that does not include out-and-out loonies or lunatics. Even today one hears a Cumbrian happily calling another a 'cloot-heed' and in return, equally happily, accepting the label of 'neddy' or a dozen other semi-affectionate terms for weak-headedness.

It doesn't seem to mean much but it is easy to imagine the slanders that were perpetuated around Cumbrian fires on long winter nights as they sought through their copious vocabularies to find a word to suit a particular neighbour or some erring villager.

The choice was wide, from gowk, neddy and feul, to cofeheed and cuddy, bung and bumweller; dunderheed, garrack, gommerel, hofelin, ledderheed, havral, gawmass, cat-wittit, makison, mell-scoped, nedlin, ninny, spaskull, sillikan and steuk.

A person could be called 'nut aw theer', 'short o' leet', 'nick't at heed' or 'hofe thick' and it speaks for the isolation Cumberland has suffered or enjoyed (it depends on which way you look at it) that anybody who was regarded as a queer customer would in some parts of Cumbria be called a Britainer!

Sentiment seemed seldom to enter into Cumberland life as represented by the dialect and the fifth Commandment gets short shrift in a society which generally called its parents 't'owld feller' and 't'owld lass', and the woman next door could be 'that boddy' when she wasn't 'that owld faggot' or 'that owld frau'.

Still the dialect could be informative and descriptive, especially in the names for birds. An oyster-catcher, or sea-pie, doesn't live on oysters. On the Cumberland coast it catches mussles, so the dialect name for it is 'mussel pecker'. 'White rump' perfectly describes the wheatear, as 'Bessie dooker' describes the dipper. Dialect is full of simile. 'As hard as Whillimer cheese' was very hard indeed because it was said that strips of rind from these tough old cheeses could be used to caulker clogs. Or a person could be as thin as a rake, as daft as a brush, as old as Knock Cross (which was also a place to 'go to' or be 'as hard as').

I have an idea that 'thin as Thursday's purse' dates back no further than the days when Cumbria became industrialised and began to have regular Friday pay-days.

There was a certain dry humour too in the dialect. The dales parson was allowed 'whittlegate' as part of his living, which meant that he ate in turn with the parish families. Cumbrians coined the phrase 'run of his teeth' to describe it; they called a good appetite a 'gey twist' and when a man was doing his utmost he said he had 'aw his watter on'.

Cumbrians liked a man who was 'jannick', which means right, fit or honest; disliked anybody who was 'ill gien'; met their friends with the greeting: 'What fettle!' and exclaimed 'Goks on!' when it rained 'hyal watter', and were 'backset and foorset' when they were in a quandary.

The Cumberland dialect was no speech for romance; certainly not a language of love, and Dickinson sorrowfully notes that the word for love is 'leuve', but adds the word is seldom used in ordinary converse.

You can't write a love letter in the dialect; it hasn't got the right words. The nearest I have found is 'liking', which means fondness, but that could be for tatie pot or fadderless stew as well as for the girl next door, but to 'lilly' was to flatter, cajole or caress, and any young people so indulging were said to be 'cuttery-cooin'.

It is difficult, but not impossible, to tell a love story in Cumberland dialect. The nearest I have ever heard is the following:

A lad and his lass were cuttery-cooin' down the lane when she said to him: 'Gwordie, lad, does ta leuve muh?'

'Aye,' said Gwordie.

There was a pause, and then the lass started again: 'Hoo much does ta leuve muh, Gwordie?'

Gwordie weighed his words carefully before he replied: 'Like owt!'

F. J. Carruthers (April 1971)

CUMBRIAN FASHIONS

OULD IT surprise you to learn that many a Cumbrian farmer has 'mucked out' a byre in a Savile Row suit, not purchased from those august quarters, however, but from a humble second-hand clothes emporium?

From this same source they have chosen the clothes that need to stand up to the rough and tumble of a farming day, and their taste in *colour*, at any rate, has changed little in fifty years. 'Muck-coloured' is still top of the list!

The second-hand shop was run by my parents for over forty years; they recently passed it on to me. They noted that although men's styles in clothing alter only slightly, the materials change greatly as new and better fabrics are invented.

Fifty years ago, the countryman's working outfit consisted of a flat tweed cap and 'union shirt', made of a heavy cotton, with a neck-band, but no collar. It derived its name from the Workhouse, or 'Union' as it was known locally, which issued similar shirts to the inmates.

Trousers were made of 'fustian', a thick-twilled cotton cloth, short-napped, in dark colours. These were common among all working classes. 'Cassimer trousers', which were known locally as 'kitle trousers' or 'slape' (meaning smooth), were the fore-runner of the modern denim jeans, a thick hard-wearing cotton material which had linings attached loosely at the waist, these being made of white cotton.

The farmers preferred the 'slape' trousers at harvest-time, asking: 'As t' nee slape trooser? – aah git aah'll stuck up wid seed in them coorse trooser!'

Later on, when long underpants replaced loose linings, they pleaded: 'As t'

any lowse linings?' They were referring to long underpants.

Rough tweed waistcoats were a necessity, with pockets – 'to hod me baccy' – and jackets were specially made for the workmen in fustian material, known locally as 'drab jackets', presumably because of their colour.

'Mole-skin' trousers were popular among navvies, and for rough work, because of their thick cotton content, which resembled a fine brown-grey leather similar to the colour of a moleskin.

Knee breeches were worn by farmers in conjunction with leather leggings tied round the leg by four straps. Longer trousers worn by labourers were kept out of the dirt with leather ankle straps or, in the case of the less fortunate, tied with a piece of 'Michael String' (or John Robert to West Cumbrians.)

Footwear was either strong leather boots or clogs, the latter having wooden soles, metal toe-caps and heel caulkers, shaped like a horse-shoe.

Sometimes, after the leather sole had worn down on his best boots, a thrifty farmer would go and get his boots 'clogged', thereby having a wooden sole put on to them. Gradually, however, leather boots and clogs gave way to rubber boots and the modern wellington. It is easier to clean, and cheaper, but is not as healthy on the feet!

Ladies' fashions have changed much more rapidly, to satisfy the feminine need for a new look. At the start of the 1930s some of the older ladies clung to the old-fashioned 'chemise', which was a long vest-like garment of pure cotton cut out in a utility square edged with lace, round neck and short sleeves.

Younger ladies preferred the waist length 'camisoles', a short shapeless top, without sleeves, again edged with lace and made of cotton. This was worn with long knee-length 'bloomers', with elasticated legs in winter or shorter wide-legged 'knickers', trimmed with lace, in summer. These were made of real or artificial silk, according to income.

The modern miss who 'burns her bra' as a sign of feminine freedom, is fifty years out of date in her ideas. The brassière was not worn by the Cumbrian ladies, all those years ago!

A fellman's footwear in the Lake District.
(*W. R. Mitchell*)

Summer coats were made of a thin-corded cotton material, known locally as 'repp', while winter skirts and dresses were of woven wool and summer dresses of cotton or silk material. There were no useful drip-dry fabrics, as we have to-day.

Our beautiful sheer nylon stockings and tights were still a thing of the future. In those days, legs were coyly covered in silk stockings in summer, and more discreetly by woollen stockings in winter; these were often hand-knitted (perhaps by grandma).

Bedtime clothes were just as practical and hard-wearing. The older ladies still wore calico nightdresses, with long sleeves and frilled bodices, while the younger ladies wrapped up in flannelette night-dresses in winter and more daring silk ones in summer.

Many an old country lady has sidled up to my mother, in the shop, and whispered: 'As t' a nice white nightie t' put by t' lay me oot in?' This was a morbid tradition among the older generation.

When the shop was first opened in the 1930s, my parents were puzzled by the request from one farm woman, for an old dress 'to go to scyal muck in'. They thought it was some town they had not heard of, but it turned out that she required a garment for manure-spreading in the fields! Now jeans, wellingtons and an old anorak are more likely to be purchased.

However, styles may come and styles may go, but the old earthy-coloured jackets go on for ever. One farmer summed it up with the words: 'Oot'll dyer – the coos don't care what colour jacket thoo has on!'

Anne V. Richardson (June 1981)

[29]

4

FARMING DAYS AND FARMING WAYS

A LAKELAND FARM

THE WINDOW framed a deep blue patch of Ullswater, cut in half by a dark red larch tree by the garden gate – and a background of Silver Hows and Place Fell. It seems years since July and the lazy hours we spent there, sun-drenched. Apple wood was thrown on the fire, a delicious scent, and chairs drawn up to the blaze. Two dogs and a kitten insinuated themselves to the best place on the fender, only backing out when the kettle began to splutter and boil over.

JESSICA LOFTHOUSE, in *Off to the Lakes*

Bowfell, from Stang End Farm, Little Langdale. (*S. Passmore*)

THERE WAS a small room used as the scullery, and beyond this was a door

through which they went into the kitchen-living-room. It was a fair-sized place; there was a large open fire-place in which burned a big fire of peat and wood. On the fire were a number of good-sized cooking pots, which gave out a very pleasant smell of food. An oaken table stood in the middle of the room and on it was a coarse but clean linen cloth. There were only two chairs used by the parents; the others sat upon a settle and on small stools.

O. S. MacDonell, in *George Ashbury* (1933)

I OBTAINED A labourer from an agricultural county, as spade husbandry was a thing unheard-of in my own neighbourhood. He brought his wife; and his wages were at first 12s. a week, out of which he paid the low rent of 1s. 6d. per week for his cottage; a model cottage which I built, with the cow-house adjoining, for £130. These stone dwellings last for ever,

and need few or no repairs, so that money is well invested in them.

HARRIET MARTINEAU (1861)

IN A DISTANT farmyard a dog barks. Now, a wild bee goes bazooning by me, pleased with the spoil he is carrying home from the flowers of Silverdale and, from yon brown upland, where the ploughman's loosened horses are wending slowly from the furrowed field, a clear jingle of chains comes through the still air. Here comes a brown-faced youth round the corner of the road, with a mash-tub in his arms. He goes whistling into the stable-yard close by. Now a coatless mason comes along, under the trees, on the cross-road. He has a dinner basket on his arm, and a tin can with a wire handle in his hand.

EDWIN WAUGH, in *Rambles in the Lake Country* (1882)

(*August 1952*)

MAN AND BEAST
A Short Story

I HAD JUST reached the point where Jenghiz Khan had detached 20,000 under Chepe Noyen to pursue and capture Mohammed, Sultan Shah of Khwarazm, when I heard a car come to a stop outside the gate. Laddie set up a furious barking, and the terrier, startled from her sleep before the fire, bounded to the door to add her contribution to the din. Emm looked up from her knitting.

'Who can that be?'

I shrugged my shoulders as I put *Jenghiz Khan* down. For a moment I resented the disturbance. The night was

cold; the kitchen bright and cosy, the fire glowing in the wide grate. As I opened the door Laddie's baying rose to a new crescendo as the visitor presumed to open the gate. I ordered the Border Collie back to his kennel, at which the stranger, unlatching the gate, came through into the yard. Against the frosty sky I saw the black shape of his car. Another figure followed.

'How do you do?' I invited.

'Fair,' came a voice rather hollow. 'Murdered wi' rewmaticks———.'

'Aye,' I sympathised, 'they're bad.'

'Couldn't do a thing baht a car, varry expensive, but what can Ah do? Got ter mak a livin' tha knows.' Pause. 'This is my lad – drives muh.'

'My lad' said 'How do' and thereafter held his peace.

The old man shuffled uneasily, and I swear I heard him creak.

'Ah'm telled tha's getten a geld beeast ter sell.'

'That's right.'

'Then let's hev a lewk at it – Ah could use one.'

Laddie was dancing a fandango close behind me and was whimpering to be unleashed, so I slipped him and he completed three circuits of the yard before one could have said 'knife'. He then fell in beside me as I led the way to the mistal.

As I opened the door a rush of warm air met us. I switched the light on, and the cows, as though worked on a string, turned their heads and regarded us with large disapproving eyes. They nevertheless continued their chewing.

I went to Molly, touched her with the toe of my boot, and she struggled to her feet.

'That's her,' I said.

Silence for some seconds, during which the gaunt old man swept the animal with critical eye, and 'my lad' chewed industriously on a piece of gum. His yellow hair stood upright as though in permanent fright. The father turning to his son observed:

'Nooan a reight lot a meyt on 'er— h'm? Hardly what Ah 'ooaped for.'

I endeavoured to explain – or rather remind him – that Molly was a milking cow, still milking, and that therefore shouldn't have a lot of 'meyt'.

'H'm – Aye –.' He coughed, and his chest wheezed not unmusically. 'Ah can see seven pahnd i' that beeast.' He said this as though he were bestowing the Legion of Honour on my breast.

'No more?' I suggested. (The average price of geld cows was twenty pounds.)

'Naw, no mooer.'

'Then we'd better go,' I said, and moved towards the switch.

'There might be eight,' as on an afterthought.

I agreed there might, and put my hand on the switch. We moved out into the crispness of the night; Laddie went to see if there were any rats in the barn. From the mistal door to the gate was about ten yards.

'An' what price dost ta put on it?'

'My price is nineteen pounds,' I stated quietly, 'and if I don't get nineteen pounds she'll stay where she is.'

'Nineteen pounds!' the old man repeated in a horror-stricken voice. I *believe* he reeled somewhat. Then, suddenly, and very crisply, he said:

'Twelve pahnd young man, an' shoo's not worth a penny mooer.'

'Nineteen pounds, Mister.'

Our progress to the gate was funereal. I was keen to follow Chepe Noyen and his 20,000 Mongols.

The gate was reached at length. Like a man announcing his own death sentence my customer, very slowly, announced:

'Young man, Ah'm gooin' ter give thee *fifteen pahnd* fer that beeast, an' that's mi' final offer.'

'She's right where she is,' I countered, one hand on the door knob.

'Reight, Jooer, start 'er up.' 'Jooer' passed through the gateway and clambered into the car.

The old man followed, his gait jerky and punctuated by deep gasps. As he opened the car door he turned to me, with an arm outstretched like one pleading for compassion croaked:

'Sixteen pahnd.'

'Nineteen pounds,' I reiterated like a record whose pin was stuck in a groove.

'My lad' had started the engine; it ticked over protestingly. Father gradually associated himself with the car's interior. Then his face appeared like lightning and he glared through the open window. The car began to move slowly forward.

'Eighteen pahnd,' he shrilled.

'It's yours,' I yelled, 'come inside.'

F. Marsden (December 1951)

CUMBRIAN HIRINGS

The heyday of the hirings was in the 19th century. A yeoman from the dales would offer a school-leaver £4 for the term.

WHITSUNTIDE AND Martinmas are names no longer of importance to the majority of countryfolk, but in the old days before the 1939–45 war they could be the highlights of life when the half-yearly hirings and fairs were held in Lakeland towns.

A few years after the end of the 1914–18 war I drove down from Brownrigg, the hill farm of S.H. Cole, to the Whitsuntide hirings at Wigton. My companion had yoked *Lady*, the Clydesdale mare, between the wooden shafts of the farm-cart, intending to fetch up some linseed cakes, a few rolls of fencing wire, some provisions and a few odds and ends you need on a farm.

The farm is in Caldbeck parish, nearly 1,000 feet above sea level. The land slopes down from the moor southwards to the beck that runs from Uldale Fells, through Caldbeck village to join up with the Caldew.

The cart rattled and bumped up the lonnen that led to the moor and main road on the top. On our left was a panoramic view of the hills, Knott and Great Calva, with the crest of Skiddaw showing behind the green and purple skyline. A soft, but exhilarating south-west breeze from the direction of Bassenthwaite wafted in the tang of the fells.

A carpet of tufted grass and heather

roots covered the moor outside the farm gate, and as we jogged along a pair of peewits, uttering plaintive, anxious cries, circled around hoping to lead us away from the nest they had built on the fell. The ground was dotted with Herdwick ewes and lambs, their fleeces displaying the red registration mark of the farm.

We reached the cross-roads where an ancient, weatherworn guide post pointed a wooden finger to show that Wigton lay to the left. Reaching the breast of Brocklebank we could see far ahead the gleaming waters of the Solway, sunlit, with the purple skyline of the Scottish hills, dominated by the dark blue mass of Criffell. Down on the green chequered Cumberland plain a haze of chimney smoke advertised the presence of Wigton.

Our cart clattered along the street to the square space beside the church where we were near the auction mart owned by Willie Hope, a Wigton character of that age. *Lady* was unyoked, hitched to the cart, and given a nosebag of oats to munch as I followed my cousin to the mart office.

He had some sheep and bullocks to sell. They had been driven down earlier by a lad from the village. The streets of the old town were becoming busy. Other farm carts and traps, conveying farmers and their wives, were converging on the town. Flocks of sheep and droves of cattle were pressing into the town and being crowded into pens near the mart. There was a cacophany of sound from baaing sheep, blaring bullocks, the stamp of hooves, the thud of drovers' sticks and the hoarse voices of cursing men.

Few cars were being driven on the roads then, but occasionally you might see a Ford flivver, the driver hooting wildly as he attempted to steer through the press of animals, men, women and children packed in the cobbled streets.

Already farm workers, young men, middle-aged men and boys were standing in groups along the street from the *Kildare Hotel* to the ornate fountain at the end of the street. All were waiting to be hired.

Brown-faced farmers from the hills and low country stood gossiping in twos and threes. Here and there were farmers' wives and daughters clad in black, voluminous skirts which extended down to their ankles. They had black bodices, and hats of black straw, with austere buns of hair at the back of their heads. Many of them were already around the stalls that street traders had set up near the fountain.

A farmer would spot a likely-looking lad, look him over and ask: 'Ist tha for hire, lad?'

'Aye, maister.'

The man would size him up as he asked where he had worked. He wanted a man that knew sheep, could milk and knew something about the breeding and rearing of cattle. He must be a horseman able to plough, harrow and handle a mower or reaper.

Tractors had not yet reached the dales in those days, and cars and lorries, used only on very large farms, were often considered luxuries.

If the man's replies satisfied him, the farmer might say: 'What's tha askin'?'

'Twenty-five pun'.'

'Naw.' The farmer shakes his head. 'Ah'll gie tha twenty.'

They would eventually settle half-way.

The term was 24–26 weeks, and the wages included a week's holiday at the end of each term, agreed at the time.

Even as late as 1949 there was a fair in Carlisle when I visited it on Saturday of

Whitsuntide of that year. It took place in the market-place before the modern congestion and one-way traffic systems altered the atmosphere which had existed for so long and which seemed to be watched over by the cross of stone with its sundial and curiously-carved lion defiantly looking towards Scotland.

Even this fair was a ghost of the former hirings which had taken place down the centuries since the break-up of the feudal system gave the worker the freedom to barter his labour for wages.

On that Whitsun Saturday there had been a few agreements made between farmers and workers. Labour was scarce, and few men and girls were seeking to be hired. Full employment in urban areas during the post-war period had stimulated the drift from the land that began after the war.

This encouraged farmers and their wives to pay higher rates for their hired men and girls so that they would not leave their employment. And the technical change in farming, with the increased use of machinery, especially tractors, was having its effect.

The Cumbrian farming community had poured into Carlisle to enjoy the fun of the fair, to shop and to meet their friends; the hirings were in the background, and may have been the last to be held here.

The heyday of the hirings was in the 19th century. Many a lad left home aged 14 to earn his living. He looked forward to being hired. He would don a brand new suit, and wear a green and red tie, presents from his parents, and tramp to the nearest market town. There he would stick a straw in his mouth and stand in the market-place, often a shy, lonely lad.

A yeoman from the dales would offer him £4 for the term. If he liked his 'place' he might remain there two or three years and become a good all-round worker – a 'fine lad'. At 17 he would go to the hirings as a man and obtain £12 to £14 a year. He would 'live in', sleep in the farmhouse and have his meals with the family.

Later, in the better times, he got up to £45 a year. If he was ambitious he would aim to get his own dale farm and get a wife to help him. Many did so, for the cost of living was cheap then and the men were thrifty.

Charles R. Denton (September 1971)

A CUMBRIAN FARMER'S BOY . . .

In 1912, when he was 13 years of age, John Hind left school and became a farmer's boy. This article, based on a conversation with Mr Hind, deals with his first year, culminating with the day he attended the Keswick hirings.

WHEN HE was 13 years of age, John Hind was summoned by the Borrowdale schoolmaster, who said: 'You can go to work. We can't do any more for you here.' And so it was that he became a farm lad at Grange

Farm, the home of Jim Coates, his wife Annie and their quite young family. He began work at Martinmas (11 November), hiring for six months at £4 10s. He left the farm after a year.

The Hind and Coates families knew each other well, living only two miles from each other. Jim Coates was already aware of the boy's capabilities. Tommy Graham, the Keswick carter, collected John's tin trunk on the next visit to Borrowdale, and it was delivered to Grange Farm. In the trunk were changes of clothes and a few possessions.

The sleeping quarters of the farm lad, above the kitchen, were approached by a ladder. So constricted was the space beneath the slanting roof that John could not open his trunk unless he first slid it towards the bed.

This bed was metal-framed, and a feather mattress was provided.

There was a skylight, to admit light, though in winter the farm lad went to bed with a candle as illumination. Little time was spent in the bedroom, and at 6.30 a.m. in summer – earlier, if there was anything special – and 7 a.m. in winter, the farmer roused him with a shout.

HOME-MADE SHIRT. And so he went forth, wearing an old jacket, a shirt made by his mother (which fastened at the back), corduroy trousers ordered from Mr Huggins, of Ambleside, who was a 'bag man', and clogs made by Ernie Plaskett of Rosthwaite (they cost 10s.). At that time, many farm men had sleeved waist-coats.

The first task was to milk the cattle, by hand, the milker sitting on a three-legged stool. In summer, the cattle must be rounded up for milking; in winter, a farm lad entered a shippon kept warm and humid by the animals. Grange Farm was

a 'small spot', and there might be only four cows to milk. Attending to one cow took from five to seven minutes.

The pail of milk was taken to the farm kitchen and handed over to Mrs Coates. She had not been reared in Borrowdale but she was familiar with farm work there, having been hired as a servant girl at Keswick some years before her marriage.

It was a woman's task to make butter, which was retailed locally. The milk was poured into bowls which were left on a slab of stone in the milk-house. (The slab was actually of slate, possibly from an old quarry on Castle Crag). The milk stood 'three meals' and then the cream was carefully removed, with the lady of the house using a section of a cow's horn. The 'blue milk' was fed to the young stock. Churning day was on Thursday.

'PODDISH' FOR BREAKFAST. When the cows had been milked, breakfast was enjoyed in the big, stoneflagged kitchen. The family and their farm lad sat down to a common table: a round table 'with one big shank'. There were forms, and chairs with rush-seats. Sides of bacon and hams hung from hooks driven in the ceiling.

The essential preliminary to breakfast was 'poddish', served stiff in a basin. Though Scots folk might object, the porridge was sprinkled with sugar, not salt. Afterwards there were rounds of bread with cheese, and tea – always plenty of tea – to drink.

Food on the farm, at that time, was plain but adequate. For 'ten o'clocks' in the field there was coffee from a blue enamel can and more bread and cheese. The family gathered at 12.30 p.m. for dinner, and supper was at 6.30 p.m. This often featured duck eggs, for the Coates kept a moderate number of ducks.

Buttermaking at Gatesgarth. (*S. H. Cole*)

The fell on which the Coates family ran their sheep was unhandy for the farm, being large and enclosed, lying off the Langstrath Valley. Here the farmer and his farm lad spent many hours repairing the old walls. They took with them some food, and also a kettle, which was set on a fire mainly composed of dry heather.

In winter, hay was taken to the sheep. The men set off from Grange Farm with a horse and cart load of hay, which was stored – through the kindness of a local farmer – in an outbuilding at Langstrath. Some of the hay was placed in large hessian sheets (each sheet was some eight feet square). 'You put your head between the knots and staggered up the fell.'

The sheepdogs were vital members of the farm staff. John Hind's dog, Bob, had been reared at the farm from a puppy and was by then half broken for work.

HIRING TUPS. Jim Coates was proud of the quality of his Herdwick tups, some of which were hired out for the season. He himself needed new tups for a 'change of blood'. Keswick had its tup fair, and farmers might afterwards be seen driving the tups down the roads to the various farms.

John Hind relates that when young sheep were sent away to be wintered on the Solway flats, the operation might take a fortnight, and farmers and their men stayed the night at different farms en route: places their families had patronised for many a year. As an example, some 600 hoggs were taken to Solway shore from Seathwaite Farm.

There was a lighter side to farm work. A farm lad did not hang about the house when his work was done for the day; he might retire to a local inn, to meet his friends, or go to a dance, such as one held regularly in Borrowdale School, before the Institute was built, or in a building near the *Royal Oak* which belonged to the 'Mechanics'. Partitions were removed to enlarge the area for dancing, a shrewd move, as most of the dances were lustily rendered.

For music, Joe Jenkinson played the fiddle and blind Joe Plaskett the concertina, which was usually referred to as the 'squeezebox'. It cost a shilling to attend a dance. If supper was provided the charge went up to 1s. 6d.

John Hind remembers the Christmas he spent at Grange Farm. There was a gargantuan meal to begin with – it was a much augmented breakfast – and for the mid-day meal the diners tucked in to goose. Raised pies, which contained mutton, were a feature of the feasting. At Christmas was the solemn opening up of the parlour, which otherwise was used only for special events like funerals.

On Sundays, he had spare time between morning and evening milkings. Clambering on to a cycle, he went to Borrowdale church and took his place in the choir. His family had long been connected with this place of worship.

A SECOND TERM. When the six months was up, the farm lad was paid for his efforts. He received sovereigns and was invited to stay on for another term, which he did, for £5.

He was taught how to plough, though the field was small and devoted to growing a few potatoes for the family needs. Jim Coates had only one horse; at ploughing time he borrowed another from his brother.

At the end of the year, John Hind left the farm, clutching a few more sovereigns. He had not been invited to stay. Grange Farm was small, capable only of providing employment for a lad. The farmer and his lad parted amicably, with the farmer promising to give him a good reference.

John Hind went to the hirings at Keswick. With perhaps fifty other young people – men and women – he stood in the Top Square while farmers approached them, demanding to know their age and accomplishments, and also the names of those who might provide information as to 'character'.

Some of the girls could demand more than the boys. Where there was a large farm, or a large family, they proved their worth at both indoor and outdoor tasks. They could help with the housework – and with the haymaking. They might be employed in buttermaking – or thinning out the turnips.

A farmer called Harrison, from near Keswick, approached John Hind. He questioned him carefully, and seemed satisfied to know that he sprang from a family he already knew moderately well. He agreed to the demand for £8 for the half-year.

Meanwhile, those lads and lasses who were unsuccessful at Keswick prepared to go to the hirings at Cockermouth on the Monday. And when the brief holiday was over, John Hind was soon hard at work, helping to milk forty cows twice a day. He was roused from his bed at 4 a.m., for the milk must be available for sale by 7 a.m.

He was not yet 15 years of age.

W. R. Mitchell (August 1981)

. . . AND GIRL

I WAS BORN in 1895 and started work on a farm at the age of 14 years. I was fortunate to have a tin box for my clothes. The family was very nice to work for, and my wage was £3 10s. for six months.

If we ran away or left of our own accord we got no wages. When term-time came, we were asked: 'Are you stopping on?'

My mother gave me 2s. 6d. when I went there. I still had that money at the end of term, as there was nowhere to spend it. I lived one mile from home and was allowed to go home for two hours every Sunday.

The missis taught me how to bake and wash. There was a backstone in the wash-house, where she made oatcake. I fed the fire underneath and she allowed me to roll one piece, but it was far too thick.

I had to get up at 5 o'clock in summer and 6 o'clock in winter. Every place was white-washed, and the spring cleaning was finished by Easter. Every drawer was emptied and scrubbed out, and all the beds were brought outside and brushed and beaten. Even the baking tins were boiled and scoured, also the milking cans and calf buckets were scoured with silver sand.

There were five horses on the farm and when the farmer and his wife went to Kendal market every Saturday, they set off at 7.30 a.m. and arrived back about 3 p.m. Everything was always up to time.

It was a real treat to see all the lovely butter-boxes in the market; they were all as white as snow.

I always looked forward to threshing time. The washing boiler was used for fruit puddings and the hot pots were cooked in the large oven in the kitchen. The menfolk went to other farms to help out when the thresher went there. The owner of the machine was called Chapelow; I think he came from Under-barrow.

The day before Whit Saturday or Martinmas Saturday was called Long Friday. On Whit Saturday and Martinmas Saturday we were paid in gold sovereigns. I stayed eighteen months and then went to private service, but when I look back over the years I enjoyed the farm.

Private service was exactly like the serial *Upstairs, Downstairs*. The newspapers used to come by post with wrappers on them. The butler or head parlourmaid ironed them before the master of the house saw them.

There were prayers every night and morning and my wages were never more than 12s. 0d. a week until I left to get married.

I well remember the flood in the early 1900s. My father was a qualified butcher and went to the flooded farms and, with other men, skinned 300 sheep that had been drowned. My father, whose name was T. Firth, was very well-known around the countryside. He went to farms and slaughtered their pigs, being paid 2s. 0d. for one and 3s. 6d. for two.

When I was at school, we all lined up in the yard on Oak Bob Day and sang as the teacher came up the drive. Anyone who had no oak leaves was in for a smack from nettles.

On Ascension Day we had a holiday. The custom then was Spanish Water. We could get enough hard Spanish for ½d. to fill a bottle. We broke it into small pieces and filled a bottle of water, put the Spanish in and kept shaking it up.

A. Ferguson (May 1974)

Farmhouse Humour

LITTLE GEORGE, aged six, came from an irreligious Cumbrian household, and preferred to spend as much time as possible at a nearby farm. These farmers were staunch Methodists, and one day they invited George to stay for his dinner. The steaming plates were set before them, and heads bent to murmur the customary grace. Mystified, George eyed the proceedings, then asked in a

small gruff voice, 'What are yer aw talken to yer puddings for?'

(1958)

A Carlisle man went to a village 'local', leaving it in the company of a farmer. There was a weird scream out of the night and the city man jumped.

'What was that?' he gasped.

'An owl,' said the farmer.

'Yes, I know. But what was 'owling?'

J. T. S., Carlisle. (1971)

Ploughing team on Slate Fell, near Cockermouth, 1933. (*Colin Denwood*)

HARVESTING IN THE THIRTIES

The smell of newly-cut corn mingled with the aroma of hot tea or home-baked bread. In hot weather, there was also the pungent odour of horses.

SOME OLDER Cumbrians look back with nostalgia to the corn-harvesting of the 1930s. The craftsmanship of those days was superior to the speedy mechanisation of today's methods.

As the tractor and the combine harvester were late arrivals to the Lake District, the harvesting of the oats, barley or wheat had to be achieved the hard way. The weather was more important then than it is today. Harvesting took place over a longer period, and rarely was there ideal weather for the whole project.

Around August, weather permitting, the farmland of the valleys and the coastal plain were aglow with small square or rectangular fields of golden corn. Harvest-time had come. The crop was ready for the first onslaught of the harvesters. The latter were plenty in number as the recession of that time left plenty of willing and spare hands for the work.

Industrious farmers would already have their binders in good working order. These binders were the simple machines used for cutting the crop. The blades were sharpened and the twine fixed ready to bind the sheaves of corn once they were cut. Before the binder could begin its work, strong supple-limbed young men or women would 'open-out' the field ready for cutting.

Opening-out a field was done by scything round the perimeter of the crop in order to make room for the binder and its team of horses. Sometimes three or more horses were used instead of just two.

Most farms had plenty of work horses in the thirties. They could almost equal the dog for their capabilities on the farm. Such animals were well treated and shown great respect. They were fed and rested at specific times of the day.

Once the opening-out was finished, the harvesting began in earnest. The binder cut and bound the sheaves – or 'shavves' as the local people called them – which were stooked. Damp crops could rot when stacked. In the farming community there was much vying as to who was progressing best. Competition was the order of the day.

Next came the 'housing' or collecting of the crop. The making of stacks was an art. Any farmer who was adept at the job was respected by all who were attached to farming in any way. A special pattern had to be followed in order to achieve a good-shaped stack. Some were round, resembling the shape of a cob-loaf. Others were oblong shaped and resembled straw houses. A neat cluster of corn stacks was a lovely sight.

The owner of a mobile thresher was a man in much demand in the thirties. The farmer who had to depend on the travelling thresher would erect his stacks in an area big enough to accommodate this machine when it came. Those farmers lucky enough to have their own thresher would have their stacks in the yard. Another method of housing the crop was to store it in a Dutch barn, a large ventilated building often near the farm.

If the weather was sunny and slightly breezy the whole harvest could be

A hand-driven threshing machine, found at a farm in the Whicham Valley, under Black Combe.
Previously, the hand flail had been used.

[42]

Building a stack, Strawberry Howe Farm, Cockermouth, circa 1935. (*Colin Denwood*)

gathered in the short time of two or three weeks. Bad conditions resulted in crops lying in the fields even in October or later. Then the crop would look forlorn and weather-beaten.

There are happy memories such as the smell of the newly-cut corn mingled with the aroma of hot tea or home-baked bread. Older farmers remember, too, the pungent odour of the horses and the sweating men, especially if the weather was hot.

Once the final sheaf of corn was stacked away, and the stacks themselves covered by a special cover or thatch, the farmer and his family could relax a little. There was always something to do, but the hassle of the gathering of the harvest was over.

Harvest Festivals and Harvest Suppers were a happy culmination of the year's work. Many a spring wedding was planned at a Harvest Dance!

(*June 1984*)

[43]

5

THE SHEPHERD AND HIS FLOCK

A WARRIOR BREED

THE LITTLE Herdwick is in some respects the most interesting breed of all. There is the romantic legend of its originating from the sheep survivors of a wrecked galleon of old Spain. It has been said to be of Scandinavian origin. It is reputed like members of a certain Highland clan, to possess an extra rib. Lambs have dark faces that turn white with maturity. The Herdwick is a true hill breed, white-faced, horns on ram only, with rough fleece of carpet-wool class, the body deep and round. Wallace said of the Herdwick that it 'is the hardiest of all British mountain sheep'.

ALLAN FRASER, in *Sheep Husbandry* (1949)

THESE SHEEP are unique in many ways. The word 'herdwick', by its terminative, suggests a warrior breed. These hardy warriors, it is believed, came over origin-ally to our hills with human warriors of as hardy a make, the Norsemen from over the foam, and by the ruffs of hair upon their necks and the shape of their roman noses, were evidently intended to fend for themselves in snowy places, where grass was scarce.

CANON H. D. RAWNSLEY (1911)

HERDWICK sheep-farming is the basic industry of the Lake District; the whole economy of local agriculture depends upon the Herdwick sheep. All who walk the fells have their attention caught by the Herdwick ewes – by their nimbleness of foot, their heavy jackets, their efficient concern for the lamb 'at foot', and the sneeze, half friendly, half contemptuous, with which they greet the passer-by in lonely places.

H. H. SYMONDS (1937)

THE HERDWICK is a true Lakelander. Take it away from its native fells and sheep-runs and it refuses to live. Even the mountains of North Wales failed to sus-

tain Herdwicks sent there as an experiment, and when, following the first world war, sheep from the Lakes were taken to the Ardennes country of Belgium every one perished in a short space of time.

SYDNEY MOORHOUSE

AS NOVEMBER advances the sheep farmer of the Westmorland dales is faced with the difficult question of when to bring his flock down from the fells. So long as fair weather lasts the sheep find sufficient sustenance on the higher ground, but an untoward rainstorm, followed by dense mists, or an early snowstorm, always involves great hardships. On the other hand, it is essential that the stock should be kept on the hills till forced to retire, as under ordinary conditions it is impossible for the flock-owner to accumulate sufficient forage to last the sheep through a long winter.

W. T. PALMER, in *Lake Country Rambles* (1902)

(*November 1952*)

JOSEPH GREGG TALKS ABOUT HERDWICKS

Joseph Gregg of Great Langdale spent a long working life among the distinctive sheep of Lakeland. He left school at 13, 'and maybe did more work between 9 and 13 than a lot of folk do in a lifetime now.' In April 1974, at the age of 81, he was still working among Herdwicks in summer. He talked to Cumbria *about some of his experiences.*

MY MOTHER was a Bland of Flake Howe, Mardale, which is now under water. Manchester built a reservoir there. I went to the Mardale Shepherd's Meet for a few years before the First World War, driving sheep from Kentmere.

I've fetched tups from Eskdale Show, some to Mardale and some to Longsleddale, also from Keswick. I did a fair bit of droving at one time. We helped one another in those days, and I drove tups back for quite a few farmers.

Tups were hired, of course. You could get a good tup for £1, but now they ask you a fairish price. A tup with a good character will cost £5 for the season.

Eskdale Show was always the last Saturday in September (it used to be on a Friday). Keswick Back End Fair was always on the first Saturday in October. Tups were taken back to Eskdale for the first Friday in May, and to Keswick on the nearest Thursday to the 20th. And they had to be returned in good condition.

I graded Herdwick ewes in 1952, following a good spring and summer, and thirty of them averaged ł cwt. Some had suckled two lambs on the fells. A couple of gimmer lambs won at Smithfield last back-end and their live weights averaged 170 lb. I've known a hogg weigh 184 lb., though it was brought up as a pet, being run on only the best land and pinching what it could from the farmyard!

It's said that a lot of Herdwick wool is made into carpets, but you could get a

smart Herdwick cloth suit. It has only one fault – it lasts too long!

One year I got 8 lb. of wool off a sheep and sent the wool to a firm in the north that specialises in making up suits. It was as good as a raincoat.

One day I walked from Eskdale to get the morning bus at Elterwater. When I'd left the bus I'd to walk over Wrynose and Hardknott passes. It was raining all the time, but at the end of the walk I took off that Herdwick suit and just shook it. It was as dry as when I set off!

We don't want sheep with soft wool in the Lake District. And we don't want it too hard. A sheep should have a decent 'jacket' with a bit o' waistcoat in it to keep the storm out.

A Herdwick ewe clips an average of 3½ lb. through, though it depends on the sort of winter the sheep's gone through. After a good winter you might get more than 3½ lb.

A Herdwick will stand a fair amount of weather. And so does a sheep farmer! On 27 March 1919, I was helping to put some gaps up (we had to carry stones a long way up the fell before we could start walling) and we decided to have dinner. We sat down to have our packed meals.

There wasn't a cloud in the sky – you couldn't have had a finer March day – but the sheep started moving down, and they were all bleating. It was a sign of a storm not far away.

By the time we had finished dinner, it was snowing, out of a blue sky it seemed. Before we got home it had put down six or seven inches of snow and was blowing it.

OPPOSITE
Tommy Teesdale, a Patterdale farmer, carries twin lambs, newcomers to his large Herdwick flock. The hill lambing season can extend into May. (*Tom Parker*)

We'd not been long at home when we had to turn out with a dog (one that was not reputed to do good work, but was first-rate at finding sheep) and we were pulling animals out of the drifts.

On 12 May that year, one of our neighbours went to his allotment with the sheep. And he found some animals buried but still alive.

When I was a nipper, I watched men salve Herdwick sheep. Every farm had a salving house and salving would go on after dark, by lamplight. We didn't talk about eight hour days then, you know!

Muther-Lorn Lamb

A new-born lamb's bleatin' doon
wheer t'beck
Tak's a sudden bend under t'fold;
Aa! Jem, its wail like a starvin' wean's
Mak's my heart turn steean-cold.

Nae woman 'ats lost a weeny bairn
Can bear sike a lile sad cry!
·It mun be nigh t'fold wheer t'roans grow,
Wheer i' t'summer, Sled syke runs dry.

Happen its muther is lyin' rigged
Or happen she's nigh t'far-end;
Jem lad, it's bleatin' is more nor I
Can thole; it's at t'river bend.

Heart's wae! but our yan should be
waulin' like yon;
Let's gae to Sled syke an' we'll finnd
Lorn cratur 'an bring it back tiv
our hearth
Safe fra' t'bitter east wind.

DOROTHY UNA RATCLIFFE
(February, 1953)

[47]

A sheep-salver, pictured in 1880. The salve – a mixture of grease and tar, was applied to the skin of a sheep, the wool having been parted or 'shedded', and a good salver could complete a single sheep in about an hour. The whole flock had to be salved by tupping time.

Salve was made out of so much tar and mutton fat. The mutton fat was fetched to the boil in a large boiler, and the tar was put in it. You had to see there was no splashing, or you'd burn the place down. It was then ladled into barrels. Salving time was generally November. Doing this work left the hands black and greasy.

Herdwick flesh is the best you can taste. Particularly if the sheep is fat off the fell. Many a Lakeland family lived off sheep; they had their own meat and their own bacon.

My mother made a favourite dish of ours with bits of fatty Herdwick mutton. It was called sweet pie. We always had it at Christmas, and we didn't want much at a time. It's the best pie I've ever tasted. Mother used a big dish, and she put a thin crust over the pie.

It's sad to see so much good sheep and good cow land taken over by forestry. It's sad to see fewer Herdwicks.

I once did a lot of work for Mrs Heelis (Beatrix Potter, you know), who loved Herdwicks. I helped her in March 1919, when I came out of the Army.

I sometimes wonder what she would think of the present situation.

(April 1974)

IT'S CLIPPING TIME IN LAKELAND

THE SHEPHERD'S year creeps on apace. By now this season's lambs are no longer the white-coated, fluffy creatures of a few weeks ago. Days spent on the fells have brought some of the peat to stain their fleeces. The older sheep, too, are already looking hot and uncomfortable in their thick wool coats, now to be lost as the greatest event of the fell farmers' summer draws near.

The time of the annual sheep clip – the boon clip as they still call it in Cumberland – is an occasion that looms large in the Lakeland farming calendar, for the profit from the fleeces is still the most important item in the fell farmer's economic system. From the fells and heights away 'back o' Skiddaw', where John Peel hunted 150 years ago and where John Richardson and C. N. de Courcy-Parry still give chase to the fox today, to the grimmer heights of Western Cumberland, from the more urbane heights above the wide valley of the Eden to the wooded fells of the old Hundred of Furness, where the monks of old had their sheep-runs, there is work to be done in bringing the flocks down from the hills and removing the valuable fleeces.

Lakeland sheep runs are no small affairs. They extend over acres of rough fell country and reach to the skyline of the highest hills. There are places where the sheep population can be assessed in acres to the sheep rather than the other way round. But the great gatherings for clipping are times for co-operation. The farmers of one dale combine and the flocks of a whole fell are brought down in one day and sorted out when they reach the valley.

The work can be strenuous on occasion, but well-trained dogs reduce some of the ardour. Indeed, the dogs are entrusted with clearing the higher parts of the fell and, often enough, they will even cross the watershed and bring back odd sheep that have strayed towards the next valley.

Sheep dogs are, of course, trained to work the sheep from above, so that time has developed a parallel tendency in the sheep to move downhill as they hear the collies' approach. Hence those that have crossed the ridge might easily, were it not for the intelligence of the dogs, make down to the wrong dale.

There are few workers who can maintain a more complete silence than the sheep dog, and as long as things are proceeding normally only the bleating of the sheep and the occasional call of some bird will break the silence of the fells. Any mishap, however, will soon cause the collie to give mouth. Some sheep might have stumbled into a gully and be 'cast' on its back, and the dogs give news of their find. Sometimes, the shepherd will arrive in time to prevent disaster; on other occasions, the sheep will have perished and raven or carrion crow begun the work of complete destruction.

Once the sheep are down, they are sorted and taken to the farms of their various owners, and now it is a question of getting them back on the fells as soon as possible. The amount of pasture round a Lakeland farm is limited and has probably been used for the lambing ewes. Now it needs as little grazing as possible so that it can be ready for next winter when, once more, the breeding flock will be wintered there.

In clipping, as in so many other things connected with hill sheep farming, a deal depends on the weather. A spell of rain or drenching mist immediately preceding the clip means clogged fleeces and things are difficult for the shearers. Under ideal conditions, however, it takes little time to deal with each animal and some of the experts, like Jack Bland, the ex-postman of Kentmere, can dispose of a sheep in five minutes or so. Even with such men as

these doing the work, clipping is a full day's job, especially on the larger farms where something like a thousand animals have to be dealt with. The clipping machine is virtually unknown on the Lakeland hill farms and all the work is done by hand – and the men who do it are adamant that the result is much better.

Clipping is more than a task for the regular farm workers, and there are many folk whose daily work takes them away from sheep that are expert when it comes to handling the shears. These rarely miss a clipping, and give their help freely, their reward coming when the flock has been dealt with and the tables literally groan with food. Even in these days of austerity I have seen mountains of food miraculously make their way on to the tables and disappear in double-quick time. Some of the older hands have recalled the days when they danced through the night and then went on to the next clipping.

The old spirit of co-operation among farmers and helpers still remains. One man's clipping immediately follows his neighbour's, so that the helpers are able to spend two or more days at consecutive clips in the same dale. The dates of the various clips never change. In fact, in the calendar of a Lakeland dale clipping dates are just as important as those of the great sports meetings or even the recognised Bank Holidays.

While clipping is the most important item of the day, the opportunity is taken of marking the sheep while they are down from the fells and as soon as the fleeces have been removed. Stripes, rough blotches, or 'pops' as they are called locally, and initials are marked on the fleeces by red ruddle or tar, and although the use of these has often been criticised by the wool brokers who find it somewhat difficult to remove the substance from the washed wool, it is difficult to see what else could be done. Indeed, the majority of farmers declare that they would rather take a lower price for their wool than run the risk of losing their sheep.

In the fields outside the clipping yard, the lambs have been left to their own devices, but when the last fleece has been removed the yard gates are opened, and there is a frantic rush of the ewes to re-unite with their offspring. For a time chaos reigns. Lambs dash here and there; ewes sniff at first one and then the other, rejecting many until they find their own. The confusion among the lambs is greater.

Mother may recognise her own youngster by the smell, but her own appearance has changed so much that often enough recognition is not mutual and it takes time to sort the whole business out.

While family re-unions are taking place in the fields outside, the clippers are busy cleaning their shears and the womenfolk are rolling the fleeces into compact bales. Time was when the brokers' represent-atives came along and bargained on the spot, but now the bales are sent direct to Bradford and Carlisle where, in the autumn, the great wool sales will take place.

Sydney Moorhouse (July 1952)

The Flockmaster's World

A sheepman from Westmorland looked over the promenade at Morecambe when the tide was high and remarked: 'If yon sea were nobbut grass, thou could git a thumping lot o' sheep on it.'

A farmer stared critically at a baby for three minutes, then asked: 'Is't a tup or a gimmer?'

The sign at the roadside proclaimed: 'Beware of sheep'. Said an American visitor to a local farmer: 'Gee, you must have some mighty fierce sheep in these parts.'

The farm lad, asked to count the sheep, said: 'There's either 286, 287 or 288.' 'Don't worry about it,' replied the farmer. 'There should only be 280.'

(October 1963)

Dipping at Loweswater.

[51]

T'OWD DAYS

IN THE PAST as soon as the back-end came, shepherds began to think of 'salving' their flocks against the dreaded scourge of scab. The discovery of effective sheep dips in the early part of this century and the compulsory dipping of sheep, almost eradicated the scourge.

The mite that causes the disease is persistent and resistant. Now and again there still is an isolated outbreak of scab. 'Saving the ship for a ha'porth of tar' is a misquotation. It originated as 'Saving the sheep . . .', not ship.

For centuries salving, the only known safeguard, was universally practised, for the losses due to the affection were serious. The only definite figures we have are from the records of a group of manors of Merton College, Oxford. These show that in the four year period from 1333–1336 the losses from 'scab' and the 'rot'

Sheep shearing at Fell Foot, Little Langdale.

were 20 per cent of the flock. 'Rot' was probably fluke.

John Faulder, for many years head shepherd for the Leconfield estate flock of sheep on Skiddaw once told me rather sadly: 'Ah don't think there'll be many left as can mak' a shed now.' With amazing dexterity he parted the wool the length of the sheep, and he dipped his first finger into the salve in his salve bowl. With a flick up the 'shed', he applied the salve. The operation was done over every inch of the sheep.

Eighty years ago he was one of many who went round in salving gangs. They received fourpence a sheep and a good man could do no more than twenty in a day. The salve was a mixture of rancid butter and tar.

An old advertisement of 1869 reads: 'To agriculturalists, etc. Christopher Mayson, Seedsman, Tallow Chandler, Dealer in Butter and Tar, Market Place,

Cockermouth. Always on hand for the season. Butter and Tar Skinner's grease.' The latter made the salve set after it had been mixed hot.

Tar was called 'the tailor's aggravation'. It made the cloth hard and nearly waterproof. The fell and hill sheep were proofed against the winter storms, and hill shepherds were reticent to accept dipping as a substitute for salving.

By 1850, efforts were being made by the south country shepherds to get rid of the staining effects of tar upon their finer wools. Fluid dips were evolved. The hill men accepted these only when they were made compulsory at the turn of the century.

Tar did preserve the wool. I have a 'hodden grey' overcoat, the 'coat so gray' of the song *John Peel*. The coat was worn by a relative in London for sixty years. Now aged over 100 years, it is as sturdy as ever.

S. H. Cole (November, 1977)

HERDWICK 'TIPS' FOR HIRE

Cumbria *joins the Lakeland flockmasters round the pens at Eskdale Show, known as the* 'Herdwick Royal'.

Whoo's ta gooing on today? Hesta any
tips to part wid?
Well, ev yan or two.
This 'esn't mich coat on it.
It's reight enuff.
Whoo mich ista wanting fer it?
Thirty bob.
Ah's gooing to gie thee twenty five bob.
Split it.
Reight.

THIS CONVERSATION, with variants, took place a score and more times at Bridge End, Boot, when the Eskdale Show brought flockmasters from all over the Lake District together to talk about Herdwicks.

Business blends with pleasure at Eshd'l. Before the foot races are run, and the hound trails get under way; before, indeed, there are many visitors to the tents where produce and handicrafts are neatly arranged, there are hours of judging and bargaining around the pens of sheep – pens which, I was fascinated to see, are labelled with the names of farmers and not the numbers which are commonplace at most events.

Eshd'l, in fact, is a show held at the threshold of another farming year where Herdwick tups – locally known as 'tips' – are hired out for the winter. There is another event here in May when they are returned and the monetary settlements are made. The hire charge is usually between 25s. and 30s. It has not varied much during the last decade or so.

A tup which comes on to the market might bring between £10 and £30. Some have been known to cost £40. Outright sale is still exceptional. The Herdwick breed is probably the last where hiring is commonplace. There is the curious situation that to ensure a regular change of blood in a comparatively small and self-contained population of sheep, a Herdwick flockmaster raises tups that will benefit the flocks of other men.

'We like to see a bright-eyed sheep,' said the tall lean farmer, who was clad in his best 'selling off' suit and carried an ornate crook which had never seen service on the fells. He pointed out a good example. A tup was doing its best to break through into the next pen.

This was not carried out in a frenzy of heated destruction, but slowly, thoughtfully, systematically. The tup charged, the pen shook and creaked. It backed again, and stood glaring at another tup beyond the barrier. A few minutes later, it charged again, and the wood splintered. More thought. Another charge. The wood gave away. The tup allowed a slight expression of satisfaction to flicker across its hoary white face. It did not seem to be troubled by a headache.

'They stands up to some awful battles in t' mating season,' I heard. 'They backs away and meets full smack with their heads. Sometimes kill each other. Brokken necks, or feaster o' t' head when one's punctured an' t'germs gets in.'

Farmers were breaking packets of reddish powder, letting the powder down with a light oil, and applying the mixture to the coarse fleeces of their Herdwicks, the result being a rusty tinge which has no practical purpose, but reputedly gives the sheep a better appearance. I asked several farmers why it was carried out. They replied that it has always been done. 'It's just same as when ladies daub themselves up,' one remarked. 'It improves t'look of 'em.'

A young farmer confirmed that there was no practical benefit in applying the dye, and added: 'One might argue that it was the reverse. If wool has too much colour there could be a reduction in the payment made by the Wool Board. At the moment it has not reached those proportions, but it could.' I noticed from the programme that the National Trust had offered a prize for one of the sheep classes, the emphasis being on 'natural colour.'

The faces and legs of the Herdwicks were being washed with detergents or soap. I admired the strong, bony well covered legs of the tups, and was told that when a lad visited Eskdale from the country of the Swaledale sheep, he looked for a long time at a Herdwick tup and then said, with wonderment: 'Yon tewp's getten booits on.'

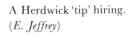

A Herdwick 'tip' hiring.
(E. Jeffrey)

Mr E. Tyson's ram, Dick's Permission, winning the Gosforth show championship for the third successive year. (*Ivor Nicholas*)

Though genetically identical there are some noticeable differences between the tups which appear at the shows and which command the keenest attention at hiring time, and those tups which live on the fells, with little limelight. The best tups are specially fed or given improved grazing so that their full potential is brought out.

Farmers watch the progress of these outstanding tups from the lamb stage right up to their time of greatest utility. Many of those on view at the Eskdale show were already 'spoken for', being brought along to be picked up at this convenient place. There is an old tradition by which some farmers used to make the rounds of the farms where suitable tups were bred, on the Sunday before the Eskdale Show. It became known as Tup Sunday, but it is not observed much today.

About twenty years ago the *Woolpack Inn* was the venue of the dale show. I heard that 'mine host' used to riddle the sand strewn on the floor before throwing it away. It might contain some lost sovereigns! Among the crowds at this year's events were men who remembered when sheep were walked here from all parts of the Lake District, some men spending three, four or more days away from home. Occasionally a man was out and about for a fortnight. 'We started off travelling at about four miles an hour, but it was down to one mile an hour towards the end,' one veteran told me.

Wasdale sheep came over Burnmoor. Those from Langdale used the great passes of Wrynose and Hardknott. Broughton stock walked across Birker Moor. As I chatted with William Wilson, better known as Herdwick Billy, he recalled his days in Wasdale, and said that on the morning of Eskdale Show he would be out of bed about 4.30 a.m. to complete the farm jobs before driving stock across the moor. It was rarely that he reached home again the same day. Joe Teasdale, of Caldbeck, brought a tup to Eskdale in a horse-drawn cart.

The pens are put up by Committee members several days before the show, and those accommodating tups for hire or sale are charged for at the rate of 10s. for every 20 tups.

I was astonished at the number of sheep which grind their teeth, and asked a farmer about it. 'It's just because they're standing idle in pens. They've nowt to do so they grind their teeth a bit.'

This farmer had just been admiring a tup with spirit (reflected in the way it rattled the pen with its head), and he told me some of the points to be taken into account when 'kenning' a Herdwick tup. A good head was important. The face should be white and hairy and the nose broad. The back should be 'good and strong', with a coat well suited to turning the storms.

Horns, I gathered, were not all that important, though some 'nice horns helps them a bit.' A first prize card had just been handed to an aged ram which had only 'bits o' stumps.' It was a 'cowed' ram. Some 'tips' sheep never develop horns and are known as 'cowies.'

In these days the best tups are registered and their pedigrees are carefully noted. They are not likely to be lost for long if they wander away from their winter quarters. If a tup dies, then there is usually no come back on the part of the owner. The hirer must keep a tup in quality and condition during the winter, for the sake of future relationships with his farming friends and also with the hope of winning a prize at Eskdale in May with the best wintered animal.

To the farmers round the pens, these impressive animals had personality, each being as distinguishable from the others as members of their own family. 'Herdwicks are naturally good and quiet,' one man told me. 'But tips vary. Ower there's a real nettled one, and here's a tip 'at's soft. Looks a bit slow. We like to see 'em sharp in the eye.'

By now the tups which were bunched together on the showfield at Bridge End, are scattered throughout the Lake District, each attending to fifty or sixty ewes.

W. R. Mitchell (December, 1963)

Sheep's Eye View

'So much for low flying jets keeping to 250 feet.'

A SHEEP'S EYE VIEW

A blustery, shivery Lakeland night and a small flock of sheep make their way down the fellside to the farmhouse. The leader of this woolly gang has discovered that the curtains are not drawn in the parlour and it's possible to peer in through the window and watch the television. It's the programme that intrigues them most – 'One Man and His Dog'.

'What sickens me about this charade,' ruminates an elderly ewe, 'is that it's the dogs that get all the publicity. The commentary is all about Shep and Jesse and Bob and Fred. The sheep get no credit at all and yet, to my certain knowledge, that's old Myrtle from Borrowdale refusing to go in the pen again . . .'

That's the sort of fleecy fantasy I spin to myself when I'm embarked in producing another skein of 'Sheep's Eye View' cartoons. Seven books and a couple of thousand newspaper cartoons later and I realise that I've been drawing these things for ten years.

It started when I read in a trade magazine that a new weekly paper was to be launched in Lakeland. I approached the editor to ask if he'd be interested in using a topical cartoon in each issue. 'We'd already thought about that,' he said. 'Can you draw sheep?' Although the real answer was 'No' I responded in the affirmative and set about learning a bit about the animals that are so much a part of Lakeland life.

It seemed to me the answer was to humanise them and let them comment on the foibles and follies of us mortals. And, then, why not take it a step further and, instead of confining their existence to the fields and fells, let them pop into town,

Barry Knowles with his sketch pad.

shop at the Co-op, drop in to the local and queue at the post office? Unlikely as the premise was, 'Sheep's Eye View' proved popular.

POSTBAG. A postbag of letters started arriving at the newspaper office weekly. Correspondence from clergy assuming I was trying to put over a religious message, irate comments from shepherds saying that I was putting my make-believe characters through the sheep dip in the wrong month. A nice old farmer from Coniston told me I'd got the phases of the moon all cockeyed and feeding blocks were not at all as I'd drawn them.

I was invited to the wonderful Vale of Rydal sheepdog trials and my hosts pointed out that the hour upon hour of lashing rain was all part of the day's entertainment. It's easy to see the popularity of this pursuit. It combines serious intent, sheer excellence and a great deal of high comedy. I witnessed a wonderful few minutes of canine incompetence when a much-fancied dog couldn't get his act together at all and managed to drive his foolish flock off the showfield and into the main car park where they gambolled about among the Fortnums picnic hampers and sandwich remains.

When the cartoon feature had been running for a year it was decided to foist on the public an annual collection of drawings and the publisher suggested that on the back cover it would be a jolly wheeze to have me standing in a flock of sheep, pretending to draw them. The Herdwicks thought otherwise and refused to take part in any of this journalistic nonsense.

My photographer friend Tom came up with a solution. 'Why not draw some big cartoon sheep on pieces of card and we'll go to a field and do a picture as pure fantasy?' That's what happened – we headed to an Ambleside fellside laden with cut-outs, propped them up in a field and, of course, real sheep then started lolloping over to have a look.

The following year we did the picture on, for some reason, a Windermere steamer. Another day of lashing rain and it was almost impossible to explain to the curious passengers and crew what two lunatics with cardboard sheep were doing getting soaking wet through on the deck of the 'Swan'.

PROPHETIC. It's odd how many of the 'Sheep's Eye View' cartoons have, in later years, become a reality. I did a sequence of drawings about low-flying jets destroying the drystone walls. That, regrettably, has become a fact. More unlikely was when I formed four of my little cartoon mates into a pop group called 'The Bleatles'. Three years later

there appeared in the charts a record by 'singing' sheep called 'The Bleatles'.

When asked to explain the popularity of 'Sheep's Eye View' I can only guess it is because the cartoonist has a great deal of freedom denied to many other communicators. He can comment wildly on absolutely anything as long as the views are broadcast by his characters.

I'll explain that Cumbria is faced today with more troubles and controversy than probably any other area of the country. Overcrowding, spoliation of the landscape, the proliferation of tourist entrapment areas, timeshare complexes springing up on every vacant acre, the pollution of the sea, worries about nuclear power plants, aircraft noise, and can the locals afford to live here any more? A hundred other issues – all a great worry.

The use of a cast of barmy sheep making comment and reacting to all these matters – in an idiosyncratic and perhaps even lunatic way, can take the edge off things and, hopefully, raise a smile. It also means I can say whatever I want and pretend it's not me at all but 'Herd and Wick and the Swaledale gang' who are creating. I shouldn't have told you that.

A councillor friend of mine tells me that he recently attended a committee meeting and the first subject on the agenda was 'What are we going to do about these flocks of sheep coming down off the fells and demolishing the council house gardens?' My friend admits that he closed his eyes for a few moments (an established procedure at council meetings) and when he awoke, he stood and announced with confidence 'I've got the answer – we build cattle grids!' This was met with stunned silence until the chairman unravelled the trouble and said 'I think the councillor is still referring to the sheep menace. We have in fact now moved on to another item – the problem of providing a new ladies' loo in Coniston.'

Yes, the sheep books will continue, as long as people enjoy them and, as you've probably noticed, they've finally found their way into the august pages of *Cumbria* where they'll be grazing till somebody shoos them away.

Barry Knowles (December 1988)

A Shepherd and his Dog

Yonder a shepherd stands, a sturdy man,
With grizzled head and weather-beaten face.
His eyes, far-seeing, through all seasons scan
The fells, where roam his sheep, a hardy race.
They are his life: unceasing is his care
For them in lowland pastures, and at need
He climbs steep frowning crags and
    hill-sides bare
For them. Good shepherd he, a friend indeed.

Yonder his collie stands, poised on tip-toe,
Eyes riveted upon her master's face;
Impatient for the sign that bids her go,
And sends her down the field with
    sinuous grace.
A lovely creature she, his faithful friend,
Bright eyed, intelligent, loyal, and wise;
Dauntless, she'll follow him to the world's
    end,
Content to serve him till the day she dies.

The shepherd and his dog are closely bound:
Two beings they, with but a single heart.
Day after day together they are found;
In all their labour each must play a part.
When spring is here, and young lambs dance
    and play,
And daffodils tremble in the breeze.
When thrush and linnet sing the
    live-long day,
Both man and dog for once may be at ease.

But when December's cruel north winds blow,
And pools freeze iron-hard at winter's behest;
When fields lie deep in drifting, dreaded snow,
For them, through night and day, there is
    no rest.
Feeding the hungry, ravenous and cold,
Lifting the strengthless, searching for the lost,
Guiding the wanderer home to the fold,
They serve the flock, and never count the cost:–
A Shepherd and his Dog.

An etching by D. Binns.

STANLEY FINCH *(December 1985)*

[59]

6

DAYS ON THE LAKES

WINDERMERE 'LAKING'

'Is thoo cummin owt lakin' tamorra?'
'Aye. I's gine ta lake wi mi lile boat down bi't lake.'
'I'll si'the thear then.'

THESE words come back to me over almost forty years from Winder-mere boys of the past. I was born in a cottage high on a hill above the lake in the middle of the First World War. I lived not more than 200 yards from Bowness Bay for the first eighteen years of my life, and since then I have never been really happy away from water.

As a small boy my grandmother took me to play by the lake and to paddle in it. Nine times out of ten my paddling ended

Teal on Windermere.

with a wet seat and wet trousers for my walk was still wobbly, the bed of the lake was stony, and at some point it became easier to sit down in the water and carry on my activities at a lower level.

When I was 10 years old I learnt to skate on the lake. This was in January and February of a very hard winter when the water was frozen almost from Amble-side to Newby Bridge. My skates were old-fashioned wooden ones and I envied the owners of the sharp, shining, steel affairs. But mine were safe and easy, and I was soon away. It was splendid to be able to take off from the pier in Bowness Bay and push and glide myself round Belle Isle and in and out of the bays and creeks behind the islands.

Another excitement was to set off from Bowness and skate northwards, delaying as long as possible my southward turn to reach home before all the winter light went out of the sky. I don't think I ever reached Ambleside, but Millerground, where I learnt to swim in summer, was a reasonable target.

After tea and a warm up at home I would be back on the ice of Bowness Bay for as long as my father would let me stay out. The darkness was broken by street lamps, car lights, braziers, torches, and the windows of houses all round the bay. It was a fairy tale winter, never as yet repeated. I can't think how I got through my work at school, how my prep was done. Fortunately we had a very human headmaster who, on more than one morning during those six weeks, said 'Physical education on the ice this afternoon, my lads.'

Although as a child of two I sat in the water, I was in no hurry to swim. In this element the lake was hard to master and I remember standing shivering on the stony bottom and moving my arms, or hanging on the side of a rowing boat and kicking my legs, thinking all the time that this didn't really compare with a game of cricket in the field nearby. Eventually I was off, and the enclosure at Millerground was only my base. I could swim out into the open spaces and look down through the exciting depths of the lake.

As with skating, a new world opened for me. I went side stroke, back stroke, breast stroke or crawl through cold water that took the breath away. I dallied in the warmer patches, feeling the soft water like silk around me. There came a day when my friend the lake took me finally into her companionship and allowed me to swim the mile or more from her western to her eastern shore. This, al-though I could not know it then, was as romantic and final a union as when a loved fiancée becomes a loved wife.

I rowed on the lake, I sailed on it, I fished its water, I picnicked on its shores and islands, my dog swam ashore from the boat after rabbits on Furness Fells. I woke in spring time and from my bedroom window saw the living green of the larches on the Lancashire fells. I woke in autumn to look at the glory of green and gold, of russet and terra-cotta, as the trees on Claife Heights blazed their thanks to summer and prepared for winter. I stared at those fells as I romanticised over my first girl friend; I mourned with them over their bare patches when the trees were mobilised, as I was, for the Second World War. I crossed the lake by ferry and walked the fells with my dog, following the tracks of Jemima Puddleduck as, like her, I sought to exchange the world of folk for the world of hills and trees and water for a while.

G. E. Martin (March 1967)

Overheard recently on a Lakes steamer was the following conversation between a small group of elderly Lancashire day-trippers.

Fred was standing at the prow which commanded an excellent view northwards up the lake, when his friend's wife came up behind him and said:

''Av yer spotted "Loch Ness Monster" yet, Fred?'

Before Fred could reply, the lady's husband cut in with: 'Naw, 'e hasn't; but if tha turns round sharp, Fred, tha'll see it behind thee.'

Mrs M. Rodgers (1972)

THE LAST DAYS OF DONALD CAMPBELL

Early on 4 January 1967, Donald Campbell's boat Bluebird, *travelling at the fastest speed a human had attained in a boat, left the water, somersaulted and sank in Coniston Water. Arthur Knowles, who knew Campbell well and was a spectator throughout the trials and record bid, writes of 'Campbell's last throw'.*

DONALD CAMPBELL, last of the colourful line of British world speed record contenders, was determined that his boat *Bluebird* – now powered by a Bristol Siddeley Orpheus jet engine – should put the water speed record out of the reach of the Americans. In early November he came again to Coniston, and established his base camp at the slipway used by his father, Sir Malcolm.

From the start, the project was bedevilled by snags, not the least of which was the weather, and miracles of ingenuity were performed in the plastic-sheeted boathouse by his engineers Leo Villa – veteran of a dozen record attempts – and Maurice Parfitt.

The first snag was when the engine was given a 'static test' run on the slipway – shackled fore and aft to prevent her moving under the jet stream. As the engine reached peak revolutions, 'expensive noises' were heard and it was found that the Orpheus' consumption of air was greater than the air intakes would stand. They collapsed, rivets were drawn through the engine, and it was badly damaged.

When a new engine was installed, it was found that because it was some two hundred pounds lighter than the original, *Bluebird* was nose heavy, and would not lift into the planing position. This was

solved by giving her a run with sand-bags tied to her stern, and, when this proved successful, lead castings were bolted beneath the engine to put her trim in the water right.

I was privileged to be with Donald throughout the whole of his time at Coniston. All of us, press and cameramen, were roped in at some time or another to give a hand with this and that. Much of the work was done by supernumeraries – although we could not help him with the weather, which played a big part in delaying the final record bid for some nine weeks.

Donald achieved some very fast runs when conditions permitted, and on 13 December, *Bluebird* got up to 267 miles an hour, at that time the fastest in Great Britain. She also hit a seagull, and sustained damage to her port spar.

The team were sent home for the Christmas break, and most of the pressmen left for their homes, none of us expecting *Bluebird* to be out on the lake. However, on Christmas Day, when Coniston Water looked like a mirror, Donald whipped together a scratch team, took the boat out, and achieved two very fast runs in the region of 280 miles an hour – which, had the timekeepers been present, could have been recorded as beating his own existing record of 276.33 miles an hour.

Again, on the Tuesday of Christmas week, with the same scratch team, he shot across the surface of the lake at what was heard to be 305 miles an hour – although Donald only admitted to it being 'very fast indeed'.

It was on this run that *Bluebird* again went wildfowling, and hit a duck, sustaining yet more damage to the same port spar.

On Tuesday evening, 3 January, the Met. office gave Donald a favourable forecast for the following morning, and I believe that he, having heard this, determined that Wednesday should be the day when he really gave *Bluebird* her head, and went for the record, with a target of something over 300 miles an hour.

We all duly received our stand-by calls. We were down at the slip-way at 7.30 a.m. to find a lake settling down to a reasonably good surface. I would not have thought the surface as perfect as Donald would have wished. A few weeks earlier, he and Leo Villa asked me to drive to the south end of the lake to advise on surface conditions there. I asked him exactly what he was looking for, and he pointed to the water near the boathouse, which was glass smooth.

'I want it like that, old boy,' he said.

Leo grabbed my shoulder, and pointed out into the bay, where there was a gentle ripple.

'It will do if it is like that,' he told me.

Looking at Donald, he nodded agreement to me, so it would seem that there was a degree of tolerance in surface conditions. I found the south end with a similar ripple on it, duly reported to Donald, and out he went, to do a very fast run.

On this, his last morning, Donald slipped *Bluebird* down into the water. She was edged round the pier, and her pilot – giving those of us watching him his customary nod and wink – started up the jet engine. With his face masked, and on his head Neville Duke's old jet pilot's helmet, Donald was alone. Somehow the atmosphere felt different this morning. There was none of the usual chatter and joking. We seemed to sense that this was it – the end of a long trying period of waiting. Today we should see the record broken, or . . .!

Donald maneouvered *Bluebird* out into the deep water, set his sights down the lake to the buoys marking the measured kilometre, and increased power in the boat. She threw up her usual spectacular sprays of water, rose to her planing points, dropped again, and then, with more power applied she lifted, and began to streak down to the south end of the lake.

To those of us on the beach, she looked slow, and someone said she was doing around 160 to 180 miles an hour. We were to learn later that in fact she had achieved 297 miles an hour on this first leg of the two runs necessary for a record attempt.

Donald usually waited for his wash to subside before doing a second run back to the north of the lake. This time, he seemed to start his second run very, very soon. We learned later that he allowed only four minutes' pause.

I watched through binoculars the start of this second run, which proved to be his last. *Bluebird* lifted up on to her sponsons and streaked towards me.

The previous evening, up at the local pub where he and the press made their headquarters, Donald had played Russian patience with a green-backed pack of cards – a colour he superstitiously hated. He turned up the Ace of Spades, and the Queen of Spades followed. Turning to

David Benson of the *Daily Express*, he said: 'Mary Queen of Scots turned up these two just before she was beheaded. I pray to God I am not going to get the chop.' He remained convinced all night that tragedy was at hand.

The radio telephone had advised him of his speed – 297 – for his first run, and he knew that he must do 6 miles an hour faster to achieve an average of 300. So Donald put his foot down.

Bluebird was like a projectile as she came towards me, her jet engine screaming, a thin comet-tail of spray behind her. As she came to within 100 yards of the second and last kilometre marker, she seemed to take off – as a jet fighter plane would take off. Fifty feet into the air she soared vertically – flipped over on to her back, and crashed down. For a few seconds she floated still, and in those seconds I said, 'Thank God he's all right.'

But *Bluebird*, water pouring into her jet pipe, sank in 125 feet of water, and Donald Campbell, brave, an intensely superstitious man, died, doing a job he felt he must do.

'We each of us have a mountain to climb,' he told me one day. '*Bluebird* is my mountain.'

As we all left the boathouse in the early dusk of that evening, I looked back at *Bluebird*'s trailer, still waiting on the slipway. At Donald's E-Type Jaguar in the yard. I looked at Donald's second engineer, Maurice Parfitt, standing white-faced and with tears in his eyes.

Maurice looked at me for a long second.

'They're not coming back, are they?' he said.

(February 1967)

The Last Time

Beside a watery mirror a freezing yet
    determined group
Is preparing in the dim sunrise of an early
    January morning.
Checking, fueling, working among his
    friends.
He walks about silent and calm.
The Chief and closest to Bluebird – his
    ruler.
The Ace and Queen of Spades shown on
    the previous night
Do not appear to lend themselves to much
    thought,
But a primitive excitement is stirred –
    again a fear
Lies hidden in him alone.

Slowly and beautifully the fish glides,
    breaking the still surface of
    Coniston Lake – more speed.
The trial run up and then down to break
    the world record.
He guides his whale, down she spurts –
    the speed
And tension rises as the foam, walling
    him from vision, thrusts upwards
    and pounds back.
Jumping, throbbing she lifts but sinks
    down again,
Rears and is whisked into the spray air –
    over and plunges
Into a roaring, vibrating explosion of
    water.
The wreckage encircles the grave of
    Donald Campbell.

K. E. CALLAGHAN *(4 January 1967)*

7

MEN AND MOUNTAINS

MOUNTAINS ARE THE BEGINNING
AND THE END

Reflections by John Wyatt (Lake District National Park Warden)

AN ARMY sergeant on exercise, who I met once on the storm-swept Scafells asked me if I had climbed the summit for pleasure. When I told him that I had he stared at me with disgust and incredulity, and shouted against the gale: 'You must be stark raving mad!'

Scafell and Mickledore from Scafell Pike. (*Vivienne Pooley*)

Mountains are all things to all men. To try to explain one man's madness is almost impossible. Some mountaineers try to show that a mountain is nothing but a large open-air gymnasium. But there are better gymnasiums elsewhere. To a true Lakelander they must mean more.

John Ruskin said: 'Mountains are the beginning and the end of all natural scenery.' They are basic, they are the bare bones of nature. They were the making of the Lake District scene. They shaped it, they created its lakes and influenced its climate. When we are attracted to our mountains we are attracted by their simple, basic truth. Water, trees, heather, bracken, foothills and farmsteads must set their tune to their compelling rhythm. To most lovers of the Lakeland scene they are a splendid backcloth. To the Lakeland mountaineer they are much, much more.

The attraction can only be partly physical. Uppermost in this is the challenge – they are *there*. Peaks are there to achieve – new rock routes to try. A successful ascent is the peak of pleasure – and what is to surpass the heady joy of climbing in hard white snow – as crisp as Kendal mint cake! There is so much to see – particularly on leaving the well-trodden tracks. In the Lake District there is little of the long distance monotony of other mountain areas. Divided as the fells are into so many crags, gullies, hanging valleys, and ravines an exploration is always rewarding, particularly so if one has learned a little about geology and botany.

There is also a mystical attraction. The Lakeland mountains have contributed much to our poetry and literature. Nowadays it is less fashionable to enjoy poetry.

A lot of us, alas, after youthful labouring in airless classrooms have perhaps sometimes harboured hard thoughts about Wordsworth and his tedious daffodils. Scorn the thought as he will, the true Lakeland fell-walker and climber must feel something of a mystic attraction.

In search of recreation he is drawn to creation itself in its primary shape – the beginning and the end. In retreat from civilisation's maddening complexity, he seeks the essence of simplicity. He cannot remain unmoved at the sight of Wasdale's splendid head. Small wonder that the view should become the National Park's emblem.

Kirkfell, Gable, Lingmell and the Scafells – before men were, they were. Among them in silence, and particularly in solitude, it is possible to feel something of the gigantic time scale. In their time man is an upstart – a few minutes old; one man's lifetime a tiny microcosm. If, when standing in the ampitheatre of Hollow Stones, or better still camping on a summit on a starry night, one feels a chill of awe and it could be a sense of our frail mortality confronted by the immensity of eternity.

There is more. Beyond the expressive reach of words – even beyond poetry and beyond music is the great hypnotic promise that draws men into mountains, never quite to find it but often to return to the valleys elated by the merest glimpse.

I know few mountaineers who would admit to being religious. I know none who are atheists. All true mountaineers, though, know that mountains have always been the haunts of holy men and seekers, and the favoured sites of monasteries. Religion was born in nature, of which mountains are 'the beginning and the end.'

On a mountain a man can find nothing

– or everything. He can alas soon lose himself, but he can find himself, find the true measure of himself, find joy and also great humility. When a man faces a mountain, he faces truth.

Climbers near the summit of Scafell Pike. (*Simon Wilkinson*)

(*September 1966*)

ANNUAL ASSAULT

THIS MONTH, April, sees the opening of that annual combined assault on the mountains and peaks of the Lake District which we take for granted but which would have so greatly puzzled an earlier generation.

When Wordsworth, himself no mean walker, ascended Scafell Pike with a pony and guide at the beginning of last century, he observed that the arrival of strangers there 'can seldom happen'. He thought it likely that there would be visitors to Scafell itself, but he did not visualise climbers on the Pike. Yet on most fine days this summer there will be groups and individuals – without ponies or guides – on most of our Lakeland peaks. Youth hostellers and others take the big peaks in their stride, often in the scantiest of garb and with no more sustenance than a few sandwiches.

Wordsworth was an exceptional walker, and part of his reputation for madness probably arose from his habit of going immense distances on foot where more ordinary folk either stayed at home or, if they did go up mountains, made it into an expedition.

Mr G. S. Sandilands, in his *Anthology of the Lakes*, published some years ago, provided an account of one of these pioneer trips – to conquer Fairfield, in the Helvellyn range, a mere 2,800 feet hill. The party was cheered out of Ambleside as if on a journey to the Atlantic. The impedimenta, described by the leader as 'necessaries', included a horse, a large tent, four bearers as well as four friends, thirty-six bottles of beer, two of sherry, two of gin, two legs of lamb, two fowls, one tongue, half a pound of cigars, and two packs of cards.

Even this well-fortified expedition failed to reach its objective. There was a storm on the way, the tent blew over and all the gin and cigars did not give them courage to continue. That was Lakeland holiday-making in the days before Ordnance Survey maps, before hikers, and when mountains were usually described as 'horrid'.

(Notebook, April 1952)

A MOUNTAINEERING RECORD

WHAT IS the greatest climbing feat ever performed in the Lake District either by a native or an 'offcomed 'un'? I doubt if anyone has equalled the performance of a Keswick mountaineer, Mr Robert Graham, in June 1932. Walking to a programme worked out with the assistance of Mr G. D. Abraham, the rock-climber, Mr Graham covered practically all the Lakeland peaks in one day.

Starting from Keswick Town Hall at 1 a.m. on Sunday morning, Skiddaw was climbed by the ordinary route. Then, descending into Skiddaw Forest, Great Calva was surmounted on the way over to Saddleback, when the descent was made to Threlkeld, and so up to Wanthwaite Pike to begin the long stretch over the Dodds of Helvellyn. These were all taken in order over the summit to Dollywagon Pike, Fairfield, and Seat Sandal to Dunmail Raise. Thus far Mr Graham had been paced by Mr Martin

Walkers above Far Easedale looking towards cloud-capped Helvellyn. (*Geoffrey Berry*)

Rylands, a skilled mountain walker.

After a short halt here the central Lakeland mountains were climbed and crossed in the following remarkable order, and numerous new sections were added to former attempts. Mr Phil Davidson, of Keswick, was Mr Graham's companion on this trying section. First of all Steel Fell was scaled, and so over Calf Crag, High White Stones, High Raise, Sergeant Man, Harrison Stickle, Pike o' Stickle, Rossett Pike, Hanging Knotts, Bowfell, Esk Pike, Great End to the cairn on Scafell Pike, England's highest mountain. By Mickledore and Broad Stand Scafell was gained, and so down to Wasdale, where a twenty minutes' halt was made.

Then, with Mr Deans, of Aspatria, as pacer, Yewbarrow was tackled, and so on over Red Pike, Steeple, Pillar Mountain, Kirk Fell, Great and Green Gables, and Brandreth to Honister Hause. Oncoming darkness made the final section trying, but, paced by Mr Hewitson, Dale Head was climbed, and by Hindscarth, Robinson, and High Snab the vale of Newlands was finally gained near Mill Dam Inn at eight minutes short of midnight. The four and a half miles to Keswick were covered in good time, and at 12.39 a.m. Mr Graham passed the Keswick Town Hall.

Very little nourishment was taken during this astonishing record of mountaineering skill and endurance. The distance covered was practically 140 miles, and the height climbed was over 30,000 feet, or better than climbing Mount Everest in one day.

B. M. (April, 1951)

[70]

THE LANGDALE PIKES

AN OLD coachman of half a century ago who came from outside the district to drive tourists around had neither knowledge of the fells nor any inclination to learn the names of places. Whenever he passed the Pikes and was asked, 'What is the name of that mountain, driver?' he would invariably reply, 'That's Sheep Fell, sir.'

The ease of access, plus the fact that they lie on the main route to the giants of the Scafell group, make the Langdales a favourite mountain with ramblers. It is only a two and a quarter hour climb to the top for the slowest person, with no hint of danger if the path is used. Rock climbers, however, can have all the thrills they want on Gimmer Crag or Pavey Ark, while archæologists have long been interested in the so-called Langdale axe factory.

Thousands of years ago, stone axes were started around the shores of Stickle Tarn – a few hundred feet from the top of the mountain, and overshadowed by the cliffs of Pavey Ark – and then taken into the valley below to be finished off. From time to time examples of these half finished implements are found on the mountain, especially near the tarn.

Stickle Tarn has had several narrow escapes from commercialisation. Attempts have been made to purchase it as a source of water supply for power to drive a hydraulic electric plant, but only once has it been used privately. That was when the long defunct Elterwater Gunpowder Company used it as a water supply.

'Ambleside to the Langdales' was always the most popular horse-coach trip. There used to be an 'understanding' between the two hotels at the end of the valley whereby each served the same tea – ham and eggs, as much as you wanted at no extra cost. The tourists enjoyed the tea, but long before the end of the season the drivers came to loathe the sight of ham and eggs!

In Queen Victoria's reign, little hiking was done among the remoter mountains and the hiring of guides and ponies was a profitable side line. George Bennett (guide to the famous Baddeley) was attached to the Old Dungheon Ghyll Hotel in those days and his capacity for speed of climbing and powers of endurance, earned him a nickname in the Press – the Langdale Antelope. He is mentioned frequently in the hotel visitor's book – almost as often as food.

There are amusing entries in the old register, as for example:–

Hungry and thin we staggered in;
Happy and stout we waddled out.

or,

Oh whence the name of this hotel
The awful name of Dungheon Ghyll,
A fitter name for it would be
The home of all who want their tea.

F.G.T.

The 1887 Jubilee was a great occasion down Langdale for there was keen local competition to build the largest bonfire. It also gave the strong men of the valley an opportunity to show their mettle. The *Chronicle* of 24 June 1887, states that 'one man carried his load of sticks and tar barrels for the bonfire up the Pikes seven times in one day and would have gone twice more if he had not had to attend a party in Ambleside. Another man carried up a plank as big as a weaver's beam – so heavy that an ordinary man could not lift it.'

One wonders if he had been training on ham and egg teas?

Without the Langdale Pikes, the Lake District would lose much of its charm. From time to time the crags claim toll in human life but it is always the fault of inexperience. By sticking to the normal route there is nothing to worry about, and children need have no fear. You can even dispense with the beloved, heavily studded climbing boots, but after a wet spell it pays to have well-soled boots for there are some swampy patches on and near the top.

Evyn Thomas (September 1951)

QUARRYMEN WHO SMUGGLED

AROUND THE western flank of Great Gable winds a track known as Moses' Trod, or Sledgait which, starting at the head of Wastwater, climbs the steep slope of the Neese, round the base of Gable's peak, across the fountain head of the river Liza, past the 2,000 foot bulk of Brandreth to the edge of Honister Crags.

It is not one of those trods made by the pattering hooves of sheep that meander in all directions up and down the fells, but a man-made track following the contours of the fell.

In the early years of the last century one might have seen trudging along it, as twilight fell, a gaunt, shaggy man dragging a laden quarryman's sled behind him. He was Moses, the most famous of the wadd (plumbago or graphite) smugglers, whose name the track bears. A quarryman at Honister he, like numbers of his fellow quarrymen, smuggled wadd from the mine at Seathwaite as a profitable sideline that could realise then, it was said, up to £500 a journey.

The Honister slate quarrymen were a wild set of men, a law unto themselves, akin to the navvies who, on a diet of beef and beer, seared the face of Britain with railway tracks. The green slate was obtained from tunnels or caves high up the crag face, reached by the workers in a climb up an almost perpendicular path, their sled strapped on their backs.

Having loaded the sled with nearly a quarter of a ton of slate they would slither down, with the sled sliding behind them; slowly and cautiously at first, then faster and faster to avoid being overtaken and crushed by their load, until they finished up in a rush at the foot of the crag.

They made seven or eight such journeys daily, taking about half-an-hour for the toilsome upward climb but only a few minutes for their head-long descent. To a man accustomed to this kind of herculean effort, pulling a sled of valuable wadd 2 or 3 miles round Great Gable down to Wastwater would have been but mild exercise.

The then plumbago mine at Seathwaite in Borrowdale, the wooded valley of the infant Derwent, was reputedly first

Tale of an Echo

Echoes have gone out of favour, although it was once a common form of entertainment among our Lakeland fells for visitors to compete among themselves for the longest continuing echo they could obtain from a shout. When distinguished visitors stayed at Storrs Hall on Windermere they were taken on boats on the lake, a miniature cannon was fired and they all counted the number of times it echoed.

A reminder of those days came from a reader's letter when he tells the story of an event which he declares happened in Wasdale.

The guide accompanying the party in a horse-drawn brake announced that there was a wonderful echo there, and he stopped the vehicle.

'Now, you will have to shout very loud. Just yell at the top of your voices "A pint of beer, please," and then listen carefully.'

They all shouted and waited.

'I don't hear any echo,' said one man at last.

'But here comes the landlord with your pints of beer,' said the guide.

(1972)

Charles Turnbull of Coniston on his 100th ascent of Coniston Old Man in the summer of 1986. E. A. Bowness, who took this photograph, commented 'This is the view most walkers would see! When I climbed with him for the hundredth ascent, we passed all other walkers except two, leaving youngsters gasping behind!'

worked by the monks of Furness Abbey. For many years the shiny black lead-like mineral was simply used for marking sheep, although there was a pencil factory at Keswick in the reign of Elizabeth I. Then it was used in potions for curing 'all manner and maks o' ills,' and later still for casting 'bombshells, round-shot and cannon balls' and the blueing of gun-barrels.

At this time it was the only mine of high-grade plumbago in Europe, and its products of sufficient value and importance to smuggle on to the black market.

A special Act was passed by Parliament in the reign of George II for its protection, providing for an armed guard at the mine and armed escort to take the wadd down to Kendal on its way to London. In spite of these precautions, and the stripping and searching of the miners as they left work, smuggling developed in a big way with a ready market among the illicit traders who foregathered at the *George Hotel*, Keswick.

Fracas between guards and smugglers were frequent, often developing into pitched battles as the quarrymen, ensconced behind boulders and trees, would pour a murderous fire upon the guards coming through Honister Pass to search the quarry workings. Moses was, however, a lone worker, taking his wadd in the opposite direction to Keswick, meeting his contacts coming up from Ravenglass at Wasdale Head.

A thriving port of Roman Britain, Ravenglass today is a small village on an almost landlocked creek, but cargo vessels could dock there as late as the middle of last century.

Moses paid for the wadd with moonshine

whisky, and the still in which he distilled it is said to have been in the now roofless stone hut in the central gully of Gable Crag.

From here he descended Sour Milk Ghyll with his poteen, and exchanged it with the miners for wadd in the shelter of the woods behind the mine. Then, loading it on to his sled in his mountain-top hide-out, he would proceed along his Trod to rendezvous with his customers in some isolated homestead at the head of Wastwater.

The heyday of the Seathwaite mine was in the early years of the 19th century when, in 1803, a seam was opened that yielded 31 tons, netting some £100,000. This was its swansong, for not many years later it closed, its productivity exhausted.

The pencil industry still flourishes in Keswick, but the graphite no longer comes from Seathwaite.

J. C. Marsh-Edwards (May, 1974)

A party of ramblers descended to a small village after tramping the fells.

'See that hill?' said one.

'Aye,' replied another.

'I can tell you it isn't as tall as it used to be.'

'How do you make that out?'

'Tramped it scores o' times – and look at the muck I bring down on my boots!'

J. P. Sinclair (1950)

8

FOLK OF LAKELAND

BILL TEASDALE

King of the Fells

SOME YEARS ago, when I interviewed Bill Teasdale for an article, I needed to see the fell racing trophies and to get all the dates. I got so much more from the thin, craggy, sinewy shepherd who was then in his forties – a man who was weatherbeaten, but with a glowing health that shone in clear, dark eyes.

The man was a legend and had been featured prominently by the media but he was shy – and just a bit reticent in telling of his victories all over the country and far beyond. The written records were placed in my hands with a sigh of thankfulness, as if he would say: 'There now! She's got the lot and that lets *me* out,' but courtesy was always uppermost.

All the warmth and glow of natural Cumbrian hospitality bloomed like roses in summertime as he took me to meet his marvellous mother at a Cumbrian tea table I shall never see the likes of again! As we ate the mouth-watering repast, Mrs Teasdale's natural kindliness had everyone feeling to be at home. 'Come on,' she said to me afterwards, 'I'll show you the cups and everything – in the sittingroom.' Bill winked at me, his crooked grin plainly saying: '*Now* you've started her off!' Blessedly, I had!

She told me of cleaning the mass of silver trophies. It was like shining up the image of her son. The story of every item was faithfully impressed upon her lively mind. When we re-entered the living room Bill raised an eyebrow and remarked

to me: 'Well – it serves you right!' His mother laughed and said: 'Well, folks can get nowt out of *you* when it comes to talking about fell racing. Frightened to death he is that they'll think he's bragging! He nivver has,' she ended, tartly.

She was so right. The quiet modesty of the remarkable man shone through everything. Readily he explained his job, combining shepherding on the wild fells around Caldbeck with a certain amount of gamekeeping, the while maintaining himself in rigorous training for the next gruelling fell race. He was at home up there on the wide, wild, open heights, being a splendid piece of human mechanism in its natural habitat.

He told me of the wildlife, and I detected a deep understanding of the powers of survival of bird and beast up there through the winters. He made special efforts to alleviate their suffering. His dog gazed at him with worship in her soft brown eyes. He ruffled her ears and remarked: 'Aye – she's like me, she's gitten a bit past it, but neebody would loss either on us up yonder.' His eyes strayed to the sun as it placed his 'training ground' in perfect silhouette and in all its awesome majesty.

He had made the fells of Grasmere his 'Hall of Fame' and the Lakeland Peaks Race his weekend's 'stroll', but here around Carrick was the cradle of Cumbria's great hearted sportsman – a

Bill Teasdale. (*Yorkshire Television*)

legend for generations to come and a reminder that tenacity of this calibre was developed where the challenge was greatest.

I approached the last question with trepidation. I knew retirement from fell racing was upon him. 'Bill – when you don't compete any more – will you miss it? Will you mind seeing someone else coming in first on your old stamping grounds?' For the first time he smiled widely. The sunlight invaded his eyes as he replied with a warmth I hadn't heard before. 'Nay lass – I've iverythink I want right here – here at home, and I've plenty to look back on. Jos Naylor'll mek a grand substitute.'

Our 'King of the Fells' accurately predicted his successor.

Edna Cass (June, 1985)

SON OF LANTY

I THOUGHT I had no company by the remote hill tarn except the few pairs of oystercatchers piping on the shingle, the wagtails swinging on the sheep fence, and the gruff-voiced grouse on the ling-grown fell. I was wrong.

Presently I spied an old man in a dark jacket and fustian breeches ambling beside the shore in my direction. I looked up from my perch fishing, as he paused a few yards away from the rock on which I was sitting. I beheld a slim old fellow, whose hawk-nosed face and craggy jaw had the mark of the Norseman about him.

I judged the old dalesman to be in his seventies. He must have managed the stern upland climb from Staveley village to reach the tarn. He spoke to me: 'Hev you a spare hook, mister? I've lost mine and the perch are just starting to take the worm.'

I produced my tin of hooks and lead-weights, and offered to tie one to the gut at the end of his line, tied to a hazel wand, that served as his rod.

'Thank ee, mi eyes aren't quite as sharp as they used to be,' he remarked.

'You've done well to walk up the steep track from the village.'

'Aye, I suppose I'm lucky to be sae lish at 95.'

I looked keenly again at my companion. 'You must be Adam Slee,' I exclaimed, smiling back at the old man. 'He's the only man I've heard of game enough to walk up the brant fellside at over the eighty mark.'

He was indeed Adam, son of Lanty Slee, the legendary Lakeland quarryman, farmer and poteen maker, who was born in 1802 and died at Greenbank, Little Langdale in 1878. His son, Adam was then a lad of 15 years.

Lanty worked in the slate quarries of Langdale by day and at night he brewed his whisky in secret stills hidden away in various old abandoned fellside quarry workings. When the Excise men were hot on his trail, he shifted his activities from one dale to another.

Adam Slee.

At the height of his secret 'business', he lived in a cottage at the foot of Tilberthwaite Ghyll. He had a whisky still concealed in a pit beneath his pony's stable adjoining the cottage. The pipe from his stove was cunningly joined to the cottage chimney and so the tell-tale vapour from the still escaped in an innocent manner mingled with the peat fire smoke.

If anyone called at the cottage when Lanty was busy making potato whisky in his underground den, his wife gave the alarm by knocking on the hearthstone with a poker. Lanty generally sold his poteen for 10s. a gallon.

He also established a trade in tobacco and brandy with smugglers who traded with France and Ireland. They occasionally landed contraband on the Cumberland coast, near the low coastline at Ravenglass, the lost little seaport started by the Romans who built Hardknott castle or fort.

Several times Lanty was pursued over the wild fells by the Excise men as he led his packponies over the steepling fell passes of Hardknott and Wrynose. The last time they caught him, he was fined the large sum of £150 at Hawkshead Court. The fine was later reduced by half. It was rumoured that certain of the magistrates were numbered among his best customers.

In the end, Lanty made enough money to achieve his ambition of becoming a 'statesman', farmer. He died owning his own smallholding at Greenbank, Little Langdale.

I was delighted to meet his son. 'You must have been about 15 years old when Lanty died. Do you remember your father well?' I asked.

'I remember mi fadder weel; he wor

A portable still, once used by Lanty Slee. (*R. D. Humber*)

about five feet ten tall, broad-shouldered an' a hairy chin. He wor as hard as an otter, an' as strang as a lion. A barrister friend, who used to gaa fishing wi him, yance tell't him that if he'd hed some schoolin' he'd ev bin the cleverest feller in aw England. I've bin in aw his caves and quarry hideouts where he med his whisky,' Adam told me.

Adam lived to be 101. When past the century mark, he still enjoyed watching the Coniston fell foxhounds hunting over the hills near his last home by Windermere. He scorned the use of spectacles. He lived to be the oldest inhabitant of Lakeland and died at Matson Ground, Windermere, in 1965.

R. D. Humber (April 1976)

VIVIAN FISHER, THE MAN AT THE GATE

WHENEVER I see a picture of Ashness Bridge, in Borrowdale, I think of Vivian Fisher. He used to 'man' a gate, not far from the old bridge, on what was then the rough and peaceful lane to Watendlath. He was always ready for a few words and, of course, appreciated the money which passers-by gave him for opening the gate. He was something of a naturalist and loved feeding the birds which came fearlessly around him. He always seemed to be at peace with the world and to be a truly happy and contented man.

We invariably stopped to chat to Vivian. Just after the war, my father persuaded him to have his photograph taken and later sent prints to Vivian in Keswick. Vivian wrote a charming letter of thanks in return and my father treasured this for the rest of his life, as indeed I do today. Vivian wrote:

'Many kind thanks for the beautiful photographs you have sent me. They are excellent studies of me, poetical in their expressions and which you have caught me in an elegant mood, which your artistic eye hath caught. You have harmonised me divinely in a natural setting, which is in tune with the rustic scenes around, whom now is robed with all the gladdening hues of Autumn, that would give to your sight constant delight. Again let me thank you for the photos with all my soul and wishes for your earthly happiness and the same to them that are dear to you.'

Vivian's letter is dated 22 October 1946. The one time lane to Watendlath has been 'made up' for some years and those on foot share it with cars. But nothing can take away the memories of

Vivian Fisher. (*F. Davison*)

Vivian Fisher from those of who were privileged to know him and who remember our conversations with him whilst he fed the birds.

W. Philip Stirrup (September 1988)

A Lakeland farmer went to market and on his return home called at a public house and asked for a glass of beer. As he was drinking the landlord said, 'Looks like rain.' 'Aye,' replied the farmer, 'an' it tastes like it too!'

(*1965*)

[79]

A MILLION WAINWRIGHTS

When he started to draw pictures of the Lakeland Fells, he had discovered a fascinating pastime. He could actually build a mountain on a blank sheet of paper.

A friend living in the North-East is elated at being appointed honorary guardian of a Wainwright gate. For years, he has found pleasure in motoring across to the Lake District at weekends to spend as much time as possible trudging above the 1,000 feet contour line. He has now done 'all the Wainwrights', the peaks mentioned in the famous hand-written, hand-illustrated climbing guides by A. Wainwright, of Kendal.

Not long ago, he was photographed beside a 'Wainwright gate' – an iron gate, with substantial stoops, but with no supporting walls or railings: an isolated structure in the wilderness. The old barrier has gone, but the gate endures, to be solemnly used when it would be far easier to walk round it.

This friend from County Durham does not often indulge in whimsy, yet there is something about a Wainwright guide book that goes far beyond mere directions. A. Wainwright is a character in the sense of a person who has a distinctive way of looking at the world. He writes in an entertaining as well as a perceptive way. Compiling the guides was that old-fashioned occupation – a labour of love. He must have chuckled to himself when he pictured a solitary iron gate on a lonely hillside. (Wainwright has long been fascinated by gates. Like him, they are individualistic. 'There seem as many ways to fastening a gate as there are gates . . . No two are quite alike.')

Four of us thought of Wainwright recently when we climbed Great End in ice and snow. It was a day in a thousand, with a northerly breeze to provide extreme clarity. It crossed our minds that the horizons and the fine detail of the crags and gullies where the fine snow had not lingered were like lines on a Wainwright drawing.

A PAGE A DAY. It was on the evening of 9 November 1952, that Wainwright penned the first page of the proposed series of guidebooks – a venture he was to carry to its breath-taking conclusion at the rate of one page a day, more precisely one an evening, with a little time off twice a week so that he might watch *Coronation Street* and be reminded of his upbringing in the industrial town of Blackburn. 'It was a good evening for me,' he recalls of that winter's night. He spent it through his imagination, with the help of a reference photograph and through the medium of fine penmanship, on an ascent of Dove Crag. 'I was lost to all else.' Since then, over a million Wainwrights have been sold – over 200 tons of paper fed into printing presses at the plant of the *Westmorland Gazette*, Kendal. That first night on his Lakeland project was followed by many another, equally good. 'At that time I had no thought of publication. I was working for my own pleasure and enjoying it hugely.'

He is a patient, meticulous man, partly because he was trained as an accountant where vagueness and impetuosity are not tolerated. When he left school at the age of 13, he had little in the way of learning. 'But I found that if I wanted to get on I had to pass exams, so I had to study English language and literature. It made me a stickler for the correct use of language and I found myself criticising the way people spoke and seeking to use the words correctly myself.'

When, in July 1953, he had prepared 100 pages of pictures and prose, he scrapped them. He did not like the raggedness of the line ends. They were not 'justified', as a printer might say. He

At the Wainwright Exhibition at Brantwood, the life-sized bronze bust of A. Wainwright, sculptured by Clive Bernard of the C. E. Gallery at Haverthwaite and photographed by A. S. Jennings.

did the work again, fitting the lines as nearly and as neatly as he could make them. 'I never quite succeeded, but the pages looked better than before. They were neater and tidier.'

HAND-WRITTEN. Wainwright wanted every page to be exactly as he had penned it. He was also mindful of cost. He would provide books that could be printed without the intervention of a type-setter. Sandy Hewitson, a local printer, quoted a figure of £950 for 2,000 copies of the first book. Wainwright had only £35. 'He said: never mind; pay me when you sell them. I did, but it took me two years, during which he never once reminded me of the debt.'

A good friend in the early days, Henry Marshall, the Kendal librarian, attended to the distribution and despatch of books. Henry's name appeared on the title page of the first volume as the publisher.

Looking back on that time, Wainwright says: 'Subsequently, this arrangement collapsed through weight of numbers. I was having to keep records and do the invoicing and collection as well as write the books, and it was a blessed relief when the *Westmorland Gazette* offered to take over publication in 1963.

At this time, Harry Firth, the manager of the printing department, became a very good friend of Wainwright. Harry was also a great friend of mine, so on successive visits to the *Westmorland Gazette* to attend to issues of *Cumbria*, which then were being printed at Kendal, I was able to take an interest in the unusual publishing project.

I marvelled at the neatness and excellence of Wainwright's art work – and at the regularity with which books were being printed and re-printed as the demand quickened. (The pages of *Cumbria* at about this time carried extracts from the guides, with the kind permission of Wainwright).

Wainwright grew up in Blackburn – in a totally man-made environment of mills and terraced housing. In the biographical book *Fellwanderer* (1966), he was to recall the period, with its flickering gas-lamps, hot-potato carts, fish and chip shops, public houses and Saturday matinees at the cinema known, and not without justification, as 'the flea-pit'. He grew up, as did many of us, in a period of unemployment and poverty. Not until he was 23 years old did Wainwright see the Lake District.

'I had saved £5 for a week off. It was the first time I had ever been away from home. I went with a friend to see the Lakes I had heard people talk about. It was the moment that changed my life. I was absolutely captivated. I did not know there was beauty in the world like I found in the Lake District. I did not want to go back to a treasurer's office on a big town council. All I wanted was to live a quiet life in the Lake District.'

TRAVELLING BY BUS. The service buses were his transport as he toured the District. He stayed at bed-and-breakfast houses where the charge was 4s. a night. At first, he walked in everyday clothes, with stout shoes on his feet. He carried a raincoat. There followed a period when he was shod in ex-army nailed boots and wore a good jacket. He is astonished at the extent of the specialist garb available to the walker today.

As he strode across the fells, and paused momentarily on lonely peaks and looked around, the initial excitement remained with him. How could he provide himself with sufficient vivid memories to sustain him in his old age, when he would be unable to get to the 'tops'? The answer was to draw and write about his experiences. Lakeland excursions became much easier in 1941, when he obtained a post in the borough treasurer's office at Kendal.

When he started to draw pictures of the Lakeland fells, he had discovered a fascinating pastime. He could actually build a mountain on a blank sheet of paper. 'Let's do Great Gable as seen from Lingmell,' he might say. And he would do it in ink, with a pen, invoking lots of memories. The sketches were based on photographs. The camera he used had been acquired second-hand. There were 'various contrivances' on that camera, but all that concerned him was how to put in a new film and 'which knob to press to take a picture.'

He recalls: 'I was a cheapjack at the game, but I am sure fidelity to the scene has not suffered . . . It is necessary only to remember that the ordinary camera lens tends to depress verticles and extend distances, and that I must correct these imperfections. But the detail, and the relationship of one feature to all the rest, is foolproof. I wasn't aiming to be an artist anyway. My aim was to draw mountains, not in a romantic and imaginative sense, but as they are.'

ROADS AND PATHS. Maps fascinate him. He made the acquaintance of the 2½ inch scale, then the 6 inch maps which provided him with the wall patterns and the courses of old roads and paths, many of which having served mines, quarries and sheepfolds had since become abandoned. He found pleasure in trying to evoke the scenes of former human activity. 'Silence is always more profound in places where once there was noise.'

Not for him the crowds, but 'the secret

places that must be searched for, the drove roads and neglected packhorse trails, the ruins of abandoned industries, the adits and levels and shafts of the old mines and quarries, the wild gullies and ravines that rarely see a two-legged visitor.'

The seven pictorial guides were compiled for his own pleasure in the years from 1952 to 1965, 'both years inclusive as the buff forms say.' He had never changed his style, 'and if I were starting all over again, I would not change a thing. I wrote what I wanted in a guide – the route to a summit, a description of it, the way to the next one and a drawing of how to get there and what it looked like.'

Those thirteen years were 'a dreamlike procession of happy, uneventful days . . . I never had an accident or a fall. I was never be-nighted in a blizzard nor tossed by a bull . . . I always walked alone . . . It's just that I prefer my own company. There are several individuals I like very much, but people in the mass mean nothing to me.' He avoids public life as much as possible. 'I never socialise. I can't be doing with all that. There are relatively few people who would recognise me.'

ANIMAL CHARITY. The books have made a great deal of money, though when I first met Wainwright, in his treasurer's office in Kendal Town Hall, he had not drawn a penny and had incurred a debt of over £900. Most of the money has gone to his favourite charity, a Cumbrian animal rescue centre, first envisaged some ten years ago and now a thriving concern on which over £100,000, from various sources has been spent. He visits the centre several times a week.

He is deeply moved by the plight of straying or abandoned animals and delighted that something has been done in Cumbria to alleviate the distress. He says: 'When I walked the fells, animals were my own companions. They had an uncomplaining acceptance of the conditions in which they lived – out in dreadful weather all the time.'

Now, at the age of 78, he is working on what he is sure will be his last book. It will be called *Ex-Fellwanderer*. He will see it published for his 80th birthday. 'I will reminisce about Lakeland walks, the times I have experienced, and there will be a little bit of philosophising about what is happening to the Lake District. Then I will sign off for good.'

(He has had an enormous output over the years, and in addition to his guides has produced books of sketches, guides to other parts of the North Country, a book in which he devised a cross-country walk, from St. Bees to Robin Hood's Bay, two hardback books for a London publisher (which have entered the best-seller lists) and, my own favourite, a substantial book produced in 1974 about old Westmorland, at a time when the Boundary Commission recommendations would be accepted and the new county of Cumbria would come into being).

Wainwright has planned on his death, to have his ashes scattered on Haystacks, in the western fells. To him, Haystacks is 'the best fell-top of all, a place of great charm and fairy tale attractiveness . . .' He concluded his *Fellwanderers* book with the words: 'And if you, dear reader, should get a bit of grit in your boot as you are crossing Haystacks in the years to come, please treat it with respect. It might be me.'

W. R. Mitchell (March 1986)

GATESGARTH MEMORIES

I REMEMBER THE first time I ever went to Gatesgarth (and to me, the Lake District means Gatesgarth, Buttermere and the Nelsons). It was one Easter years ago, and my friend and I left Keswick station on a cold afternoon to walk through Borrowdale.

We climbed up Honister in wind and snow which worsened all the way, and when we started the descent it was in a blinding storm which blotted out mountain, rock and path. A wild, tumultuous welcome, indeed.

But when we reached the farm, and heard the soft Cumbrian voices, and sat by the fire in the stone-flagged kitchen, and were regaled with good farm fare, the bleak outside world was forgotten.

Old Mr Nelson sat in his armchair, looking like some Hebrew patriarch. Sweet-faced old Mrs Nelson smiled at our pleasure, and their daughters bustled about quietly, caring for our comfort. Outside the circle cast by the lamplight and the fire, the men sat relaxed and easy, while various favoured dogs and an assortment of farmhouse cats slept in the warmth.

Well, those days are gone long ago; but there is still a Nelson at Gatesgarth Cottage. And the same soft voice bids the traveller welcome. Still the best way to come is on foot over Honister, disregarding cars and motor cycles which rush past, taking the gradient with ease.

It is still good to sit by the beck with your back to a boulder or stone dyke and eat a meal in the sweet mountain air; to know in advancing years the strain of the climb and the compensation of the quick easy swing on reaching the level stretches at the foot of the pass: good to glimpse in the distance the clump of trees which shelters the farm and cottage and the line of silver which is Buttermere; and, best of all, to push open the gate of the whitewashed house, to know the kettle is singing on the hob, to smell the friendly fragrance of new-baked scones, and to hear Annie Nelson's soft voice saying, 'Come in. I knew you'd be coming soon.'

Annie Nelson. (*Russell Horton*)

Miss A. Lee (January 1957)

9

TRADITIONS AND CUSTOMS IN CUMBRIA

FORGOTTEN CUSTOMS

MANY OLD customs have vanished from these parts in recent years although it is good to see that rushbearing ceremonies still continue, and smaller events like the election of a Troutbeck 'Mayor' and shepherds' meets have not been entirely lost.

One old tradition was honoured at a wedding at Kendal parish church a few weeks ago; the tying of the church gates by children, only to be released by the scattering of coins to the hopeful youngsters. This custom was once widely observed throughout the north, as was another which required the bride and bridegroom to leap over a form on leaving the church.

Whether the custom of racing for the bride's garter was ever as common in Lakeland as in Yorkshire seems doubtful, but the throwing of an old shoe after the bridal carriage – or sometimes tying the shoe behind it – continued until recent times.

Most people have forgotten that the ringing of the curfew bell was once common in Lakeland, and it was often regarded as having power to keep off evil spirits in the night. Penrith church bell was nicknamed 'T'taggy bell'. It was told to children that if they were out after it rang 'Taggy'll get you'. Packhorses in these parts carried bells not merely for guidance but to keep away evil.

Old horse-shoes nailed to barn doors and even to house doors testify to an old-standing belief in Lakeland that this would bring good luck, and may be a link with an even older belief in the power of iron to keep away evil spirits. Spitting on a shilling received in payment for work done was another crude way of ensuring more to come.

But what was the origin of the phrase 'to take pot luck?' Had it anything to do with pottery or was it a form of invitation to someone to call in at a house when passing and take the luck of chance of whatever was in the pot for a meal? The term was once used widely in Cumberland so may have had something to do with a 'tatie-pot'.

(Notebook, September 1970)

THE RUSHBEARING

THE LATE SUMMER is the season of the Rushbearing – first Musgrave and Warcop in North Westmorland, and Urswick in the Furness District, followed by Ambleside on the Saturday nearest St. Ann's Day at the end of July,

Grasmere Rushbearing.

and the Grasmere ceremony on St. Oswald's Day early in August. It is a great pity that the tradition has died out throughout the length and breadth of England, and only our five Lakeland villages keep up the ancient ceremony.

We all know how in ancient times, hundreds of years ago, the churches had only mud floors covered with rushes, and how, once a year, the old, dirty rushes were swept out, the whole church spruced up, and how the lads brought in fresh, sweet smelling rushes, followed by the lasses who decorated the church with flowers.

Actually, like Christmas, this ancient floral festival was taken over by the Christian Church from a pagan festival. It is said to have been a Roman fertility drama, and is thus closely connected with our Pace-Egging Play.

In Grasmere, Wordsworth himself used to walk in procession carrying his emblem, and in his day the Rushbearing used to be followed by a merry barn dance in which he also took part. Among the many emblems is St. Oswald's hand, made of rushes, carried on a high pole, followed by the rush sheet, borne by six little girls who are even to the present day decked out in the traditional rushbearing dress – a loose, green pinafore frock and wide brimmed hat.

At Ambleside many willing hands help to prepare the large emblems in the shape of crosses, harps, crowns and Maltese crosses, decked out with rushes and flowers.

Wordsworth's niece, 'kind Mrs Harrison', who was nicknamed 'Middle Dolly', always had these large emblems prepared in her garden at Greenbank. In the memory of our older inhabitants, grown men and women always walked in the procession carrying their bearings. Now only one or two of us 'old 'uns' take part.

The procession forms near the church, from the tiniest toddlers carrying their little crosses and bunches of flowers to big lads and girls. Preceded by the town band, the procession winds up the steep crooked streets, then down again through narrow North Road which higher up leads to the Kirkstone Pass.

At last there is the halt at the market square where the emblems are raised for the onlookers to behold after we had all burst into the Rushbearing Hymn, written by Owen Lloyd, Wordsworth's friend, in 1835. Young and old, we all know it by heart:–

Our Fathers to the House of God,
   As yet a building rude,
Bore offerings from the flowery sod,
And fragrant rushes strew'd . . .

ending with
These of the great Redeemer's grace
   Bright emblems here are seen!
He makes to smile the desert place
   With flowers and rushes green.

On we go again, several hundred strong, to the Church, bringing in our emblems and leaning them against pillars and walls. After the service each child receives a large piece of gingerbread which surely points to the connection with the ancient floral and fertility festival.

On the Monday following there are the usual sports, a huge tea and games for the children, wrestling bouts, fell races and the like.

Clara Boyle (September 1961)

Facing the Opposition

Pulling a grimace which could not even be equalled by a former champion, Wyndham Taffy Thomas, of Cockermouth, is George Mattinson, of Aspatria (see page 89). Mr Mattinson retained his world gurning championship at Egremont Crab Fair. Thomas was placed second, and John Bryan, of Egremont, third.

The tradition of pulling the ugliest face through a horse collar dates back to the 13th century. Holding the 'braffin' as the gurners put on their act is Egremont farmer, Mr John S. Kirkby, president of the Fair, and third generation of a family to play a leading part in the organisation.

(November 1972)

APPLES, ACROBATS AND ANTICS

It is the gurning that sends the crowd crazy. In this, Egremont is really placed on the map, for these are the World Championships.

EVERY OTHER person in the broad street was munching apples. The cart had just passed round the site of the old cross, marshalled by smiling police. Aloft, five of the town's worthies had hurled a hail of apples down upon the laughing, grabbing, wrestling populace. These were not crab apples, small and sour as in the early days of Egremont Crab fair, but sweet and rosy Worcesters.

Since 1267, when Henry II granted a market charter to the town, the Parade of the Apple Cart has taken place on the Saturday nearest 18 September. The custom dates from the time when the serfs of Egremont paid their dues in kind to My Lord de Lucy, up in the castle at the end of the street.

In rejoicing that they had produced sufficient grain to rent their narrow strips for another year, the tenants made high day and holiday, and the lord – probably unaware of the delights of crab apple jelly – distributed his largesse to the mob.

Today, things have changed. The 12th century castle, defended by moat and steep motte above the river Ehen, stands in ruins. There, graceful arches of the Great Hall remain beside a massive keep and gateway. The people of Egremont work not so much on the land as in iron and coal, though these industries are giving way before the great power station at nearby Windscale.

No proud lord rides forth through the gateway of red sandstone, though legends linger of Sir Eustace de Lucy, an heir who was taken prisoner in the Holy Land at the time of the Crusades. His jealous brother, Hubert, hastened home to claim the castle and lands of Egremont, but took good care not to blow the magic horn which hung at the castle gate. This would only respond to the rightful owner.

One night he was feasting, as was his custom, when he heard through the castle the plaintive note of the magic horn. Eustace had returned to claim his rights, and as for Hubert, he escaped to spend a lifetime of penance within a monastery.

The castle held sway in Egremont until Tudor times when the Catholic de Lucy supported a plot to put Mary Queen of Scots on the English throne. He was imprisoned for his pains, and his fine castle was dismantled and left to decay.

FAIR DAY. The good people of Egremont do not allow their traditions to slip into oblivion. At dawn on Fair Day, a greasy pole is erected by the war memorial in the main street. The top is decorated with coloured braids, and surmounted not by half a sheep, as in more affluent days, but by a neat parcel done up in polythene, and containing a succulent leg of lamb. What a dinner for the first successful lad to scale that greasy pole!

Throughout the long morning, young aspirants climbed and slithered. Shirts were removed and thrown up to one young athlete so that he could remove some of the grease. All seemed hopeless until a group of older youths formed a pyramid, and hoisted a small boy to their shoulders.

Amid shouts of encouragement, jeers, and laughter, the pyramid toppled. Down came the boys. The leg of lamb was firmly out of reach. By mid afternoon yet another combined effort was crowned with success. How the seven young monkeys shared out the meat we shall never know, but at least they were now free to turn their attention to other pleasures.

While these urchins were entertaining the populace outside, the more pious were clad, not in climbing kit, but in scarlet cassocks. Within the Church, not 100 yards away, sponsored hymn-singing had been in progress since 8 a.m. As their contemporaries struggled and slithered

'It's the gurning that sends the crowd crazy'. An extended caption appears on page 87. (*Ivor Nicholas*)

without, their voices were raised in a somewhat less literal appeal:

> *Let not my slippery footsteps slide,*
> *And save me lest I fall.*

The singing was over at 1 p.m., and races followed. In an age when the plodding cart horse was all too thankful to be granted a nosebag while the events were in progress, these continued throughout the afternoon.

Today, the coastal road from Whitehaven to the South passes through the town. As a concession to tradition, traffic is halted while two races are run down the street, but most of the events are transferred to a field on the road to St. Bees, where a small fairground delights the youngsters. Cups and prizes are offered for sprinting, wrestling, and pole vaulting. Hound trails are the order of the day.

THE LAST RACE. For the last race we return to the main street. The crowd is agog as landlords of the *Black Bull*, *The King's Arms* or *The Wheatsheaf* bring out tables laden with half measures of ale. The pram race is due to start at any minute.

A shout goes up: 'Here they come!' Down the street hurtle pairs of men willing to make fools of themselves. The 'mother' is dressed in a variety of frills and furbelows, the 'baby' – complete with dummy and other unmentionables – its hurled along in a pram rescued from the rubbish dump, and fortunate if it stays the course. At each of the many inns, 'mother and child' down a half pint before sprinting on towards the £25 prize money.

The street is re-opened to traffic. The

crowd wends its eager way over the river to the football field where the events of the day reach their climax. In the dark night the crowd surges forward to a brilliantly illuminated dais, where entrants for the pipe smoking competition were supplied with a clay pipe, a candle, and a wad of thick twist apiece.

The exercise is to get through the evil smelling weed as quickly as possible. It is just as well that the feat is performed under a starlit sky.

It is the gurning that sends the crowd crazy. In this custom Egremont is really placed on the map, for these are the World Championships. Some entrants possess an unfair natural advantage as they slip a halter over their shoulders, and with hideously drawn mouth, contorted eyeballs, and toothless gums, vie for the doubtful honour of being able to pull the ugliest face in the world.

The crowd roars appreciation. The winner waves aloft his silver tankard. Strains of *John Peel* and other hunting songs rise between mountains and sea.

Egremont Crab Fair is over for another year.

M. Nixon (September 1981)

APPLEBY HORSE FAIR

THE APPLEBY Horse Fair is the largest annual gathering of travelling folk in this country. For a week in June, the town of Appleby is taken over by the visitors, who park their caravans on the hill and turn the sedate little town into a non-stop spectacular.

One of the most picturesque traditions is that every day the horses are ridden down from the hill to the river which runs through the centre of the town; here those horses are given a wash. They arrive in a steady procession, ridden bareback, some with rope halters, some with bridles and, once in the water, they are covered with liquid soap and then urged into the deepest part of the river to rinse off.

Riding a soapy horse, bareback, where it does not particularly want to go, is left to the younger men. It involves getting wet, and the water, tumbling down from the fells, can be icy cold even in June. Sometimes you see as many as three young children on one horse, clinging to one another and almost disappearing under the water when the horse is swimming. Then horse and riders emerge, dripping, as the horse finds its feet and comes surging out into the shallows.

They all dry off on the way up to the hill again, travelling at a fast clip to the horse trading area near the vans, where the serious business of buying and selling goes on all day. Not only horses are sold. There is a vast area where the caravans are set out with gifts, souvenirs and ornaments for sale. And every few feet there is a gypsy fortune teller anxious to promise you a long and happy life in a bungalow with all mod cons.

DEALING IN HORSES. The temporary community is divided into two camps. One

OPPOSITE
A fine display of harness as a traditional caravan makes an overnight stop on the way to Appleby. (*Tom Parker*)

A horse being put through its paces at Appleby.
(*J. Hardman*)

section contains the old families who have been coming to Appleby all their lives and whose fathers and grandfathers were here before them. Another section, 'the newcomers', deals in horses as a sideline.

One of the descendants of the old horse-dealing families was Everett Booth, who had arrived at the Appleby Horse Fair with his young son. Everett had brought ten horses with him and he sold them all on the first day. Since then he'd been buying more horses and selling those, too.

The son did the riding, bareback. When I first saw him he was riding a new horse his father had just bought, cutting through the crowds like speedboat through water, leaving a wake of white-faced spectators washed up on the grass verges behind him. The only warning was a shout of 'Hey UP!' as he shot past gathering speed all the time.

Such riders lean well back, with their legs stretched out in front of them on either side of the horse's neck to keep their balance. If you don't get out of the way in time, it's just too bad.

It turned out that this young man was the only one of Everett's children who had taken to the horses. Considering that horse dealing is a precarious business, and Everett Booth was obviously good at it, I asked him how he judged a horse when he was buying.

'It's just like looking at a woman, isn't it, love?' he said, with a quiet smile. 'You look at the legs first, then at the eyes.'

Later in the day when the trading had gathered momentum, horses were being raced along the lane in both directions, heralded by shouts of 'Hup, hup, hup!' from the riders as they came, giving the spectators in front a split-second to decide which way to jump.

I took refuge in Everett Booth's van, where I met a man called Jack Toon, a 77 year old horse dealer who, as he said himself had 'learned the hard way – by losing money.' Everett Booth was up the lane doing some business and his son and a friend were stretched out at the front of the van having a test.

Jack Toon told me that he had been attracted to the travelling folk as a boy and had spent his life with them. He believed firmly in bareback riding. He had always broken in his own horses by riding them bareback and thought nothing of conventional methods. 'Most people you see on horses today look like humpbacked rabbits,' he said. 'If you rode like that here, you'd have a nasty headache in 500 yards.'

Jack Toon believes that the more you handle a horse the better. 'They like a fuss. The more you mess about with them, the better for your own sake. And the calmer you are, the better it is. A horse knows your temperament the minute you go near him.

'You get some men; they go to put a halter on, and they throw it round the horse's neck, and some of them frighten the horses, and some of the horses frighten the men. If you get a horse that bites, you have to watch what you are doing; with a kicker, you have to have an inclination to trust them – they can tell.'

On the last night of the fair all the old-timers gathered in the pub to talk over their memories and sing their songs. An Irishman was there wearing a remarkably large, black, weather-beaten hat. He was alternately apologising for not feeling too bright after an all-night session the previous evening, and dosing himself with Guinness.

Everett Booth and his son and Jack Toon joined the group.

Last orders were called and the music from the next room was getting louder. Jack Toon got to his feet and bowed to me with old-world courtesy: 'Excuse me, my duck,' he said. 'I'm just going to sing my song.'

Josephine Haworth (July 1983)

10

LITERARY LEGENDS
OF LAKELAND

WORDSWORTH THE MAN

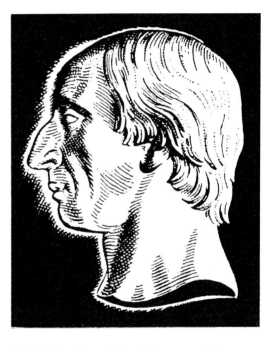

RECENTLY I heard of a graduate who asked for a book about Wordsworth, this one book to cover all sides of the poet: how his life and work were influenced by the atmosphere of peace and solitude of the Lakes, and how his work was similar to, or differed from, the work of other Lake poets of his generation.

At all events the graduate knew something of William Wordsworth. He was a Cumbrian, born at Cockermouth in 1770, one of five children of a lawyer, who was agent for the Earl of Lonsdale. He lived in what was then, and still is, the largest house in Cockermouth. What the graduate did not realise, in common with so many English people, was that Wordsworth spent quite long periods not only out of the Lake District, but also out of the country.

His school was Hawkshead Grammar School, which he left in 1787 to continue his studies at St. John's College, Cambridge. In 1783 he had become an orphan and until 1799, when he came to Dove Cottage, Grasmere, he did not live in the Lake District again.

During these years he had spent his Cambridge vacations walking in Wales and Scotland, and after graduation he spent some months in Germany, and in France during the Revolution. It was not until 1795 that the poet and his sister had a home together at Racedown, where

Coleridge first visited them, and later at Alfoxden. These two villages were where the Lyrical Ballads were first conceived as a combined volume, to be published by Joseph Cottle of the nearby town of Bristol.

Here they stayed for a short time and then went off for a walking tour in Germany. Any hikers wishing to hear of the discomforts of a walking tour at the end of the 18th century in Germany should read Dorothy's account of their holiday. In fact hikers of today are in luxury, and I do wonder how Dorothy walked in her long skirts and voluminous clothes. William's long trousers and tight jacket cannot have made for comfortable travel.

On their return they stayed with relatives in Yorkshire, but on 17 December started off for Grasmere. For the first 22 miles Dorothy rode pillion with her host, while William rode another of the borrowed horses, but at Wensley their friend returned home with his horses, and the Wordsworths walked the 33 miles over the Pennines to Kendal.

Here they bought furnishings for the cottage and then had to hire a postchaise to get themselves home to Grasmere, the centre of their beloved Lake country. Walking, while exploring their immediate neighbourhood, took much of their time while they lived alone, and they visited friends in Keswick and Pooley Bridge by walking and 'thumbing' lifts from carriers and farmers.

Their friends, with the exception of Charles Lamb, shared their tastes and William records in 1804 that Coleridge left Grasmere and walked the 19 miles to Kendal 'through mud, drizzle, fog and stifling air, in 4 hours 35 minutes.'

A 10 mile walk was quite normal, and brother and sister record in poem, journal and letters their appreciation of the scenery. In a letter to Hazlitt, William writes 'I should have liked to show you 200 yards or so of mountain brook scenery which I found yesterday above Rydale, a small waterfall, and rocks of all shapes. I passed under Nab Scar; it is infinitely finer in winter than in summer.' I wonder when 'brook' became 'beck'.

Rydal Mount is supposed to be haunted. The only ghostly incident I experienced could have been connected with the family's habit of taking quite long moonlight walks, often returning in the early hours of the morning. I wakened to hear voices on the drive below my bedroom window. I thought some hikers had lost their way on the path down Nab Scar. I looked through the window but could see no one in the bright moonlight, although the conversation continued.

Then the voices seemed to be coming into the house, and with a decidedly nervous feeling I went out on to the landing. There was not a sound. I remembered that during Wordsworth's tenancy there was a door from the drive into the room below my bedroom. It was an eerie experience, for I could not refrain from thinking I might have heard the ghostly echoes of a returning party of moonlight ramblers.

Talking of the Wordsworths' walking habits has reminded me of an incident which occurred in 1803. They and Coleridge started off for a tour of Scotland. Actually on this journey they took with them an 'Irish dog-cart'. After a few days Coleridge found that the noise of the wheels grated on his nerves, and that sitting in an open carriage in the rain was death to him. 'I begin to find that a horse and jaunting car are an anxiety,' he writes. 'The chances of rainy weather and damp beds daunt me.'

After a fortnight Coleridge returned home. One must agree with him regarding anxieties about the horse, which proved a very nervous animal. It bolted at various times and for various reasons, on one occasion rolling itself and the cart down the bank of a loch. In her *Journal* all Dorothy reports is that 'we leapt to the ground,' and after being helped by a passing man to get the poor creature to the road again 'with the help of strings and pocket handkerchiefs we mended the harness.'

Throughout the tour food was simple, almost primitive, and in one lodging the sheets were so damp that they could not dry them for hours round the sulky peat fire. But the scenery enchanted them and when they were back home Dorothy wrote a most entertaining account of the tour. William's poems, such as 'To a Highland Girl' and 'The Solitary Reaper', were two of the results of this tour, although not published until 1808. Apparently scenery outweighed any discomfort where the Wordsworths were concerned.

It is surprising how little is to be learnt of the clothes they wore at any time. Presumably clothes were for warmth not adornment. In Dorothy's *Journal* very little is said of what they wore, though she did once mention that while William was away she was binding carpets and mending old clothes.

As William's family grew Dorothy spent her time helping to care for the children, or acting as secretary to William, whose eyes were troublesome. He composed while walking about the garden or in his study and then Dorothy wrote the work out for him. He could do little writing at all by candlelight and, incidentally, his sense of smell was very weak. He seldom refers to a flower's scent in his writings.

Mary Wordsworth must have had a very busy time at Rydal Mount. It was a large house and there were constant visitors, either neighbours or people who came to see William. He had many American correspondents and some of these came to Rydal Mount including Emerson, who was holidaying in England.

One of them, Ellis Yarnell, describes a visit he paid the poet in 1849, telling of the poet's extensive learning, and describing the sweetness of Mrs Wordsworth, particularly her smile, and he describes the poet as a tall thin figure, his face deeply wrinkled, a large nose, but the eyes still bright and kindly. As the poet walked down Nab Lane with Ellis Yarnell a child ran to them to ask for money. This Wordsworth tried to find, but when he had none remarked, 'I must have given the children all I had in my pockets.'

The children of the district were always welcome at Rydal Mount and the poet's family and friends used to celebrate Wordsworth's birthday by giving a treat to children from Grasmere and Rydal at Rydal Mount.

He was a charitable man and in maturity a deeply religious one. There were morning prayers before breakfast, which was at 8 a.m. This was usually porridge. The heaviest meal of the day was at 2 p.m. and supper, again very often of porridge, came at 7 p.m.

But, and this a very large but, there were frequent intervals for cups of tea and biscuits. Dorothy Wordsworth was particularly fond of home-made oatcake with lots of butter (and so am I, and now I can never find the real home-made variety). Housekeeping was chiefly of the home-made kind in Wordsworth's time and although Mary Wordsworth was said to be a good manager she was also said to keep a close watch on household accounts.

The poet sometimes became lost to all thoughts of mundane affairs while composing and at such times the only way to bring him to a meal would be to break a bottle near him, which the poet would think to be a plate for, said an old servant to Canon Rawnsley, 'Wudsworth was a careful man, varra, and he could nat abide the brekking o' his chiny.'

At the same time, when speaking to an old man who remembered Wordsworth, Canon Rawnsley reports that he said 'They were both plain-faced people.' Perhaps this was noticeable in a district where most inhabitants were, and still are, comely.

Wordsworth was not appreciated as a poet among the peasantry of his time. Canon Rawnsley's inquiries among those who remembered him chiefly speak of a shy, quiet man, who had little to say although he was usually seen to be 'murmuring and mumbling to hisself' as he walked the lanes. One man said that while he was engaged in building Fox How – a house later to be occupied by Dr Arnold and now the home of the Bishop of Penrith – he used to see Wordsworth walking almost every day along the Pelter Bridge road to his stamp office in Ambleside. He usually wore a dark blue cape and a Jim Crow hat, and carried an umbrella. He (usually) walked with this whether it was wet or fine.

Wordsworth was appointed Stamp Distributor for Westmorland in 1813 and continued in office until 1842 when his son, William, took over the duties. Wordsworth at this point became a reluctant but pleased-with-the-honour Poet Laureate. The £300 a year paid for the Stamp Office was a great help to the poet. His duty was to receive stamps from London and to distribute them to the sub-offices in Westmorland, and quarterly accounts of the sales had to be sent back to London.

At this period dealings with Death Duties were also part of the Stamp Distributor's work. This was known as the Collection of Legacy Duty. Forms were supplied to executors to be filled in and returned. Once a month these filled forms were sent on to London, stamped if deemed correct. Wordsworth engaged a young man, John Carter, as his clerk, a young man who was to live with the family as a friend for life.

Considering William's travels in the British Isles and on the continent it was strange he should have opposed the continuation of the railway line from Windermere to Keswick. Wordsworth persuaded people to come from the towns and admire nature, yet refused them what was then the cheapest means of transport. In fact, according to F. W. Bateson, 'Wordsworth never succeeded in resolving this logical contradiction between his belief in equality and his belief in the spiritual benefits to be obtained from an intimate communion with wild nature.'

Apart from walking he was not an athletic man, his only sport being skating. At this he was outstandingly proficient. He never drank and was not a smoker, even when visiting his literary circle in London. His last visit to London was in 1849. Previous to this he often 'ran up to London,' sometimes for business, sometimes to see friends.

He was definitely not a recluse, though his heart was always in his beloved Lake District, where still today are many of the round chimneys he so favoured, saying 'there is a pleasing harmony between a tall chimney of this circular form and the living column of smoke ascending from it through the still air.'

On 23 April 1850, William Wordsworth died at Rydal Mount as his cuckoo clock called noon. How is this man remembered? As Poet Laureate of England; as an official of the early post and inland revenue offices; as the author of one of the best guides to the Lake District; or as a man with contacts in France and the U.S.A., and with an intelligent interest in national and inter-national politics?

Or was Sir Walter Scott right when he said to Dorothy Wordsworth, who was comparing Scott's popular novels with William's mostly unknown poetry: 'His time will come. Your brother's poetry will never be forgotten.' Perhaps he was right for most English people reply to any mention of Wordsworth: 'Oh yes, Daffodils; I wandered lonely as a cloud.'

Sarah Ouston (May 1965)

ARTHUR RANSOME'S LAKELAND

A HUNDRED YEARS have passed since Professor Ransome brought his wife and young family from Leeds, to spend the long summer vacation on a farm in a remote hamlet near the foot of Coniston Water. The young Arthur loved it. Forty years later, his memories of these holidays at Nibthwaite were given substance in *Swallows and Amazons* and its successors which were to make him famous. Today the farm has become something of a place of pilgrimage. Indeed recently I heard that some Japanese visitors, wearing Swallows and Amazons T-shirts, had called there.

His readers found the characters, their adventures and the setting so real that many children wrote to ask if it was true. This question leads towards the secret of Ransome's achievement. For the Swallows and Amazons (or most of them) ARE real, the places existed and if some of the adventures are imaginary, the activities – sailing, fishing and camping – were those he had enjoyed for years. Ransome simply wrote about those things he cared about – the children of a dear family, the countryside of his child-hood paradise and 'the best little boat that ever was built'.

As a boy, I read and re-read every Swallows book I could lay my hands on. The landscape of *Swallows and Amazons* and the other four Lakeland stories had such clarity, unlike the blurred images of some stories I had read, that I was hopeful that it existed somewhere. I studied a map of the Lake District again and again but none of the lakes seemed right.

It was not until my first holiday in Bowness that I was sure of anything. There I saw Rio Bay exactly as Ransome had described it, with the steamer pier, rowing boats and Victorian boatsheds full of period charm. During my week's holiday I saw rocky islands, forests, becks and the distant mountains. It was all very familiar, but since Rio Bay existed so precisely, where were the other well-loved places? Where could I find Wild Cat Island and Holly Howe Farm?

Just before we returned home to Bognor Regis, I spotted the houseboat in Rayrigg Bay, just north of Rio Bay. But House-boat Bay should be south of Rio! Puzzled and greatly daring, I wrote to Ransome and asked him to confirm my discoveries and let me know where I could find Wild Cat Island and the other places I had read about.

He was not going to make it that simple. He replied that the only way to keep a secret was never to answer questions. As I seemed good at guessing, he said that all the places were to be found but not as in the ordnance maps. Perhaps he did not want to reveal the whereabouts of the locations but, unknown to me, he had already let out some secrets.

More likely, he realised that I would find it much more rewarding to discover the places for myself. He had said enough and I was determined to be equal to his unwritten challenge and prove it by making an album of photographs. The one I had taken of the houseboat would make a start.

HUNTING FOR RANSOME. That was more than 30 years ago. Since that first visit I have returned almost forty times and when on holiday I have spent a day or so 'Ransome hunting'. Fifteen times I have brought a school party on an educational visit but you cannot start looking for Slater Bob's Mine when you have fifty 11 year olds half-way up Coniston Old Man and bursting to be the first to reach the summit.

As well as the discoveries I was able to make in the field, several books and articles proved helpful and Octopus Lagoon was located after much studying of maps. I was in no hurry, for my quest provided a purpose for exploration when on holiday and a focus for Lake District reading when not.

Then, about a dozen years ago, the Rio boatyards were pulled down and the North Pole disappeared. It occurred to me that future explorers would not find

as much as I had done and that perhaps I was making a record that one day might find a publisher. In 1984, the centenary of Ransome's birth, two major works were published which gave away most of the secrets and I realised that the time had come to complete my quest and so I wrote to *Dalesman*.

At the time I had an almost complete set of photographs of the important sites with the exception of Swallowdale, Beckfoot and The Dog's Home. For years a photograph I had seen of Mitredale haunted me. It was so like the head of Swallowdale, but Mitredale is far from Coniston. I had looked for Swallowdale in vain around Coniston and Windermere a number of times but two people had pointed me towards a particular area. When *Dalesman* agreed to publish *Arthur Ransome's Lakeland*, I planned a week in August 1985 to find the elusive Swallowdale and to re-photograph some of the other places in monochrome for publication. I took with me three ex-pupils who love the Lakes and the Swallows books and who had already walked miles looking for Swallowdale the year before.

Somewhere near Coniston Water we climbed beside a waterfall and when we reached the top Caroline let out a squeal of delight, for there was a charming secret valley, with rocky sides and a bracken-covered floor. It is not quite as Ransome described, but I am sure it is the essential Swallowdale; just as Peel Island is the essential Wild Cat Island with features borrowed from elsewhere. Fresh evidence has reached me from Ransome's grandson in America to suggest Mitredale has a part in it. Perhaps the head of that distant valley was borrowed to improve the one he had known as a child.

CONVERTED BARN. It was near Windermere that Ransome wrote *Swallows and Amazons*, sitting over his typewriter in a converted barn from which there is a superb view across the Winster valley to Yorkshire. We visited his old home at Low Ludderburn and Mrs Caldwell showed us over the barn. Some of his manuscripts are in the Ransome Collection in the Abbot Hall Museum in Kendal and we spent a happy morning among his books and possessions looking at his illustrations and reading the unfinished thirteenth novel. It was rather a wet week, but we just about completed all that I wanted and on the last afternoon we had tea with some of the Swallows and Amazons.

Five young members of the Altounyan family were the 'originals' of the Swallows and Amazons. In 1928 they learnt to sail in the 'Swallow' and 'Amazon' on Coniston Water and Ransome spent a happy summer with them, calling them duffers if they behaved in an unseaman-like way. He had known their parents as a young man and their grandparents were his adopted 'Aunt' and 'Uncle'. These were W. G. Collingwood and his wife who wrote and painted at Lanehead near Coniston.

Captain Nancy was, partly at least, inspired by Taqui, the eldest. The others kept their names: Susie, Titty, Roger and Brigit, and it seems that Ransome depicted them quite accurately. Soon, however, the characters developed in his mind and became more real to him than the originals who grew up rather too fast.

Today the family's link with the area is as strong as ever. Titty lives in Coniston and still paints. Brigit also lives in the area and has recently bought a new dinghy to· replace 'Amazon' which is really retired now. Roger told me how he spent his honeymoon on Wild Cat Island and Taqui would have taken me for a sail in 'Amazon' but for a broken mast-foot. As it was, my young friends joined some of their children and grandchildren on the lake for a row in 'Amazon'.

AROUND CONISTON. The Lake Country of the Swallows books has great charm. It is a complex combination of attractive features of the area. Coniston Water and Windermere merge to become one lake and while Rio and its islands are Bowness, most of the surrounding country is that of Coniston. Fells, rivers, woods, farms, valleys, mines and charcoal pit-steads he knew, were moved around to fit the demands of the story.

Future explorers who travel in the footsteps (or wake) of the Swallows will find that most of the places still exist. I should be pleased to hear of any ideas anyone may have about Beckfoot, which is my only serious failure. It is rather frustrating to see the 'Ransome's Lakeland' as fragments in unexpected places, but it is reassuring to know that Ransome himself found it confusing when he returned from a spell away.

Roger Wardale
(June 1987)

ENCOUNTERS WITH BEATRIX POTTER

Josephina Banner knew the famous author/illustrator of children's books when she was down-to-earth Mrs Heelis, of Near Sawrey, farmer and pioneer conservationist. 'She was the prettiest old lady I have ever met'.

JOSEPHINA FIRST met Beatrix at Eskdale Show, a celebrated event for the Herdwick men of the western dales. It so happened that Beatrix Potter (now Mrs William Heelis) was a keen and knowledgeable breeder of Herdwicks, the distinctive type of the Lake District. On this occasion, as on many others, she was among the judges.

Majestic Herdwicks, daubed with 'show red', their faces coarse and white like hoar-frost, were paraded before the diminutive lady judge, who was suitably attired in a tweedy outfit – browny-green – with clogs on her feet and a felt hat, with elastic under the chin to cheat any Cumbrian breezes.

Josephina, and her husband Delmar, were introduced to Beatrix by Cyril and Sally Bulman, who had come to help their relations at the *Woolpack Inn*, Boot. 'As a sculptor, I was wearing my usual working attire – boiler suit – and had clogs on my feet. I think she liked me instantly because of the clogs. We got on with each other because we were both straightforward people.'

The Banners watched her judging the stock. Then they saw her wander around the sheep section of the show, looking intently at animals in the pens. 'You could see that the farmers respected her.' Then a big, tall farmer approached her – and slapped her on the back as he might have done with a well-built farmer friend. 'The blow was so hard it nearly toppled her over, and she staggered. He had drunk too much and was just too friendly. He told her that his ancestors had known John Peel, the famous huntsman. Sometimes, when Peel was really drunk, one of the family had lifted him on to his horse. Beatrix was determined not to be impressed. She simply said: "I've never thought owt of John Peel." It was a brave thing to say in front of all those farmers,

Josephina Banner pictured at Isel Hall, near Cockermouth, 1989. (*Hilary Gray*)

because they all thought that John Peel was marvellous.'

CUTE AND PRETTY. When she had time to study the features of Mrs Heelis on visits to her home, Josephina was enchanted. 'She was tiny, and the older she got, the tinier and rounder she became. And she was so cute and pretty – the prettiest old lady I have ever met. The eyes were of a brilliant blue. She had lovely rosy cheeks and soft white hair, done up at the top with a little black velvet bow.'

At the time the Banners became acquainted with her, she no longer had the keenness of sight to enable her to paint delicate water colours. She cherished her original paintings, each measuring about 12 by 8 inches. Wrapped in brown paper, with a blue ribbon, they were kept behind the geyser in the bathroom. 'Even in this matter, she was completely original.'

At Castle Cottage, near Sawrey, not far from Hawkshead, Beatrix had the company of her husband, William Heelis, 'a very fine Lakeland gentleman – tall and goodlooking.' William, a solicitor, was known to the older folk as Apple Billy, his family hailing from Appleby, in the Eden Valley. There was also 'a tiny little old traditionally dressed maid, rather like a Victorian doll to look at.'

Josephina recalls her first visit to this house, and the way that she and her husband had to go through the gardens of two other houses to reach it. (Later, they became acquainted with a back door which gave access to the back lane). Beatrix cherished the obscurity of her residence, not because she disliked people but simply because fame ensured a regular flow of visitors. If she were to be well-disposed to them all, no time would be left for leisure or her ongoing interests.

Hill Top, at Sawrey, was also hers, of course, and here were many of her treasures, including a large doll's house. She kept some rabbits in a hutch in the garden of Castle Cottage so that children would not be too disappointed if they visited the place and could not find Peter Rabbit. The rabbits in the hutch, which was of the bottomless type that could be moved daily to enable the animals to have fresh nibbling, were introduced to children as 'relations' of Peter Rabbit.

'She nearly always had people to tea at Hill Top so that they would think that she lived there. Beatrix valued her privacy above everything . . .'

Beatrix Potter. (*E. Jeffrey*)

SOUND OF CLOGS. On the first visit to Castle Cottage, Josephina had to rap her knuckles on the small green door, there being no knocker to use. 'There was a long silence. Then Delmar and I heard little clogs toddling along on the flags beyond the door. They toddled up to the door. Then they stopped. We felt it was just like a little mouse, stopping to sniff the air, to try and detect who was coming.

'Then gradually she opened the door until it was 2 or 3 inches wide. We saw her little face peep through. She recognised us. She opened the door a little and said: "Coom in." And do you know what she was wearing on her head? One of those old-fashioned tea-cosies which are knitted and have a hole for the spout.' It is recalled that the tea-cosy was blue. 'She looked so cute, like one of her dressed-up little animals.'

Beatrix did not shake hands with her visitors. 'She turned and toddled off. We just followed her. Delmar shut the door behind us. We found ourselves in a flagged hall. There was no mat. Two beautiful old guns, with silver mountings adorned a beam. Then, on the right, there was a door into this lovely old room.'

It was not over-furnished. 'There was a fireplace, with two easy chairs, comfortable in Victorian red velvet. I remember an old-fashioned dining table. We saw some chocolate wrappers – what Delmar later declared was "a naughty amount of chocolate paper."' Some straight-backed chairs were available, and the visitors sat on these. 'We sat here, rather politely, because Beatrix was very awe-inspiring as well as being sweetly pretty – like the little dog Duchess!'

She began to ask questions. 'As we answered, and she discovered that we knew the Lakes, and a number of local farmers intimately, she began to open up and became very friendly. She said something very funny: I laughed, and as I laughed I snorted. My husband said: 'Oh, Pig-wig!' a nickname that made Beatrix laugh. She opened her brilliant blue eyes very wide, stopped and looked from the one to the other, then said 'Do you call her Pigwig?' After this it amused her to do so also. She very often used this name when she wrote to me.' (The letters are now in the care of the National Book League).

Josephina had a clear recollection of that first visit to Castle Cottage, to the extent that she can recall fine details of a Girton that hung here. 'It was so suitable – a shepherd, also sheep running for shelter from an approaching storm.'

TWO LETTERS. Josephina's letters from Beatrix Potter include one dated 20 October 1938, when Beatrix returned a book about rural crafts and expressed sadness 'that the old strong honestly-made hand crafts are dwindling. Labour-saving and laziness are nearly allied. It seems impossible to find apprentice black-smiths now. The smithy in this village is closed, and not for want of work.

'There are still a few good wheel-wrights left: but I observe with disgust the increasing use of rubber motor tyres on carts and wheelbarrows. They offer some advantages, but no one can call them lovely on a farm horse-drawn cart . . .'

On the subject of children, Beatrix observed: 'It's curious how graphic children can be, up to a certain age, and then they lose it, or it is wiped out by teaching. A shepherd's child about 5 years old showed me a remark-able crayon scribble of two lambs . . .

remarkably capering lambs kicking up their heels. I asked for another specimen. Now six months later she gave me a "picture" done at school; outline traced from an elaborate scene in Kate Greenaway style, little boy and girl, cottages, etc., all carefully coloured; and consigned to the fire by me . . .'

In a letter written on 9 November 1939 Beatrix referred to what had been 'a most lovely autumn for those who had leisure to enjoy the beauty of the peaceful valleys and fells. For my part, between arrears consequent on being laid up, and wanting to do as much as might be before petrol is scarce, I have hardly known which way to turn during October.

'I have been up three times in Little Langdale about repairs. There is not much ploughing to be done on sheep farms. But timber and pit props are a pressing need. A lot will have to be cut; it wants careful choosing . . . It's not a cheerful time. A most peculiar war; for those of us who lived through the last one, it seems different; "bad to reckon up" as the saying is. And everything in a muddle. There is no use thinking; keep working and make the best of things!' The letters were signed Beatrix Heelis.

MEETING THE FARMER. Delmar and Josephina Banner were at the *Woolpack* when they met a professor of agriculture at Durham, who mentioned the circumstances in which he came to meet Beatrix Potter. He had sent a questionnaire round the district, seeking information about sheep diseases, and one of the most helpful replies came from a farmer called B. H. Heelis.

He made an appointment to see this farmer, and in due course he arrived at the Cottage in Near Sawrey, where 'their little maid' took him upstairs to a tiny room. In an enormous bed was this tiny, pretty old lady – B. H. Heelis, the farmer. He had tea with her and was enchanted by what she told him about sheep complaints, and with her unique and delightful personality – her unpretentious realism . . .

Beatrix had toured the Lake District in 'an antiquated, strange-looking black car, very much like a taxi, and driven by a very ancient chauffeur.' When attending outdoor events she often carried an umbrella which had belonged to Mr Warne, a partner in the publishing firm, to whom she might have been married but for his untimely death. (Mr Warne gave her an engagement ring and, to her sorrow, this was lost in the hayfield.)

'She was very naughty – went and tossed hay when forbidden such frolics by the doctor. "Then, my belt-support slipped off, and down I fell!" She told this with a twinkle. "I felt such a *fool* – they had to carry me in!" '

When Josephina and Beatrix last met, it was a garden occasion. They walked beside the flower garden, then the apple trees, then the vegetables, to where a strip of ground housed local wildflowers she had collected and planted. 'Among them was "zig-zag clover", of which she picked a leaf to show me . . .'

Beatrix and her friend walked to the very same little iron gate set between mossy posts where clover had been featured in the tale. 'She pulled my head down to her level and she kissed me. Neither of us spoke. We knew, as we parted company, that we would never meet again. When I turned round, there was Beatrix, waving a clover leaf at me. Just like Timmy Willie.'

W. R. Mitchell (June 1986)

OWNER OF BRANTWOOD

Walter M. Johnston writes about John Ruskin, who was born 150 years ago.

FROM 1871, until his death in 1900, Ruskin's home was 'Brantwood' on the edge of Coniston Water. He was a man of many parts; poet, philosopher, artist, writer, designer and critic. By the age of 4 he had started to write rhymes, even if not poetry. By the age of 11 he had started drawing and sketching, and his poems 'Derwent-water' and 'Skiddaw' were written on a visit to the Lake District with his father.

On his return home, Ruskin yearned for the Lake District hills. Anyone who has visited *Brantwood* will know of the magnificence of the view which overlooks Coniston. The fells were to look over Ruskin and be his guardian in old age and infirmity.

Ruskin's work was first published when he was 15; it was an essay on the formations of mountains. This was soon followed by another essay on the chemical analysis on the colour of the Rhine water. Constantly suffering from ill-health, Oxford in many ways became his saving grace and he met many eminent writers, painters and scientists.

After a visit to Switzerland his life was to take shape. He went intensively into painting, drawing and writing on theories of painting – he became an art critic. His message is still of much value today:

Let our young painters go humbly to nature, rejecting nothing, selecting nothing and scorning nothing and rejoicing always in the truth.

At this time he wrote his famous book *Modern Painters*. As he was only 21, he was advised not to put his own name to the book but, 'a graduate of Oxford.' The book became the talk of the art world. It created a storm due to its contents, but criticism was coupled with the remark that whoever wrote it knew his subject.

In March, 1847 he re-visited the Lake District and stayed at the *Salutation Hotel*, Ambleside. The following year he travelled to Scotland and while there married a Scots girl, who was a friend of the family, and for whom Ruskin had previously written *The King of the Golden River*. His next book was *Stones of Venice*, followed by his first complete book of poems; it was called *Poems. J. R. 1850*.

The death of the artist Turner was a bitter blow to Ruskin. Ruskin had published letters defending his work in an England which wasn't ready to accept Turner's paintings. He bought paintings to help him when his finances were low, encouraged him and wrote of his work. He left an estate of £80,000 and Ruskin was left £20 to buy a mourning ring. His father said: 'Nobody can say you were paid to praise.'

Ill-health still beset him and his domestic life was not happy. In 1854, his wife left him and the marriage was annulled. He returned to his beloved Lake District in 1867 and found great pleasure with Keswick and its district, but at Coniston all didn't please him.

He wrote to his mother: 'I was at Coniston today. Our old *Waterhead Inn*, where I was so happy playing in the boats, exists no more. Its place is grown over with smooth dark grass – the very site of it forgotten, and a quarter of a mile down the lake, a vast hotel built in the railroad station style – making up, I suppose, its fifty or eighty beds, with

[105]

coffee room, smoking room, and every pestilent and devilish Yankeeism that money can buy, or speculation plan.'

The poet J. W. Linton was selling a house at Coniston for £1,500. Ruskin bought it and wrote: 'What I found was a rough-cast country cottage, old, damp, decayed, smokey chimneyed, and rat riddled, but 5 acres of rock and moor and streamlet. I think the finest view I know in Cumberland or Lancashire with the sunset visible over the same.'

He got to work drawing up plans and spent a further £4,000 on its extension and furnishing. He formed the St. George's Fund to which he gave £1,000. Old property was bought and converted for the needy. Six houses his father had left him he gave for the use of unfortunate people and a tea shop was bought for the people in London by Ruskin.

He continued writing and after a visit abroad, brought out books on birds and botany. After a visit to Greece he brought back samples of Greek lace and started a Greek lace industry in Coniston. Classical vases he had brought back influence the shapes of English pottery of these days.

In 1878 Ruskin was seriously ill with inflammation of the brain. On 4 March the exhibition of Turner paintings opened in London. Ruskin had spent six months arranging and cataloguing the exhibition. Each day Ruskin's condition was reported to visitors. As he recovered he carried on writing and enjoyed friends being with him at *Brantwood*. Among them was Mary Wakefield.

The company would sing some of his own compositions and the Christy Minstrel songs, and Ruskin would joyously clap his hands to the music. By half-past ten his day was over and as no lamps or gas were allowed at *Brantwood* he would take a candle, and after a look at some of his favourite pictures he would climb the stairs to his bedroom which was lined with Turner drawings.

One Christmas he gave a dinner for 315 young people in Coniston. He was often called an atheist, but he spoke to the young people on: 'Jesu here from sin deliver.' *Pretorita*, his autobiography was now written, and in 1899 a complete volume of poems was published due to public demand. He gave most of the profits from his books to needy people.

On 18 January 1900, as he was going to bed, he turned at the bottom of the stairs to look at the painting of his father by Burne-Jones. He stopped and nodded to the picture and said: 'That's Ned, that's my Ned.' During the night Edward Burne-Jones died. Burne-Jones had stood loyal to Ruskin at all times. He took his criticism and gave his friendship.

It has been said that Ruskin had a mental breakdown. At times he was ill, but never violent. A flu epidemic had hit Coniston; on 20 January 1900, Ruskin complained of a sore throat. When the doctor arrived his temperature was 102 degrees. Suddenly he collapsed and became unconscious. There was no struggle, he fell asleep in his own room with his beloved Turner drawings.

During his lifetime 134 of his works were published. While at Coniston he mixed more freely with the villagers than Wordsworth had done at Grasmere.

He was buried in Coniston churchyard on 25 January 1900; his friend, the fine singer Mary Wakefield, sang at the service. Among the many wreaths was one from the village tailor. The card said:

'There was a man came from God
  His name was John.'

(*November 1969*)

[106]

11

ON THE COAST

ACROSS THE SANDS

IN THE MERRY month of May, the first of many large parties of walkers is conducted across the Sands of Morecambe Bay by the Guide, Cedric Robinson, who says: 'It's a walk to be enjoyed; there are hundreds of acres of firm sand where I can allow people to spread out. If we walked in military style, they wouldn't enjoy it at all.'

Elsewhere on the Sands, extreme caution is needed. 'Then I blow the whistle, get them all together, and tell them what to expect.' Cedric always carries a whistle and a stick. The party sets off from Hest Bank about four hours after high water, and 'we're very lucky with the weather. Very seldom did we have a bad day last year.'

The route can be used for only half the day because for the remainder of the time it is covered by water; the tide erases all traces of the previous party's passage from Kents Bank to Hest Bank. A fairly brisk pace is maintained, and no one lags. It is enough to know that this 'wet Sahara' will soon become a shallow sea.

Cedric has been Guide to the Sands for many years; he does the work for the Duchy of Lancaster, and he occupies the Guide's cottage near Grange-over-Sands. Trains on the old Furness line thunder by at a range of a few score yards, and the railway blocks an immediate view of Morecambe Bay.

Cedric has the walk well organised. Parties are taken across by appointment.

Between now and the end of the season the total number of walkers will exceed 5,000.

For Cedric, familiarity with the Bay has not bred contempt. No one knows

Cedric Robinson, Guide to the Sands.

Arnside. (*J. A. M.*)

better than he the several dangers that lurk on the hundreds of acres of mud, sand and rippling water. He has an almost daily excursion on to the Bay as one of the all-weather fishermen who seek shrimps, cockles and flukes, conveying themselves and their equipment by tractors and trailers.

Shortly after our conversation, on a day of penetrating cold last winter, Cedric and his daughter set off looking for cockles. Ten minutes after they had left dry land, they were enveloped in a blizzard.

KENT CHANNEL. I asked him about the main channel, the course taken by the Kent, which has the reputation of being the swiftest river in England. When it has broken free from the confines of the dale, to join the sea, the Kent can vary its route.

Cedric said that at present it was to be found mid-way between Kents Bank and Silverdale, but for four years it was on the far side. 'It's done a lot of damage and made it hard work for me. I haven't been able to keep my eye on it.'

History repeats itself. 'Seemingly, it's quite a few years since it was on this side

Walkers crossing the sands. (*E. Jeffrey*)

of the Bay. It's much easier for travellers when it is running central, because once it gets in near any rocks, it gets a hold. It may be a few years before it moves again.'

When I last strode across the Bay, we seemed to be well clear of the shore. The precise route depends on the river's course and the attendant quicksands. Last year, there were days when 'we walked the sand to Silverdale, and then took to the footpaths and continued to Arnside. It became a long walk.'

The Kent, gouging the sand, has disturbed an old embankment near Jenny Brown's Point – a structure made during one of the many abortive attempts to reclaim sections of the Bay. 'In my lifetime, that embankment has shown itself about three times. Normally, we've walked over it, because for years it was covered by sand. When the channel went to that side, it undermined it.' Avoiding the hazardous areas, by taking to the marshland, 'puts mileage on to the journey.'

AT MORECAMBE LODGE. Inquiries about the walk reach Cedric as early as December, for the following season. He arranges to meet the parties at Morecambe Lodge, north of Hest Bank, having travelled there by train to Carn-

forth, and by bus connection to the shore of the Bay. 'Sometimes I'm lucky enough to get a lift by car.'

For years, the starting point was on the marsh near Hest Bank railway station. It became very popular with day-trippers, some of whom tended to join the walk unofficially, hence the decision to assemble further along the shore.

The first major snag is the river Keer, which 'looks straight forward, but never is!' It is an area where quicksands are likely to be encountered. Cedric organises his party into several groups, and tells each person what lies ahead, and of any action that is needed to prevent 'miring'. Some areas of the Bay would 'mire a cat'.

The members of the party are kept moving, for the first reaction on reaching soft ground is to stop, and this is unwise. Beyond the soft spots near the Keer is a stretch of 'nice firm sand'. Vast areas have a rippled appearance. Cedric explains that the state of the sand depends largely on the speed of the tide. 'If you are in an area where the tide has lapped in very slowly and the weather has been quiet, it leaves the sand ridged.'

The Kent offers a special challenge to Cedric's knowledge of the Bay and, as related, a considerable detour may be needed to find a crossing. He has a pair of binoculars of great power with which he scans the Bay, but visual inspection alone is never adequate; he must go on to the

Bay to check on his observations.

Traditionally, the fording places have been marked by 'brobs', pieces of bush set in the sand, but 'when a river is moving, it's pointless to do this, for the water just goes with them. You can put an odd "brob" in where an area is stable.'

Cedric still uses brobs to mark the routes to his cockling and fishing grounds, which can be up to 10 miles from home. Pieces of laurel are ideal, for the leaves do not drop off when they are dead.

A FICKLE BAY. Not many weeks before – and I met him in December – there was an especially wet spell. 'Three very experienced fishermen from Flookburgh lost their tractors in quicksands, within a week of each other. And those men had followed the Bay all their lives.'

One tractor that was claimed by quicksands near the Keer was shifted by the next tide for a distance of half a mile. 'The tide eased it out of the quicksands, scouring round it, and rolled it up the Bay.'

There is danger for the unwary, yet most people have a healthy regard for the swift tides of Morecambe Bay. Cedric is an auxiliary coastguard – there is a colleague at Arnside – and at the bathing pool, Grange-over-Sands, is a hooter used when a tidal bore is imminent.

That bore continues to impress Cedric Robinson though he has seen it many times. A wall of water approaches with a roaring sound and runs far up the Kent to dash itself against the railway viaduct. It is yet more evidence of the fickle nature of a Bay which, on a sunny and calm day, can look invitingly safe.

W. R. Mitchell (May 1982)

A SOLWAY ADVENTURE

ALMOST EVERYONE who lives on the shores of the Solway goes fishing. Where I live we stake out a long line far out at low tide and bait perhaps a hundred hooks. Then at the following low tide we collect the catch, a mixture of plaice, flounders and rough-backed dabs, and we hope for codlings in the autumn. These codlings are prized as a change from the summer flat fish, but short daylight hours create difficulties.

In the middle of last November I had a memorable morning's baiting. It was dark – darker than I thought it should be, but a break in the clouds showed the complete disk of the full moon low over Criffel. A yellow beam of moonshine glinting over the blue-black sands showed me my landmarks, and I kept two rocks, a near and a far one in line with a particular curve on Criffel.

Drifting clouds made me doubt the way, but in time the familiar stakes were there. I had reached the line. As I had not baited for some time I had some repair work to do, and still there were only fitful gleams of moonlight to work with. I was, perhaps three quarters of a mile out, and the sea beyond sight. The water of innumerable pools lapped gently on the shell-encrusted rocks, and as the first grey streak of dawn appeared, something akin to the dawn chorus of land birds awoke.

There was the high pitched squeaky note of densely packed flocks of oyster-catchers, and the lonely wild notes of gulls on the wing. One of the large dark-winged gulls was circling me in ever narrowing rings – perhaps eyeing my tin of bait. At one time I fancied I felt the whirl of air from the slow beat of its wings close to my face, and as I moved I heard the raucous laugh with which that type of gull mocks us in bad weather.

It seemed that quite suddenly the line of hooks became visible. Then, in the western sky there were flushes of pink reflected from the eastern dawn. The pools and gleaming sands sprang to vivid life, and the day had dawned.

Familiarity with the ways of the Solway brings scorn of ever getting lost. Then, one November afternoon the experience came with appalling suddenness. I was baiting as many as seventy hooks with boiled mussels. Standing astride the line I worked my way along slowly, for my fingers were stiff with the cold. My eyes were on the line and hooks.

Usually I straighten my back and look around from time to time, but that afternoon I kept on with the task until the last hook had been baited. Then, straightening up I realised that a fine drizzle of mist had descended, making both land and sea invisible, cutting off indeed all landmarks. Of course I should have retraced the footprints of my rubber boots, but I could not find them. Perhaps I could tell the position of the land and sea from the line – but then I realised that I might not have staked it out parallel to shore or sea.

It should be a simple matter to start walking with my back to the line. I counted my strides until they mounted into some hundreds. Then I remembered that in a novel I had read, one of the characters says that a normal right-handed person lost in the desert circles towards the left. At the time of reading it seemed a point of merely academic interest, but thinking of it now I deliberately took a half turn to the right.

Soon I saw a stake, one of two lines marked out for firing practice during the First World War. I was surprised and frightened for I knew that just beyond the far line was the edge of the channel towards which I had been walking unknown. I turned my back on the stake, and set off again determined not to panic, and yet very near to the verge. And now I was on a part of the sands unfamiliar to me, for the pools and channels were unrecognisable.

To the right I could see a long line of hills with what seemed to be a clump of tall trees. I knew there were neither hills nor trees along the whole shore. Then I remembered having read somewhere of the magnifying power of mist. I had never believed it, but I wondered now if it might be true.

I turned deliberately to the right again, and then realised that I had been walking almost parallel to the low sand hills of the shore, and the tall clump was the only two-storey house on that stretch of coast. I made landfall about two miles from home but thankfulness made short work of that distance along the high-tide line.

My wife said nothing at all when I got home, for she had long since drawn the curtains and put on the light, shutting off all knowledge of the world and the far-reaching sand flats.

E. R. Burnett (June 1968)

LIFE ON ROA ISLAND

Roa Island! Fancy you living there! Isn't it awful in the winter? But I suppose the summer makes up for it.

I'VE LOST count of the number of times this has been said to me. Certainly, living on Roa Island, one is aware of the weather. Rampside, barely a mile away, is much warmer and calmer. The island may be joined to the 'neighbouring island of Great Britain', as the Act for the construction of the embankment put it, but it is still three-quarters of a mile out in the sea.

I have a regular visitor each year who listens to the seagulls crying overhead and says: 'Bad weather when the gulls come inland.' The visitor does not realise that we are the ones who have gone out to sea. Perhaps this can be accounted for by the fact that, from Roa Island, Morecambe Bay seems more like a huge lake than the open sea.

When visibility is reasonable, whichever way you turn, there is land, from Coniston Old Man in the north to Blackpool Tower in the south, from Walney Island in the west to Ingleborough in the east.

We are still in a very exposed position. The wind is the climatic feature with the most influence, and this can be as strong, though not as cold, in June as in December. A completely windless day is fairly uncommon. This is particularly noticeable if you want to spray part of the garden without getting drifts on to other plants. The only calm days are wet, or you are at work!

Low-growing shrubs, especially the grey leaved ones, planted close together for protection, do well. So do medium-sized roses. Foxgloves and honesty stand up to the winds, but lupins don't.

I do well with root vegetables: sage, mint, thyme and parsley flourish, while an azalea is happy in a tub in the yard. But each year, just as the daffodils are coming to their peak towards the end of March, the equinoctial gales blow them all down.

I have not yet had the experience of an uncle who planted rows of lettuce in my great aunt's garden on Roa Island. A gale blew up that night. Next morning there wasn't a lettuce to be seen!

Sometimes I dream of having a beautiful sheltered, walled garden away from salt spray.

Contrary to what many people think, summer is not necessarily the best time on the island. One reason is that while the island is not exactly picturesque, it is quaint and different, and visitors come, especially on Sunday.

This is the day when I feel I am living in the middle of a large car park, and I retreat to the bottom of the back garden away from it all. If I want to go out I must get the car out early in the morning, otherwise I may find a car, whose owner is out fishing, parked across the garage door. People who belong to the large and flourishing boating club have a car park and launching facilities on their own ground.

The summer is full of other people driving around with boats on trailers looking for some water. They launch their boats down a slipway at the end of my back street. It isn't a good beginning to the day to set off for work at 8.25 a.m. and be unable to get out of the back street because someone is rigging a very large boat across the end, between the cars left by people who are out cruising, or camping on Piel Island. It isn't much better when you can't get home at night for the same reason.

The season is fairly short, and the rest of the year, particularly during the week, can be extremely beautiful. This is when, if there is no wind, the most noticeable thing about Roa Island is the silence. These calm still days seem more frequent from December to March. Time after time we say: 'Why are there so few days like this in the summer?'

Living out at sea can cause problems in the winter. It can be raining gently when you leave Roa Island in the morning, sleeting at Rampside, and as you get closer to Barrow the snow is looking very settled and quite deep. Sometimes you drive through a thick sea mist as far as Rampside Road, and suddenly come out into brilliant sunshine.

Most strangers to the island want to know what it is like on the causeway in bad weather and if we are ever cut off. Occasionally traffic has been held up for a short time when the tide has come over, but this doesn't happen very often. The Coast Road to Ulverston floods more often.

About eight or nine years ago, there was a week of very low barometric pressure and high tides. Walney Promenade and Roa Island embankment were inundated more than once. It was interesting to see boats lashed to the lamp-posts on the causeway.

Last September there was an exceptionally high tide, but the sea was like a mill pond. With a wind we would have been a true island once more. The wind worries me less when I am driving myself

across the embankment than it does when I am being driven.

The wind affects us less now that the electricity and telephone lines have been put underground. In the days of telegraph poles and overhead wires, the electricity went off quite often in bad weather. My oil lamps, the open fire and camping stove still come in very useful, for Roa Island has no gas. In the days of gas lighting the island had its own small gasworks. When electricity came, the gasworks closed. We are among the few communities in the country not affected by North Sea gas and the conversion problems.

The gulls and waders are the commonest feature of birdlife here, but there are other birds which I always associate with particular seasons. In February and March, a shelduck seems particularly noticeable.

In late summer, large families of female eider and ducklings bob up and down over incredibly large waves. Occasionally in spring I look over the back garden wall and see a magnificent eider drake, pink, green and white, floating on the tide.

Swallows usually arrive in Rampside about 23 April, and in some years they and the house martins come to the island. Whether they nest or not, there is always a day at the end of September when the swallows flock on the overhead wires twittering and preening before their journey south. And there is always at least one October morning when I put the milk bottle out and hear the wild geese flying over.

The sound of summer is the harsh cry of the terns. Another sign of the times is the arrival of the Lake District Naturalists' Trust caravan on Foulney Island to protect the nesting birds.

We have plenty of starlings and sparrows, some thrushes, blackbirds and robins. There is at least one family of wrens, and in some years we have goldcrests. Goldfinches visit Rampside. Sometimes there is a stray blue tit, willow warbler, chiff-chaff or redstart.

Along the embankment, as well as all the waders you would expect, there are wheatear, pied wagtail, linnets and skylarks. A cuckoo calls in spring. A kestrel may be seen hovering at any time of the year.

Lately there have been more hedgehogs, and I have had both a lizard and a weasel in my yard, as well as seeing them on the embankment.

When autumn comes, and it is the season for going to amateur musicals and plays, or signing on for evening classes in Barrow, Dalton or Ulverston, it is easy to feel enthusiastic to start with. But on a windy, wet January night the temptation to leave the car in the garage and settle down with a book is great. I suspect it would be just as great if I lived in a town.

It's worth a gale now and then, when you have to block up all the little cracks to keep the cold winds out, when sand is blown in the yard and the windows are coated with salt, to be able to see the sun rise over the Pennines and set over Walney: to look at the Howgills and Whernside, a picture in the snow, or the flat top of Ingleborough rising out of a morning mist over the Bay.

Late on a summer night, the Lakeland fells are a black frieze against a clear opal sky. And all I have to do to see all this is step out of the door, or look out of the window.

There's nowhere like Roa Island.

Pat Jones (January 1978)

12

SPORTING CHANCES

LAKELAND YOUTH 'TAKS HOD'

Since the war, wrestling academies in the three Lakeland counties have led a revival in this skilful sport.

HOD, HYPE, hank, clicks: these words will not mean much unless you are familiar with wrestling, Cumberland and Westmorland style. Yet hundreds of Lakeland people use them daily, for the sport is popular and has an enthusiastic following.

Supporters would have you believe that the style dates back to the day when Jacob wrestled with the Angel!

Just before and during the war, interest in wrestling was flagging, but the post-war years have seen a tremendous revival, largely through the efforts of academies which exist during the winter and, apart from teaching lads the tricks of the sport, entertain hundreds of fans with league competitions.

For instance, there was a crowd of 1,000 people in Carlisle Drill Hall for special contests held in 1951, an outstanding 'do' at Egremont Market Hall one night attracted 1,200 people, and even a quiet village like Gosforth was able to pack the Public Hall with 450 people when South v. North finals took place in 1950.

Although the high peak of popularity seems to be past – there has been a slight slackening of appeal during the last two years – the position is still much better than before the war. It is impossible to estimate the number of visitors to Lakeland shows in summer who enjoy watching wrestling bouts in the open air.

From May until October the wrestling fans congregate at the shows to see the lads take hold, and the grass season usually ends at Wasdale Head Show. Then the sport continues under cover. At the academies young lads start to climb the ladder which leads, they hope, to the holding of world championships.

These championships are for various weights – 9½ stone, 10 stone, 10½ stone, 11 stone, 12 stone, 14 stone and heavyweights. Some years ago Billy Bragg held the all-weight honour, and he weighed 20 stone. The present holder is Desmond Ward, of Wolsingham.

Some wrestlers have had the distinction of being treble champions. J. T. Richardson, of Kendal, has won a world championship every year since he was 15; last season he won two – for 9½ stone and 11 stone – and this year claimed the honour at 10½ stone. Cyril Bragg, of Wigton, is a treble champion. In 1952 he came out top at 10, 10½ and 11 stone.

Toughness and science combine in Cumberland and Westmorland style wrestling. The lads usually have the first quality, for they are engaged in farm work or forestry, jobs which develop their muscles until they are like bands of steel. The best wrestlers keep their fitness by not touching tobacco or alcohol.

Five teams take part in league com-

Drawing by E. Jeffrey.

petitions, and they are from Carlisle (present champions), Bootle (runners-up), Gosforth, Gilsland and Kendal. Home and away fixtures are arranged, and the league is run very much like association football, with two points for a win, and one for a draw. The academies wrestle boys under 14, under 16, 10 stone, 11½ stone and all weights.

Traditional costume for wrestling consists of silk vest and slips, with coloured trunks (often elaborately embroidered) and socks.

A contest is judged on the basis of three falls, and there are two umpires and a referee to supervise. Two wrestlers enter the ring and shake hands. They then grip each other round the back. Wrestling starts when both have taken a fair hold.

The first wrestler to touch the ground with any part of his body other than his feet is declared the loser. Sometimes the outcome of a bout is in doubt, for both men fall side by side. This is declared a 'dog' fall, and they wrestle again. If a man breaks hold he loses the fall.

The 'hod' is most important, and the wrestlers try to grip each other as low down the back as possible. It is not easy. Both bend their bodies so they are almost horizontal and their legs are wide apart.

The bout commences when the referee shouts 'hods'. Then the wrestlers try to throw each other. A fall may come in 10 seconds, or the contest may take 10 minutes.

There are special names for the standard throws, including inside and outside hype, the right and left back-heel, twist off the breast, swinging hype, right and left leg hank, full buttock, half buttock, cross buttock. Skill and experience soon tell.

For this story of modern wrestling I chatted with Mr J. R. Wilkinson, vice-chairman at Gosforth, which was formed in 1946. As an official umpire, Mr Wilkinson has journeyed to Kendal, Gilsland, Brampton, Carlisle, Bootle, Waburthwaite. The Temple family have contributed a good deal to Gosforth's success, and the six sons of the late David Temple wrestled at one time.

In Lakeland, wrestling is not confined to the academies or the summer shows. Not all wrestlers wear the traditional costume. It is not an unusual sight to see two schoolboys 'tak hod' on a village green, emulating the older lads and yearning for the day when they, too, will be able to take up the sport seriously and aim for a world championship.

W. R. Mitchell (August 1956)

HOUND MAGIC

To A CUMBRIAN in any part of the world what is sweeter music than a pack of foxhounds in full cry, or to hear and sing that grand old song *John Peel?*

I well remember as a lad hunting with the famed Blencathra Foxhounds. Before joining the army in 1914 I worked at the bobbin mill near Keswick. When the pack was hunting Brundholm or Latrigg it was always a good excuse for lads at the mill to take a day off work.

It seems only like yesterday that I heard, coming out of Brundholm just

Cumbria's Mighty Huntsman. From a colour study of John Peel by Edward Jeffrey, showing the huntsman as he might have looked in his later years, with his beloved Skiddaw Fells in the background.

above the River Greta, a low murmur not unlike the humming drone of a swarm of bees, that kept rising in intensity as it neared the road above the bobbin mill to resemble the gaggling of a flock of wild geese. On they came, closer and closer. Now the running foxhound pack surged over the crest of the hill into the valley opposite the railroad tunnel.

That day I heard and saw a pack of foxhounds in full cry. It was like a rushing river of melody rolling to a crashing crescendo, a mighty cascade of savagely, spine-tingling and primeval music, that thinned to a rippling ribbon of high-pitched hound cry, which gently faded out as they trailed the fox.

If there be those too sophisticated to believe in witchery or sorcery, let them regard the authentic magic of good foxhounds. For here is a genuine wonder just a little above our comprehension. Their intelligence is more than that of ordinary dogs. They are sagacious past human understanding, and the sense of smell is the master agent in a foxhound's uncanny performance.

A tired fox will for a while run here and there, pausing, listening. The trail he leaves is a very criss-crossed affair. Good foxhounds will wind their way through any mazy trail, and very soon, with triumphant yowls, will announce that the mystery had been solved, setting off again in the right direction.

Down in the Arkansas Ozark foothills of America I have heard old foxhound hunters declare that a hound on a very hot scent gets more than the scent, that

he actually gets a delicious taste as well. Yet, even granted that these two powerful senses of taste and smell are at work, the abiding element of mystery centres around the foxhounds' wonderful feat in taking the right direction. Often indeed, good foxhounds will make a temporary false start down the wrong end of the trail, but are usually swift to correct their error.

A foxhound possesses the artistry of high discriminative powers. The well-trained foxhound can be taught to run a fox and nothing else, be it a deer, an otter, or a rabbit. It will enter a dewy maze of cover, reject allurements in the way of tempting scents. He will be turned aside by nothing from the urgent business of finding the trail of a fox.

ABOVE

Tommy Dobson with some hounds and terriers in Great Langdale.

BELOW
John Richardson.

Far be it for me to say that all foxhounds have the same abilities. One hound will have a phenomenally cold nose; one will always tell the truth of right direction; one will have the ability to follow implacably a single trail; one will be gifted to unravel the snarls of a tangled skein of scent; another will have the stamina to run all day.

All this is very human, very appealing, having in it elements of the whimsical. But, to me there is always a deeper element of mystery. For, after all the explanations of conjectures for a foxhound's excellence have been made, there still remains the exciting possibility of something just a little beyond our immediate ken. We might call it sorcery, because, no matter what breed of hounds, the foxhound knows no superior in any hunting scene for versatility, nose, stamina, natural hunting intelligence and gameness. No dog commands more respect or welcome.

What is more heart-warming to a foxhound hunter than, after a successful day's hunting on the beautiful Cumberland fells, sitting in the inn with his hunting friends on a crisply cold night, when the stars seem a little closer, and the fire glows a bit brighter, reminiscing of the hunters of bygone days, and singing all those grand old hunting songs. Above all the friendly talk and singing, the voice that sings in your heart is the trail-cry of a pack of black and tan, white and tan foxhounds.

Fred Newton (August 1957)

HOUND TRAIL IN SPRING

There was that indefinable aura of anticipation and excitement which emanates from race meetings anywhere, writes Mrs J. Gowan.

MY HUSBAND had been away since early morning trying to photograph red deer in Martindale. I had promised myself an easy time after long hours on the fells the previous day, but now after lunch I was wondering how to fill in the afternoon. The old man passing by made up my mind for me. Beaming, he called out, 'Off to t'Trail', as he stepped out smartly down the road. After momentary hesitation I decided to follow. I'd never been to a Trail before but knew that, with nearly 1,000 meetings during the season, hound trailing could justly claim to be 'the Sport of Lakeland.'

I was thankful to escape from the hectic holiday traffic on the Windermere to Keswick road into the comparative calm of the trail meeting. The scene was typical: a large green rolling meadow, bisected by a low iron railing, with odd cars already parked on either side of the entrance; around the field a high, dry-stone dyke, with rooks cawing in tall beeches in one corner, and beyond the chequerboard of fields and odd trees rising sharply to the horizon, to be merged with the russet bracken carpet and grey rocks of the fellside.

It was quite early but there was still that indefinable aura of anticipation and excitement which emanates from race

Hound Trail at Pooley Bridge. (*J. Hardman*)

meetings anywhere. Tweed-clad officials stood around enjoying the sunshine. The trail secretary sat side-saddle at the open door of his car taking entries on a small folding table.

Several owners were already walking their hounds up and down the field, most of the latter sporting colourful tartan coats. Bookmakers, standing by the boards on their cars, were busily chalking up the runners in surprisingly clear script. A vociferous pack of small boys, led by a tousled urchin who had the competent air of a hunt terrier, swooped joyously on each new arrival and showed a remarkable knowledge of each hound's name, pedigree, and prospects for the day.

The field was becoming busier as more vehicles appeared, and the hounds came spilling out eagerly. Land Rovers, shooting brakes and vans were abundant, and several had been converted into 'dog-boxes', with wire partitions and straw-lined interiors. Two young puppies stood on the seat of one van, gazing out wide-eyed and excited at a scene with which they would become very familiar in the next few years.

The trail secretary read off the entries, and the crowd, swelling with holiday-makers, surged around the bookmakers, who were now shouting the odds: 'Three to one Ullswater Princess; Five to one Fast Harry; Seven to two Troutbeck Glory . . .'

My own fancy was a newly arrived black and tan hound with an almost supercilious air of confidence about it, echoed in the appearance of its master, a rubicund gentleman dressed impeccably in Glenurquhart check. Both were rather larger than their rivals and had the appearance of having been fed upon the best of everything since their youth.

Seeing no odds shown against this hound I approached a friendly-looking bookmaker. He gave me a rather knowing look: 'That one, Ma'am? For you only mind, two to one *on*.' And in a more confidential tone, 'Compared with *him*, now, those others are just a lot of dogs!'

It transpired that my hound was the reigning champion, having won fifty-nine trails during the previous season! I felt that this was sufficient justification for the superior look about it, not to mention those meagre odds.

The crowd jostled by the railings as the hounds were led to the nearby hillside, and there they lined up by a rugged old oak, yelping and baying as they strained frantically in their owners' grips, their muscles rippling under smooth coats. The starter checked the entries, earmarked the hounds and motioned to a waiting figure 50 yards away.

As the trail layer came towards the field with his 'drag' of sacking impregnated with aniseed, paraffin and turpentine, they were released in a great crescendo of barking, to race past him and into the country. The hounds strung out over the fellside in a loose pack of white, tan, fawn and black, running strongly by a rocky outcrop and over a stone dyke, where, through my binoculars, I could see one unfortunate scrambling desperately to regain several lost yards.

Smoothly they flowed through the rough dead bracken to turn right-handed along a boulder-strewn slope, down a deep gully, out again at the far side, past a scurry of sheep and finally out of sight over the shoulder of the hill. The tremendous murmur of hound music died away slowly, and from the distant road came again the faint drone of traffic. I realised to my surprise that I had been at the Trail for an hour, and feeling slightly fatigued, was glad to avail myself of the joy of a shooting stick.

An extremely well dressed woman, escorted by a pair of elegant miniature poodles, walked languidly through the crowd, fully conscious of all turning heads. She was happily unaware that the focus of all eyes was the dogs, a state of affairs which could happen nowhere else in the country!

Fascinating fragments of conversations drifted past:

'. . . owd lass got cramp in t'legs through getting wet. Dosed her with hot milk and whisky. She's grand now . . . Happen she'll win today.'

'. . . Get away man! I tell ye one o' them poodles 'ud come in afore that dog ye backed!'

'. . . been walking them thirty miles ivery weekend since Christmas. Tell ye, man, I feel fit enough to run t'trail meself!'

The terrier-like boy, who had been perched on the railings, suddenly let out a shrill cry of 'TRAIL' and the crowd pressed forward with a burst of speed which would have done credit to the crew of Captain Ahab upon sighting Moby Dick.

On the fell top I could see a tiny moving speck, 2 or 3 miles away; just between the bracken and the scree, followed shortly by three or four others, and there came the main field giving tongue as they poured over the skyline.

Though binoculars I could see that the leading hound was black and tan. *My* dog! The excitement increased and when they were still streaming down the fellside through a birch wood, and across a network of dykes some half-mile away, the air pulsated with the blast of whistles, roars, screams, shouts and yodels from the owners, lined up 30 yards behind the finishing line, jumping madly up and down and waving handkerchiefs, scarves, and flags.

The same dog held its lead and came loping powerfully across a ploughed field, over a dyke, across a meadow and another dyke, and finally sprinted the hundred yards to the tape, past the waiting officials and towards its owner, to gulp a rewarding titbit, and be immediately swathed in a blanket.

I proudly collected my winnings. I was right about the feeding too – the dog's owner was a well-known Kendal master butcher!

(*May 1966*)

THE ART OF RACING TERRIERS

I lay flat on my stomach in the mud, trying first to persuade and then to force Bloggs into one of the traps. Bloggs thought otherwise.

'THERE ARE going to be terrier races', said my husband, unavoidably detained at a far part of the Grand Arena. 'You must enter Bloggs,' he added. Bloggs is our terrier. Of indeterminate parentage, he is, uncharacteristically, the quietest and gentlest of dogs.

I obediently set off with him for the starting point, easily identifiable by the amazing chorus of high-pitched yapping as terriers and owners mustered at the end of the arena among a crowd of supporters shouting advice – they had, perforce, to shout to be heard at all above the din – and the placing of bets.

The more partisan milled about near the start and lined the rails, while the general public – interested but less passionately involved – sat on the grass in the sunshine to enjoy the fun.

Being a newcomer to this sport, I hovered on the fringe of the gathering, trying to find out what to do. The owners were, on the whole, tough-looking types, the few women among them being rather tougher than the men. The form, it seemed, was to gather up one's terrier – and what a remarkable variety there was, dogs of all ages, colours and degrees of shagginess – and hold it struggling and yelping under the arm.

When so hoisted, Bloggs soon got the idea, and I saw with astonishment our quiet, well-behaved little dog turn into a yapping, snapping, struggling, demon before my very eyes, adding his mite to the general cacophony and, for good measure, taking a swipe at the backside of the dog in front. It, perhaps fortunately, was too shaggy and, anyway, too occupied in doing the same to the dog in front of *him* to notice this dastardly attack.

To my surprise, I saw the terriers were being started, as in greyhound racing, out of traps, five at a time. I also observed strong men lying on the ground behind the traps trying to force reluctant competitors through the narrow entrance into the darkness of the trap and sometimes, despite helping hands from friends, having to admit defeat and give way to owners with more amenable or more experienced dogs.

I learnt some interesting new Cumbrian oaths as these frustrated owners withdrew, and it is devoutly to be hoped that their terriers placed their paws firmly over their ears.

A BIT OF FUR. In front of the traps the 'hare' – a bedraggled bit of fur attached to a cord – lay inert on the grass and, as the traps flew open, it suddenly came to life as it was winched along at high speed by an energetic man about 150 yards away at the finishing post where, in each heat, he was joined by the owners of the entrapped terriers.

However, not all the terriers appreciated that they were expected to dash after this desirable and provocative quarry and some, when the trap suddenly opened in front of them, bounded out and fell with zest upon their neighbours in what appeared to be the settling of old scores. Yet others, neither knowing nor caring what all the hullabaloo was about, sat down to enjoy a satisfying scratch, oblivious to frantic signals from their owners, now trying to attract their attention from the finishing post.

But in each heat, some of the dogs knew exactly what to do; they set off after the 'hare' at high speed. As it reached its destination, the intrepid winchman, foolishly un-gloved, reached down and snatched it up before any of the competitors could actually lay paw upon it. Although he worked like lightening, once or twice, when he held the prize aloft, a terrier was attached to his hand and had to be shaken loose.

Sometimes when the terriers arrived, only to be defrauded of their prey, they turned on each other and some bonny fights ensued, owners urging on their dogs with cries of encouragement. Once or twice, during the actual progress of a heat, a large greyhound was mysteriously unleashed and dashed after the hare, scattering the racing terriers to right and to left and inspiring the winchman to new heights of energy.

SECOND ATTEMPT. Heat after heat, the races proceeded: The entrants seemed to get no fewer and the noise was deafening. I decided to call it a day and returned to my husband to say that this was really not for us and that I wished to preserve my eardrums intact. I got no sympathy. 'Don't be feeble; give the little chap a chance; he runs faster than any of the dogs I've seen so far.'

So back to the start we trudged, the same transformation coming over Bloggs as we neared the noise and the excitement. Eventually we reached the man who was collecting the 20p entry fee; his pockets jingled as he moved.

He eyed us dubiously and asked if we had done this before. When I said No, he said, even more dubiously: 'Well, you can try'.

Try we did, but Bloggs and I had different ideas as to exactly what we were trying to achieve. Soon I, as others before me, was lying flat on my stomach in the mud trying first to persuade and then to force Bloggs into one of the traps. Bloggs thought otherwise.

The technique adopted by terriers who do not intend to enter traps is to place one hind leg firmly behind the partition on each side of the entrance. The owner, working at ground level, with one hand must hold the dog by the scruff of the neck, now inside the trap, so that it cannot back out and run amok among the crowd; with the other hand he – she – must seek to release the hind legs from their grip.

Alas, one has one hand too few. The entrance is just too wide for it to be possible to gather both hind legs in one

"Got anything for somebody who just wants to loaf around?"

hand, and one dare not let the scruff go. As fast as one prizes one leg loose and shoves it into the trap, out pops the one already in and resumes its grip outside.

I learnt that terriers have springs on their hind legs; and that they are amazingly strong animals, not un-advisedly, lightly or wantonly, to be compelled to enter small, dark cages where they have no wish to be.

A HUMILIATION. No one came to our aid; the ground was sodden; Bloggs screamed deafeningly from the interior of the trap and was, I suspect, using in his own language some of the oaths earlier learnt from the frustrated owners. I, too, had to admit defeat.

My 20p was re-funded and we with-drew humiliated, from the field. At least, I was humiliated but as we returned to base, I could swear that Bloggs was grinning in a nasty, new, smug, self-satisfied way.

As for my husband, when I explained why our little treasure had not carried off the prize, all he said was: 'Do you mean to tell me that you couldn't get that little scrap into a trap? I never heard such nonsense in all my life.'

Elizabeth Delmore (June 1982)

Brute Strength

ROBERT DODD, commonly called 'Miller Robin', who lived some years at Brough, was possessed of such bodily strength as to be able to take a bushel of wheat (a Carlisle bushel of 96 quarts) between his teeth and toss it over his shoulder. He would also lie down and, with six bushels of wheat placed on his back weighing some-thing like 950 pounds, rise up with apparently little exertion. Robin was also an expert wrestler and very few who knew the man would contend with him for the annual prize belts. Robert Atkinson, the Sleagill giant, carried a conveyance called a 'carr' out of a dyke-back on to the turnpike road near Kendal. This unlucky vehicle had defied the efforts of three or four persons to drag it out by tugging at the shafts and wheels. Very big men, since Atkinson's day, have somehow ceased to be wrestlers.

from *Wrestling and Wrestlers* (1863)
(August 1956)

13

WORKING WORLD

MY FIRST DAY IN GREENSIDE MINES

Joe and I peered into the gloom and saw two big red eyes swing from side to side. Joe pulled me by the coat. 'Com' on, let's git back till't shaft,' he said.

I COMMENCED WORK in the Greenside Mines just after Easter in 1937. I drew my lamp and the miner who was put in charge of me got me a stick to help me walk in the mine along the Lucy Level, which was a mile long. The reason one needed a stick was that miners walked along the rails to keep their feet dry because water poured down the level from the old workings above Lucy Level and from the pumps from the Lower Level, and a stick provided some guidance. It was no easy matter for a beginner to walk the rails and until I learned to walk them dryshod I often got my feet wet. We arrived at the Smith shaft top. Before us was a white-washed chamber cut out of the rock and a shaft that was 90 fathoms deep. Groups of miners stood about awaiting the cage to take them below. The foreman came up and said: 'You go up South end with Joe.'

I went with Joe some distance up 90 South end, where a few miners were preparing to 'muck out' a driving. They began filling wagons with the grey-green rock, known as 'deads' because there was no metal in it. Joe and I had to tram these deads to a hole near the shaft and tram the empties back. We went back and forth until 'bait time', when we put our coats on and walked to the shaft top. Here we sat and ate our sandwiches. The foreman, whom we called Primer, came up and said: 'You two, go to 120 North

after bait.' He departed. A miner who was sitting nearby said: 'I wadn't gah up theer if I was you.' I asked: 'Why. Is it dangerous?' He said: 'It's warse nor dangerous – it's haunted! There's a girt ghost powney we' big red eyes like saucers and it rattles its cheeans. I tell thee – ask Primer to let thee gan some-wheer else.'

MEETING THE GHOST. Primer was nowhere to be seen. Joe said: 'Come on, Arnold, they're nobbut trying to flay us.' We got in the cage and descended the shaft to 120 level, got out, rang the cage off and set off up the level. We had gone some way, talking as we went, when Joe said: 'Didsta hear owt?' I said: 'No.' He said: 'It's theer agen!' This time I heard a distant rattle of chains and a snort. As we peered into the gloom, we saw two big red eyes swing from side to side. Joe pulled me by the coat. 'Com' on let's git back till't shaft.'

We departed, our lamps casting grotesque shadows on the walls of the drift as we sped and stumbled along. Soon the lights of the 120 landing came in sight. As we arrived we met Primer who said: 'What's the matter we' ee?' Joe told him about the ghost. Old Primer laughed and said: 'Get back up there – tis no ghost it's only old Bobbie.' He led the way and we followed.

We did the same work again, tramming

wagons to a dead hole until about 3.15 when miners came down from their working places in the stopes shouting: 'Fire! Fire!' We went to the 'baitspot' and awaited for the shots going off. The miners counted them – one, two, three and so on until all the shots had gone off. We lit our carbide lamps, for the detonation of the shots had put them out, and made our way to the shaft.

Soon we were riding upwards, and went homewards down the Lucy Level. We emerged in the daylight, dirty and wet. I was aching all over. How sweet the air seemed as I made my way home to the village. My first day in the mine was over.

Arnold Lewis (October 1986)

CUMBRIAN BLACKSMITH

Recalled by David and Margaret Sibley

IN ONE OF the loveliest valleys of Lakeland, twenty years ago, Tom Colthard followed his trade of blacksmith. He and his wife, with a rising family, lived in one of those old stone cottages that in their simple beauty add so much to the charm of the district. Tom joined his father in the smithy as a lad, and for half

a lifetime had done all the blacksmith's work for the neighbourhood.

This ancient craft, requiring strength and skill, was essential in every agricultural community, and until our mechanical age it offered a good livelihood to an industrious man. Even a small farm had at least one pair of horses, so that shoeing was a large part of the blacksmith's business. There was the repair of farm machinery, plough-shares, reapers and mowers; cartwheels from the wheelwright to be fitted with iron tyres; and always harness and chains to mend.

Work in the forge was all done by hand. The smith usually had an apprentice who worked the bellows and adjusted the size of the fire to the type of work in hand at the time. He also helped with the horses and gradually, through a long apprenticeship, acquired the skills of his master.

Although the usual work was on farm implements the smith would sometimes engage in ornamental work, and beautiful specimens of wrought-iron came from his hand: screens and flower stands for churches, and gates for the new tenant of the old mill or the wayside cottage.

The blacksmith's shop was a fascinating place full of old bits and pieces, illustrating a way of life now completely passed away. Horse-shoes hung from nails, and there were nails themselves, hand-made in various sizes, old sickles and scythes, hedging tools, broken pieces of ploughs and harrows, axle-shafts and wagon fittings.

A great vice was a prominent feature of the forge, and in a corner lay a heap of smithy nuts for the furnace. In the light of the window stood the work-bench; hammers great and small lay around and, taking pride of place, the anvil, that most characteristic symbol of the blacksmith's craft, with its gleaming surface, and evocative shape. Many such ancient pieces, for all we know, may still be lying in the grime of old smithies, well-worth salvaging for their interest to posterity.

What greater joy for the village children in bygone days than to watch the smith at work! Through the half-door of the smithy they stand and gaze in at the blazing furnace which lights the mysterious interior with its dancing flames. And now the smith, his face ruddy from the fire, seizes the white-iron from the depths of the furnace, and strikes it with great blows of the hammer so that the sparks fly around gloriously.

In a wonderfully short time the shoe is formed. Meantime the cart-horse stands patiently by. The smith lifts the great foot and, supporting it on a three-legged stand, places the shoe on the hoof. There is a pungent smell of burning horn as the shoe is tapped rapidly into place. The job is done, the spell that binds the children is broken, and they rush off chattering like sparrows.

By the 1940s, when horses were being replaced by tractors and farming was becoming everywhere more mechanical, the volume of work for the village smithy dwindled away. The new machinery was too complicated or too heavy to be repaired by local craftsmen. Agricultural engineers with modern equipment began to appear, who serviced the new monsters that took the place of the simple reaper and binder and horse-drawn cultivators.

Tom Colthard was troubled. He had two growing sons and when they were born, no doubt, he had rejoiced that one of them at least would carry on the family tradition, and take over the work when his own arm began to tire. But now the incentive to continue in his trade was lacking.

The smith started to think of emigration. He was probably influenced by one or two farming friends who had recently begun to make good in New Zealand, or had caught some infection of wanderlust from the schoolmaster who had sailed for America. However it happened. One day the news went through the valley that the smithy and cottage were up for sale. Tom and his family were going to Australia!

'I hadn't realised what I was doing,' said Tom to us, 'until I saw my tools coming under the auctioneer's hammer. That was a bad moment!' It was a bad moment for our village too, for Tom was really devoted to his native valley and served it in a number of ways. His wife and children took an active part in village affairs, and were well-liked and dependable. Thus the new farming uprooted this family of good Cumbrian stock, who should have been valuable members of the community for years to come.

Now the smithy fire is dead. The once noisy building is silent and deserted; new people from the city have taken the blacksmith's house. The disappearance of the village forge and similar old crafts, combined with the departure from their districts of the families practising them, make a double break with the tradition that leaves our countryside the poorer.

(March 1969)

CHARCOAL BURNER IN CUMBRIA

Choking wisps of smoke drift gently through the young larches. A mistle thrush sings from a nearby birch. In a clearing of broad-leafed woodland along the River Leven below Newby Bridge, Walter Lloyd pursues his ancient craft. He is one of an almost vanished race of charcoal burners.

NEARLY SIX thousand years ago the craft was practised in Africa. Iron Age man in this country shaped his weapons in its glowing embers. During the thirteenth century as many as nine hundred burners were at work in a single area of England, and after the Battle of Crecy in 1346 charcoal, mixed with sulphur and saltpetre, became vital for the production of gunpowder. Until the introduction of blast furnaces it was used in large quantities for smelting iron and steel. More recently its use has been limited to domestic products such as biscuits for the diabetic, barbecue fuel, or artists' materials.

Life for the charcoal burner and his family was no sinecure. As the final product was so much lighter than newly cut timber, the work was invariably carried out in the forest. Groups moving from one area to another lived a nomadic existence in conical huts built from a skeleton of wooden poles covered with turf and sacking. If timber was plentiful, and the stay likely to be prolonged, a wooden floor might be laid. Separate huts accommodated beds of brushwood and straw-filled sacks, while a metal drum, lagged with turf, represented the family's cooking facilities. It is difficult to believe that at the beginning of this century children were reared in such conditions.

A burner was welcome in the forest for he kept it clear of dead wood, and by coppicing renewed the life of alder and juniper, beech and birch. Trees were not uprooted, but felled to within a foot of the ground. Within fifteen years new shoots had sprouted from the stool, and so the mixed woodlands which latterly have

Building a charcoal pit at Grizedale, 1970.

been fast disappearing, were maintained through past centuries.

Having felled his timber, the charcoal burner set about building several kilns. Most important was the central flue, built not for the passage of smoke, but to allow lighted pieces of wood to be dropped within to start the slow conflagration. Uniform lengths of timber were then placed round the flue, and 'roof pieces' laid across them. The whole was then packed with turf to exclude air, and covered with a sprinkling of soil. Smoke rose lazily through the turf, and the long watch began.

MODERN CONDITIONS. The conditions of Walter Lloyd, a modern burner, are little different. Admittedly his kilns are of metal and a pair of bow top caravans spare him the trouble of building turf huts. A lorry replaces the traditional cart, and the bags, no longer of sacking, are neatly labelled 'Lakeland Charcoal'. They advertise the fact that the enterprise 'conserves nature's woodlands'.

Otherwise, life is as primitive as it was eighty years ago, but Walter is accustomed to hardship. Life in the Royal Navy has prepared him for the cold of winter, the long watch, and the ability to survive on fragmentary periods of sleep. He works in conjunction with the New Woodmanship Trust, and the Lake District National Park, groups more concerned with coppicing than the production of charcoal. However, this pilot scheme makes the work a viable proposition, and produces a cheaper product than that imported from Spain or Mexico.

Since the demise of the charcoal burners our mixed woodlands have been endangered. Areas such as the Wealden Woodlands, the New Forest, or here at Grizedale have been partially cleared to make room for the ubiquitous conifer, planted in geometrical formation, and presenting a sight quite foreign to the area. It is the aim of the Trust to correct this imbalance, and to preserve our natural woodlands.

But the work is demanding. It is a rare character who would choose to live in a bow topped van in the heart of a forest through all seasons. Nor would many workers be willing to bathe in a tub of painted zinc surrounded by curious woodpeckers and roe deer, or to discover that the last of the butter had been consumed overnight by questing hedge-hogs. But Walter accepts such minor difficulties in his stride. He loves the life.

As one kiln smoulders lazily, Walter fills a second with 2 foot branches of beech. Ventilators stand open to en-courage the start of the burn, and burning faggots are dropped into the flue to start the twenty-four hour combustion. The kiln needs constant attention. Perhaps it burns too sluggishly, and more air is required. Perhaps it is too hot and must be dampened with water. Clouds of white smoke drift down the forest glades.

This will turn to a transparent blue as the burning nears completion.

Another kiln is slowly cooling. If opened too soon it is liable to burst into flames and the charcoal will be consumed, but a fourth kiln had already stood for a week. Walter removes its lid and passes the brittle black coals down a sieve and into a skep of hazel wood, and the waiting bags.

Walter does not complain of his two hourly vigils throughout the night. He surveys the skies as once he did on deck, and notices the position of the Great Bear, or that Venus and Jupiter are drawing near together. He watches badgers at play, and listens to owls hooting across the valley, or the deer snuffling in the undergrowth. If daylight should bring the favoured visitor he dives into the recesses of a tent stretched between the caravans and with all the culinary art of the practised seaman, produces delicious Waberthwaite sausage barbecued to a turn, elegantly served with a spicy dip, and steaming coffee. Seated on tree trunks, we agree it tastes like ambrosia.

In his few spare moments Walter Lloyd sits splitting willow into fine sticks for artists' material, or cleaving beech for tent pegs. Whimsically, he ponders on life in the forest. On the whole he is well content.

Margaret M. Nixon (February 1989)

A CUMBRIAN 'SWILLER'

I DON'T REMEMBER WHEN I first met 'Miley' Whinfield, but to me, and many others, 'Miley' and Eskdale are inseparably associated.

Though the swill shop stands just beside the Post Office at Eskdale Green, a wayfarer could pass it by without knowing, unless it was boiling day, when the soft, sweet smell of burning wood and boiling timber permeates the sur-roundings.

It was here, at Moor Head, that Miles Whinfield set up business on his own in 1906. He had served his time at Wood-land, North Lancashire, and came to Eskdale in 1891 to work for James Grave,

The tools of the 'swiller's' trade. (*W. R. Mitchell*)

who owned the bobbin mill at Longrigg Green and also employed swillers on basket-making.

In 1917, Miles was joined by an apprentice, William Hartley, who has kindly given me the information for this article. For the next twenty-three years these two craftsmen worked together until, in 1940, William Hartley took over the business.

Fortunately for us all, Miles continued to work, and although he admits to not working such long hours as before, his output would do credit to a man half his age.

A swill, or skep, is an oval-shaped basket, with a hand hole at each end. The most suitable wood is oak of about 25 years growth which, after being boiled in a tank for three or four hours, is riven into laths whilst hot. The laths are then individually dressed to weaving thickness on a 'mare', a machine on which one sits astride, using a two-handled knife like a spokeshave, the lath being gripped by wooden jaws actuated by a pedal.

The weaving laths are kept in a pile by the worker's stool, their pliability being retained by constant damping – as in other basket-work. The swiller weaves the basket on to a rim, or bool, of hazel or rowan, the only tools used being sharp knives for trimming the length before insertion, and cutting off any rough ends when the end of the lath is reached.

Swills are made in all sizes, and have many uses on the farm, in the granary or at the mill. They are practically indestructible. My father bought a small one in 1930 for gardening, and I still use it for the same job! Bill Hartley made me a special one with a dropped side, and the cat not only spends most of her time in it, but it reminds us of good friends and happy times in Eskdale.

I have told you something of the shop and the swiller's trade. Now let me tell you of these two remarkable dalesmen – Miles Whinfield and Bill Hartley. The

Wilfred Barker, a stalwart of the Furness swilling trade. (*Evyn Thomas*)

equally welcome, for while deft fingers work on the baskets, the talk goes on – talk of current events or bygone days.

Miley, at the grand age of 86, is nature's own child. His sweet, soft voice is interspersed with an occasional quick look in your direction, a look born of the fells and open country.

When he came to Moor Head he often walked over to Grasmere Sports and back; even now he climbs the nearby fell to plant the marker on top for the local 'guides'' race.

As to the future of the craft, Bill Hartley tells me that it is dying. Most swillers are now elderly men, and young ones will not take it up, as the working hours are much too long. Though the war stimulated a demand for swills, which has since been maintained, the supply of suitable wood is dwindling, oak coppices having been felled and replaced by conifers.

Russell Horton (August 1957)

swill shop is not only a workshop but a social centre as well. Whether you are a visitor, or a fellow-dalesman, you are

---

FLYING MISSILES AND FURRY FRIENDS

These were only two of the hazards which were considered to be run of the mill . . .

I SHIVERED AS I stepped from the warm sunlight into the cool, dim interior of Stott Park Bobbin Mill. I could well believe Jim Dixon when he told me 'I can honestly say these were bitter cold places to work.' Jim, head guide at Stott Park, was talking from experience. He spent his working years as a bobbin maker, in an industry which employed most of his family and contemporaries, often under conditions which would cause present day health and safety inspectors to blanch.

The mill in the parish of Colton is the last complete example of its type – all that now remains of the original Lakeland bobbin industry. Although a largely re-equipped mill operates at Staveley near Kendal to meet the limited demand for wooden products, it was the introduction of synthetic materials that sounded the death knell for a once thriving industry.

Stott Park ceased production in 1971. 'They wanted to flatten it and turn it into a caravan site, until Dr John Marshall and Michael Davies-Shiel, who were interested in industrial archaeology, managed to persuade the Department of the Environment to put a restriction order on it, so that it had to remain industrial.' When there was no demand for the building as an industrial site, it was established as a museum and opened to the public in 1983. Had this step not been taken, a valuable segment of Cumbrian heritage would have been lost forever . . .

Jim confirms that Stott Park, despite any restoration, is still completely authentic, even down to the old cobble stone floors. 'Although these have been relaid and set in concrete, they follow the exact contours of the original cobble stones.' Clogs were the statutory footwear. 'You couldn't feel the cobbles through a pair of clogs.'

The comfort of workers, he recalls, was not a prime consideration. 'The wind used to whistle through the buildings in winter. Many a time the glass was knocked out of the windows. You had to work hard to keep warm – they always got a better production rate out of you in cold weather . . .'

Like all of the old industries, the original source of power was water, hence the Lake District provided a perfect location. Fifty or sixty bobbin mills were sited from the River Lune at Lancaster to Caldbeck.

After the first twenty-five years of production at Stott Park, the 22 foot diameter water wheel was replaced around 1860 by water turbines. 'People seem to think we're always flooded out in the Lake District but when we ran on a dry spell, that's when the steam was needed.

That was the reason why High Dam was built above Finsthwaite.' Improved efficiency by use of the steam engine was an even more important consideration than standby capacity in times of water shortage.

In 1940 came the advent of electricity. 'Prior to that, the only form of lighting was a paraffin oil lamp above each machine. Then the electricity came and if you got a 40 watt bulb, you did well for yourself. There was no spoiling you in these places.'

Another governing factor in the siting of the mills was the ready availability of ash, alder, birch, hazel and sycamore which had all been coppiced for generations. Their quality was generally suitable for 'turning', whereas the introduced conifer was unsuitable for bobbin making. 'The grain is too open and it contains too much resin.'

When coppicing, it is essential that the trees be cut at the right time of year. In other words, in winter, when the sap isn't running. The exception to that rule is oak. When oak is cut, the bark is peeled from it and sent for tanning leather. The remainder is now largely used for the manufacture of rustic furniture but it was once used for making the 'swills' or baskets into which the bobbins were collected at various stages in their production. Every time a worker filled a swill, he would put a nick in a piece of wood or 'tally stick', his record of his day's output.

Trees brought to the mill would measure 3 to 3½ inches in diameter and would be placed on a 'peeling horse', a rough log with two or three 'catapult sticks' on it. 'You dropped your trees on

OPPOSITE
Stott Park Bobbin Hill in its heyday. (*E. Jeffrey*)

[134]

them and went down them with a double-handled draw knife, taking strips of bark from top to bottom, to allow the trees to dry out.' The process of drying would take approximately twelve months.

'Peeling' was a source of income, though perhaps not particularly lucrative, for the local youngsters. 'When we were kiddies of 12 or 13, we used to go down the mill to make pocket money. A penny a score for a tree 20 foot in length, three ha'pence for 30 footers. You never made a fortune peeling trees, but it kept you out of mischief on a night, did that.'

Once dry, the trees were cut off into lengths of about a yard, then gauged into certain diameters. The smallest bobbins were produced from the biggest trees and vice versa. Birch and sycamore were generally used for the tiny silk bobbins. After the trees had been sawn into 'cakes', they were smoothed on a device known as a 'blocking' machine.

'I knew an old worker who'd been a blocker all his life. He used to say "As soon as you can knock out a hundred gross in ten hours, you can call yourself a blocker". A gross wasn't 144, either, it was 150 when you were on piece work, to allow for scrap.' The skill of the blocker was to produce as many blocks from each cake of wood as possible with the minimum wastage.

Jim held up a 'typical bobbin mill cushion' for inspection – a hessian sack. Lack of padded seating would have been the least of a blocker's worries as he watched the unguarded saws spinning on his machine at 5,000 turns a minute.

The dangers were obvious. A momentary lapse of concentration or the effects of a cold winter's day on numb fingers could spell disaster, especially when working with saws capable of cutting through 3 inches of wood.

There were plenty of other hazards to contend with, not the least of these being preparation for the annual visit of the boiler inspector. This heralded an unpleasant task for whoever was chosen to climb inside the boiler to chip off the scale. Their assignment didn't end there – all the flues had to be swept out which entailed crawling along through the main fire tube. Not recommended for anyone of faint heart or with claustrophobic tendencies.

There would be other unpleasant surprises, too. While the shavings on the floor, often 3 or 4 feet deep, had the advantage of keeping legs warm in winter, creatures other than humans were also quick to appreciate the benefits. 'You had to watch out for furry friends and creepy crawlies. What with the heat from the boilers, they couldn't have wished for nicer, cleaner bedding. We found a gerbil in the drying room only last year. Goodness knows where it came from!'

Above the workers' heads a mass of belts and pulleys would be whizzing round constantly. 'It was always advisable to wear a cap. These belts could have as many as six to eight joins in them, so if you ducked up quickly, better that it knocked your hat off first . . .'

It was a fairly common occurrence for these belts to snap but the line shaft wasn't stopped while replacements were made, otherwise twenty people would have had to halt production for 5 minutes. 'That would have meant too much money lost, so you had to develop the knack of keeping your thumb upright, out of the way, and replacing the belt while it was moving – at 4,000 turns a minute – and the line shaft at 350 turns a minute.' I paled at the prospect.

More hidden dangers lurked for

workers in charge of the machine which bored the holes through the centre of the bobbins. If one did decide to spin adrift, everyone gave it a wide berth. 'The centrifugal force meant that it could hit a wall, bounce back on to the belt and be catapulted anywhere in the mill. I've seen blocks of wood fly through the roof before today. Nobody ever tries to catch one of these once they're in flight. Let it go where it likes!'

By this time, it was becoming apparent to me that life in the mill was no picnic. But worse was to come ... 'If your sleeves touched the machine, it would pick them up and tear them right off you, a loose end of wool and you had a ball of knitting wool if you weren't careful. Some of the worst accidents I saw involved women and girls who had long hair.' Suffice to say that the machine would have to be stopped as quickly as possible in an emergency but the braking system for a bobbin machine was to thrust a block of wood under the moving belt.

All this for 10s. 6d. a week as a boy in 1939. Surely the workers must have hated their environment? 'Not at all. There was more enjoyment working then than there is nowadays. Everybody knew everybody and we would all help one another. That attitude's gone from industry now ...'

The working day had its lighter moments. If a younger apprentice was cheeky to his elders, he would be picked up by the scruff of the neck and the seat of his pants and given a few spins inside the polishing drum. Was Jim talking from experience in this instance? 'Oh,

I've been spun round in there a few times,' he admitted.

Jim first started in the bobbin industry when he was 14 years old. Apart from a short spell at Ulverston Ironworks and a stint in H.M. Forces, he worked at Sparkbridge Bobbin Mill on the River Crake until its closure in 1983.

'It was four times the size of Stott Park and I can remember as many as 170 people being employed making bobbins. That was in the peak period of wire production, in the late Forties. I can remember us sending three or four wagonloads to Liverpool alone on one occasion. The big textile bobbins were sent all over the world.' Coincidentally, Jim's grandfather was a country joiner who helped build Sparkbridge. His father, when he finished joinery, also worked in the mill, as did his aunts and uncle.

I was shown one of the machines where the same man had worked for over forty years, the wooden handle worn smooth in the contours of his hands. Like Jim, he had spent a long time in one industry. Could Jim have envisaged working in any other trade?

'It's been my life, has bobbin making. I've seen them come and I've seen bobbin mills go ...'

The machine in front of him whined and clanked into action as he demonstrated what appeared to be another highly dangerous-looking technique which seemed second nature to him. 'Any volunteers to take over?' he grinned. At that point, I bade him farewell.

Hilary Gray (November 1988)

14

TRANSPORTS OF DELIGHT

REAL-LIFE COACHES

Many Christmas cards feature the coach and four. What was it really like during the Cumbrian coaching era?

ALL OUT 'N SHUV! That used to be a familiar call in the days of horse-drawn Lakeland coach trips, according to one of the 'character' drivers, Charlie Wittam. As not all the routes were confined to valley bottoms, passengers often had to lend a hand pushing a coach up a severe gradient, especially in bad weather.

But apart from pushing – which may not have been too often – there is no doubt that on the steep roads most passengers had to get off and walk. The story goes that when the beginning of a 1 in 4 or 5 gradient was reached, the driver stopped and shouted: 'First class, sit still! Second class, walk! Third class, shuv!'

This invariably raised a laugh and the wags in each party would vie for the honour of being 'third class'. Which suited the horses at least!

In the case of the trip from Ambleside up the Struggle to Kirkstone, six strong horses went to the top, and two returned to base in the care of a postillion. After reaching the top, the flushed, hot and panting tourists had their minds taken off their physical plight by the coachman, who shouted across to Red Screes and invited his charges to listen carefully for the echo.

In those days, children were no less opportunist than they are now, and an approved way of earning pennies was to run ahead of coaches and close gates, so

Coaching days at Thirlspot.

that they could be opened again for a fee. That sort of enterprise dies hard, and it was not until around 1947 that the last 'toll' gate was taken off its hinges.

Another form of transport was also a source of revenue to the enterprising youth so fortunate as to live at the foot of a mountain. Living in Edinboro – that part of Ambleside situated at the start of the Kirkstone Pass – were children who used to waylay cyclists beginning the ascent, and regaled them with fearsome tales of the steepness that lay ahead.

Having made their point, they charged 6d. for pushing the bicycle as far as the inn at the top. Sixpence was quite a lot then, but they earned every penny of it, and not just by physical effort alone.

Their description of Kirkstone top was

worth half the fee, for they said that it was so wild that in any other country but England it would have been the home of brigands!

In Victorian and Edwardian days, coach-drivers worked a six day week, and wore wing collars, tail coats and silk hats. A typical day started at 5 a.m. with the collection of horses from Sweden Bridge, Ambleside.

They were taken to the stables – for example to the *Queens* – and after feeding, cleaning and brushing were got ready for the 10 a.m. or 10.30 a.m. start. First of all the advertising had to be done, in the shape of boards which described and timed the trips.

'Trips of Scenic and Celebrity Interest' was the favourite publicity man's cajolement in those days, combined with some drivers' personal cries of 'we shall see, ladies and gentlemen, the residences of those whom honourable toil has raised to honourable wealth.' It is more than a suspicion that these words were lifted straight out of a guide book!

The main Lakeland coach trips were run by the *Queens*, *White Lion* and *Salutation* hotels, and Brown's Livery Stables. All these were in Ambleside. By 1895, Brown's coaching business had already been in the ownership of the Misses Townson for several years. It was not until sometime later that they parted with the business to Mr Edward Faulkner, but the name of Brown was still kept.

There were also quite a number of coaches starting off from the 'outlying' areas such as Grasmere, *Low Wood* hotel, Ullswater, Riggs of Windermere, Bowness, and Bells from the *County* hotel.

The 'Sally' (*Salutation*) had its own permanent blacksmith as well as a coach-painter-builder, and both had plenty to do to keep the holiday charabancs on the road. Their trade was a development from the mail coaches, the first of which ran from Manchester to Glasgow via Kendal in 1786. By 1823 there were a dozen running daily, though the first post-chaise service operated around 1750.

The journey was considered so hazardous, especially over the wild, mountainous parts, that passengers often made their wills before setting off. No wonder, when floods, bad roads, highwaymen and drunken drivers took their toll. We have thus come full circle with our motorways!

However, mountains are there to be tamed, and by the late 1800s things had improved to such an extent that even ladies were allowed to climb the fells (more often on the backs of ponies) in the company of a competent guide, the best known one being called Bennett, who was based at Dungeon Ghyll.

Some drivers were kept on during the winter months doing various upkeep jobs or driving for private hire, but most had to look for off-season work or go back home – if they were not locals – to Ulverston or even as far away as Liverpool. Experts spent the winter mowdy-catching (moles) and lived largely on 'fatty bread' (fried bread). They probably needed plenty of fat, as the winters sounded to be rather harder than we get these days.

Lakeland coachmen were renowned for their dry humour, and had a marked flair for inventing strange and expressive nicknames, as the following may prove: 'Sigh' Muncaster. Feet Wilson. Fearing Mackay. Pill Richardson. Park Rigg. Twist Hewitt. Nutter Whitehead. Pudding Hewitt. Torch Creighton and, a real gem, Tootie Pip Aitken!

The Toll Bar, Lyth, with farmers returning from market. The last remaining Toll House in use in Westmorland at the time, charges were: Cars 1s. Motor cycles 3d., Horse and cart 3d., Horse 2d., Cow 1d., Sheep ½d., and persons on foot and bicycles free. (*J. H. Cookson*)

A popular amusement among coach-men was the 'gurning' competition usually held at some local inn where courage, in the shape of strong beer, dispelled all inhibitions at making a fool of oneself. Putting one's head through a horse halter and grinning was not enough. There had to be a strong resemblance to a horse to get a vote, and the uglier the horse the better!

The prize was 5s., and one man, appropriately called 'Sappy,' won so many times that there was serious talk of banning his performance.

T. Smithies (December 1974)

A Cumberland farmer returned his new car to the garage. 'What's matter with it?' exclaimed the proprietor. The farmer answered, 'Nut much – but it's nut rattlin' reet.'

(1975)

I was travelling by bus between Kendal and Bowness. It was a bumpy passage at one place and there was a good deal of comment.

Suddenly, a shrill voice came from the back.

'Leave t' driver alone,' said a middle-aged lady. 'This trip will cure mi lumbago!'

(Miss) J. F. Thomas (1951)

DOUBLE-DECK BUSES IN LAKELAND

OUBLE-DECKER buses have for a couple of years carried people from Kendal through Windermere Town, Ambleside, Grasmere, Dunmail Raise, Thirlmere, Wythburn, Naddle and Chestnut Hill to Keswick. The ten leagues are accomplished in a couple of hours; the road runs beside four lakes – Windermere, Rydal, Grasmere, Thirlmere – and has distant gleams of Derwentwater and Bassenthwaite as Keswick is approached.

I was born in the Lake Country many years ago and have used every method of progress except the aeroplane. As railway fares constantly rise and never descend, I have become an enthusiastic top-decker with much 'practice' south of the Thames.

The trip from Kendal to Keswick and back was on successive days of autumn clearness and glory. The double-deckers give excellent outlooks over fields and walls and hedges, from bends and hills. From them you admire colourful villages and tiny market towns. The first lake-glimpse comes 8 miles out from Kendal where from the shoulder of Alice Howe the southern section of Windermere stretches from Belle Isle, past the Ferry, between Gummers Howe and the Furness woods.

For the next mile there is hide-and-seek; the lake's silver and blue flashes here and there among leafless trees. Above ancient Calgarth there is a charming vision. The next mile dodges over low ridges. Then comes that memorable and haunting terrace-view across the lake with Coniston Old Man and other fells. The road drops to lake level at Lowwood and continues with magnificent views to Waterhead. In the autumn afternoon the fells are limned in clear glory; crags are tinted with fallen leaves, fiery bracken, crimson-touched bilberries and gold of sphagnum moss. The bus passes through Ambleside, with its corkscrew corners.

The next lake, Rydal, is less than three-quarters of a mile long and a quarter of a mile wide. The road dances along the foothills and once touches the lake. From this upper-seat, the outlet flashes as it passes through the meadows. To those in lowly inside-places and on foot, a garden wall hides the Rothay. Along the pool backed by mighty rocks, the afternoon lingers in delight. There is more of sepia scree and rock, of reedy shallows than about the head of Windermere.

Grasmere, double the size of the other lake, has a green glory partly from the pines planted to enrich gentlemen's grounds. The meadows flow up to the farms at the foot of the fells. A few minutes halt at Grasmere (where the poet Wordsworth and his family rest between the green yews and the clear Rothay river), and the bus twists among hotels, lodging-houses and cottages. Clear of these, the deep gap of Dunmail Raise where the Keswick road crosses at 782 feet above the sea, is obvious ahead. Then the approach is masked by obtruding ridges, several rattling ghylls or water-courses are crossed; the road climbs pitch by pitch passing great sheep farms until Town Head hamlet is deep below.

Beyond the cross-road there is a sharp ascent, up which the bus's engine thrums a little. Beyond the climb eases, jogging along the comparative level of Dunmail Raise into Cumberland. Thirlmere, 3½ miles long, soon dominates the north, with Helvellyn on one side, Armboth Fells on the west, and the bristling Blencathra or Saddleback on the northern horizon. Thirlmere's surface has been gradually raised to 583 feet; narrow zones of conifers grow bleakly on former cattle and sheep pastures.

Of the communities along the old road to Keswick, only the church of Wythburn remains inviolate; south of it the bus road was lifted to avoid the brimming reservoir. The inn, closed many years since, has been used as a cottage. So has the former school, but Manchester Corporation has powers to clear all dwellings and place its workers in Legburthwaite, where a new school, many dwellings and a tree nursery have been established.

From this upper deck seat, the view along the lakes is interesting. The gentleman at my elbow asks me to locate the 'Rock of Names,' the trysting place of the poets of Grasmere and Keswick, on which the initials of William Wordsworth, Mary Hutchinson, Dorothy Wordsworth, Samuel Taylor Coleridge, John Wordsworth and Sarah Hutchinson were cut in the stone. The fractured pieces were salved and placed in cement on the Helvellyn side of the road half a mile or so north of the Straining Well.

The bus route continues to rise steadily. At one point the cascade of Launchy Ghyll (except in long drought) is visible, riven among the rocks of Armboth Fells, across a pretty wide stretch of lake. This is the last to be seen of Thirlmere, for the road sweeps through a narrow 'neck', descends into Legburthwaite, and crosses the outlet from the lake at Smeathwaite Bridge. The occupier of a top seat certainly finds pleasure for the road keeps near the centre of the dale, following the beck

which carries down the overflow of the Cumberland (lower) Helvellyn. The sharp ridges of Blencathra or Saddleback are well seen in front.

After Naddle Bridge, Skiddaw's 3,000 foot peak becomes more prominent than Blencathra. The last 2 miles are mostly descent, some of it steep and even twisty, with a view first of Bassenthwaite Lake in front, washing the north-western foot of Skiddaw. Near the Old Toll Bar Cottage, Derwentwater becomes an exciting view to the left. Both are lost to view as Chestnut Hill is descended, and the river Greta followed through Brigham to Keswick.

The return journey (made the following day) was just as memorable. The autumn tints were one moist, cold night more mature, and the carmine glow of wild-cherry foliage rose in all its charm. I was quite alert to the pageant of woods and pastures, the rattle of Greta when the bus halted at Brigham, the panorama of Latrigg and Skiddaw as they retired and lowered slope and summit; the sun-jewel of Bassenthwaite creeping over its broad plain; Derwentwater with Causey Pike and Catbells was radiant for a minute, then lost to view.

Helvellyn took the place of Blencathra or Saddleback when Nest Brow was descended to Naddle. For half a dozen miles it towered higher and higher, and was lost to view when the bus route climbed over the 'neck' and trickled along the shelf above Thirlmere. At Wythburn church a party was dropped to climb Helvellyn, and one of equal strength picked up, having accomplished the crossing.

From the north Dunmail Raise was a brief rise; at the top Grasmere's bright lake soon became a wider patch in the green meadows. Rydal lake had more golden delights this day; Windermere, as ever, puzzled with its constant change of shadows among the fells and the tumultuous dales.

This double-decker service across Lakeland will render its charms more accessible. The unobstructed outlook from the upper seats will stay with us, and many others who travel in that direction in time to come.

W. T. Palmer (March 1952)

'RATTY'

Cumbria's Little Railway with the Big Heart!

Since it was opened in 1875 the Ravenglass and Eskdale Railway has twice had the threat of abandonment hanging over its head. Today it is supported by a preservation society, and is again thriving. Many thousands of people a year enjoy the thrill of a journey from the shore of the Irish Sea to the foot of Scafell behind a miniature steam locomotive.

A JULY MORNING at Ravenglass, headquarters of the only passenger-carrying narrow gauge railway in Lakeland. A stiff breeze is wafting the tang of the sea inland. It is sunny but heavy clouds are hanging over the peaks of Scafell, less than 10 miles away, and looking even nearer.

People are everywhere. 'Ratty', as the Ravenglass and Eskdale Railway has always been nicknamed, has no high platforms or barriers to keep passengers in check. A queue has formed outside the booking office. The tea room is doing brisk business and the series of aerial photographs of the line mounted on the wall are attracting many a glance. In a hut opposite a till clicks in musical-box fashion as happy holiday-makers buy souvenirs ranging from mint-cake to pottery.

Several coaches are idling in the nearby car park after disgorging their complement of day-trippers. Other intending passengers are relaxing, recovering their aplomb and soothing their nerves, after driving in mountain goat style over the primeval passes of Wrynose and Hardknott. 'Ratty's' big brother, British Rail, has added to the number on the platform; several full-sized trains connect with the miniature service.

A variety of rolling stock forms the first train of the day up the line. It is just turned eleven and the train is now almost full. The crowd is a remarkably varied one. Young children, impatient to be off, jump in and out of the coaches. Teenage girls, accompanied by their parents, seem bored and uninterested. Adults stand on the platform clinging faithfully to their cups of tea. A schoolteacher tries valiantly to keep an outing of his pupils under control. Railway enthusiasts, armed with a battery of cameras and notebooks, are lost to the world as they faithfully commit to posterity their visit to the line.

At the far end of the station the exciting sound of steam can just be heard above the hubbub. The *River Irt* is, in railway parlance, preparing to move off shed and head the morning train. Her green paint and polished brass glisten in the sunshine. An almost translucent column of smoke rises into the sky. Coke is burnt on 'Ratty' so as to avoid covering the passengers with dirty coal smuts.

The engine has already taken on water from the nearby column and Driver Cyril Holland makes a few last minute adjustments to the mass of levers inside the cab. Then he climbs onto the footplate. Squeezes is perhaps a more appropriate term, for the *River Irt* is little more than 4 feet in height and Mr Holland's head protrudes way above the top of the cab. This locomotive has a long history, being rebuilt at Ravenglass in 1928 from an engine that had been originally constructed as long ago as 1894.

Soon all is ready. Mr Holland touches the regulator and with a loud hiss from the piston valves the 'Irt' moves obediently forward to the fan of points at the very end of the station. Then she slowly backs down towards the platform and couples up to the now crowded train. A green flag is unfurled in the breeze, whistles sound and the journey begins.

Mild Cumbrian accents contrast with raised Cockney voices, but both are soon lost in a cacophony of sound as the train gathers momentum to the accompaniment of tiny wheels passing over rail joints and a deep-throated roar from the engine chimney. A youth remarks: 'We'll be touching 2 inches per hour in a minute.' Someone replies: 'The wheels have come off.'

But once past the popular camping coaches owned by British Rail and clear of the station *River Irt* soon attains a respectable speed. For a few moments there are glimpses out to sea, although little remains to indicate that Ravenglass was a thriving port when Liverpool was unheard of. Nor is it easy to imagine that

the village was once a centre of the smuggling activities in the area.

Away to the north can be seen the towers of the Seascale atomic power station, but very soon the line swings towards the east and a wonderful panorama of the Lakeland hills opens up ahead. The train seems like some puny toy when contrasted with the mountain backcloth which is made up of all the high fells between Ennerdale and Wastwater as well as Steeple, Pillar, Great Gable and Scafell.

The pattern throughout almost the entire journey is one of mountains coming closer and the valleys opening out. The line now drops steeply down to Barrow Marsh and the left bank of the River Mite. It dives under the bridge carrying the main coast road and passes Muncaster Mill.

For the next 3 miles the line climbs continuously, hugging the precipitous slopes of Muncaster Fell and remaining aloof from tarmac roads. This section is well-wooded and the blast of the engine's exhaust echoes back from the trees. The rails, as usual, are damp and greasy, and Driver Holland brings the 'Irt's' sanding gear into operation to prevent wheel-slip. Trains can weigh up to 25 tons, but it is seldom that the locomotives are completely defeated. In the early days, however passengers often had to get out and push at this point. They felt cheated when the engine topped the climb unaided!

The sense of remoteness increases as the plains are left behind. Today, there are no buzzards or kestrels hovering above, waiting to dive on their prey, but they are nevertheless seen frequently in this region.

The former stone crushing plant, now a permanent way depot, at Murthwaite is passed, and before long Irton Road is reached. Although the first intermediate station, it is more than half way up the line. It is also the only point at which two passenger trains can pass, and as it is the summer season a voluntary station master is in charge of the operations.

Little more than half a mile separates Irton Road from the next station, Eskdale Green, but during this distance the line switches from Miterdale to Eskdale. For the remainder of the journey the views are dominated by Harter Fell which despite its imposing stature is only 2,140 feet high.

The rails pass under a bridge carrying the main road up the valley and immediately afterwards the steepest gradient on the whole journey begins – it has a maximum of 1 in 36. The surroundings are now extremely picturesque. A luscious carpet of vegetation is overshadowed by both deciduous and evergreen trees and in the middle of it all stands a water tank, now only used in emergencies. This is a much photographed location.

The line now hugs the Eskdale road. Beckfoot Quarry and the long established C.H.A. holiday centre at Stanley Ghyll House are passed. The engine is working hard as she attacks the final gradient. As soon as she has breasted the climb Driver Holland closes the regulator and *River Irt* and train drift gently to a stop at Dalegarth station, the terminus of the line. The 7 mile journey has taken 40 minutes.

There is a mass exodus of passengers. Many of them go into the cafe before taking themselves off into the mountains for the day to return to Ravenglass on a late afternoon train. *River Irt*, though, does

not have time to spare. She runs onto the turntable and within minutes is pointing downdale.

Quarter of an hour after arriving she pulls out with the 12.15 p.m. departure, a train that is lightly loaded when compared with its counterbalancing working. The run is almost entirely downhill, and the locomotive is able to recuperate after being left a little breathless by the long drag up from the coast into the mountains.

A stop is made at Beckfoot to pick up some holidaymakers from Stanley Ghyll House, but little of incident happens on the journey and Ravenglass is reached well before 1 p.m. Many of the passengers have dozed off, but they soon come back to life as the train grinds to a stop. A young cynic remarks in a voice heavily veiled with sarcasm: 'That was a lovely run wasn't it, go and say thank you to the driver.'

A lot of people do dismiss 'Ratty' as a toy. They regard it as a holiday camp line, elongated and transported into glorious surroundings. But they are wrong, for several reasons. The railway was built not just for pleasure purposes, but primarily to serve industry. It was opened in 1875, a time of prosperity in

'Ratty'. (*E. Jeffrey*)

the iron and steel industry, to carry deposits of haematite from around Boot village and Ghyll Foss to the main line of the Furness Railway at Ravenglass.

Unfortunately, only two years later, the price of iron ore began to fall and the Whitehaven mining company which had promoted the venture failed. The line passed into the hands of a receiver, but managed to keep going through catering for tourists which even then were invading Lakeland in considerable numbers.

There were only four passenger coaches and cleaned-out ore wagons were used to provide extra accommodation when necessary. The short tourist season did not bring in sufficient money for satisfactory renewals or repairs and by 1912 the two locomotives, *Devon* and *Nab Gill*, which was the nearest the Yorkshire manufacturers could get to Nab Ghyll, were worn out. The track was unsafe and the rolling stock more suitable as hen huts. The line closed and it seemed like the end. But by a remarkable change of fortune it was to begin operations again.

Mr W. J. Basset-Lowke, the famous model-maker, was wanting a long length of line on which his fine engines could really be tested. He decided that the Eskdale railway would be ideal and promptly set about converting the gauge from the old 3 feet to the present 15 inches. By 1917 the task was complete.

'Ratty' now entered upon a period of prosperity. It carried all the Mails for Eskdale and goods traffic reached quite sizeable proportions. Coal, fertilisers, food-stuffs and stores of all kinds went into the valley and out of it came wood, timber, potatoes and all the produce of the dale.

The line was owned by the Brocklebank family and its registered office was in the Cunard building in Liverpool. A steady flow of traffic resulted from the opening of the Beckfoot granite quarry in 1922. London's Waterloo Bridge is built on concrete containing this granite and in the north of England the roads of many towns have been paved with granite sets from Beckfoot.

By the 1950s 'Ratty' was in trouble again. Increasing competition and problems of transhipment had made the quarry uneconomical and in 1953 it closed. The last big firing, when 4 tons of explosives dislodged at least 60,000 tons of granite, was a record at the time.

Once more it was found that the line could not survive on passenger traffic alone, and in September 1960 it was offered for sale by auction. It seemed that the rolling stock would go to seaside fairgrounds, the track for scrap and some of the land to form caravan sites. But 'Ratty' was to confound the sceptics.

Over the years scores of people had come to love the little railway, and were not prepared to see it go without a struggle. The Ravenglass and Eskdale Railway Preservation Society was formed and subscriptions and donations started to pour in. Clergymen, doctors, stockbrokers, railwaymen, nurses, lawyers and housewives were among the many who gave generously.

Almost £7,000 was raised and Mr Colin Gilbert who had long been interested in the railway undertook to provide the balance. The new cutting is named after Mr Gilbert who is now chairman of the Company. The auction was held at Gosforth Village Hall and a successful bid of £12,000 cheated the scrap merchants.

David Joy (July 1966)

15

MAN, BIRDS AND BEASTS!

PIGS IN POSSESSION!

I AM FOND of pigs, but enough is as good as a feast, and a feast I certainly got one golden autumn day.

For my set of colour slides illustrating Lancashire landmarks and legends I needed pictures of the site of the Hill Fort on Warton Crag, and the prehistoric stones – the Three Brothers – that lie between the Fort and Leighton Hall.

As I left the Fort and crossed the bracken covered fellside towards the Brothers I became increasingly aware of roughly turned earth, as though an army of untrained gardeners had been spasmodically tilling the rocky ground.

Then I saw them – a few at first, then in family groups, then in foraging parties of healthy young warriors. Pigs! Big pigs, little pigs, stout pigs, lean pigs, strong silent pigs, rude aggressive pigs; and all impelled by a common bond – to defend the Brothers against all comers.

I retreated to the main path that crosses Warton Crag, and took stock of the situation. I would try the nonchalant approach – the ignore them altogether attitude. I strode out firmly, straight for the crest on which the Brothers stand.

I passed the first few groups without incident, but a stronger band ahead split  into two spearheads and advanced, one to my right and one to my left. It was clearly a pincer movement. I made for the right hand slope and over a low stone wall into a wood, and thence back to the path.

Next I tried an outflanking manoeuvre, through the wood once more. For a time this met with success, until I emerged into a clearing just beyond the Brothers. There, accompanied by several huge sows, was a horde of lusty youngsters. They set up an appalling clamour.

I raised the camera for a quick shot, but before I could frame the Brothers in the viewfinder a chorus of disapproving grunts announced the arrival of a strong force of assorted sizes, mostly large. The young pigs yelled encouragement as they closed in!

Even as I made for the safety of the wood I could see the headlines –

'CLUES TO LOST PHOTOGRAPHER

Tripod found on lonely fell – Pig coughs up lens hood.'

Where on earth did they come from? Were they protégés of George Orwell, emulating *Animal Farm*, or had they like Topsy, 'just growed'?

I left the enemy in undisputed possession. The Brothers have been there a long, long time, but I doubt if they were ever so well guarded. No doubt by now the pigs are in command of Warton village, and laying siege to Leighton Hall!

Harry T. Hampson (1960)

SHEEP SHOCK

MANY ARE the perils which lie in wait for the unwary wanderer in Lakeland, but my 'moment of danger' brings to light yet another hazard.

Ramblers in the Helvellyn area will be familiar with the delightful walk from Tongue Gill via Grisedale Tarn to Patterdale, and may remember the long narrow wooden bridge spanning a stream about halfway down the valley. Here it was that we, a party of three, paused for a rest. One crossed the bridge, one drank from the stream, while I sat on the end – or rather the beginning – of the bridge, with my back to it.

Suddenly our peace was shattered by a thunderous clatter on the bridge, and before I could make a move to investigate, I was struck violently on the head and shoulder, and a huge object descended from above and in front of me. All this was accompanied by shrieks of laughter from my two companions.

My first thought was that a boulder had rolled from the mountain-top. But why the unseemly mirth? Then I realised that the 'object' was a sheep, now disappearing at the gallop! Apparently it had ventured on to the bridge, and finding itself caught between two fires, had made a panic-stricken rush and vaulted the 'obstacles' at the other end. Could it have mistaken my inert body for a wall?

Very funny, no doubt, to the onlookers but to be knocked almost unconscious was not my idea of a joke! However, despite a headache, a buzzing ear and a bruised shoulder, I could not resist joining in the bursts of hysterical laughter which continued all the way to Patterdale.

After all, it could have been worse and at the thought of serious injury and newspaper headlines – 'Lady hiker injured by flying sheep!' – our mirth could not be suppressed.

Mabel Plant (1960)

HE MADE FRIENDS WITH A HORSE

SOON AFTER the First World War I spent a walking holiday in Lakeland when 'hikers' was an unknown term and rucksacks on the back were a rare sight.

Setting off from Keswick I passed, in the main street, a horse-drawn milk cart (then a still familiar object). A few moments later I heard the horse and cart following me. I glanced round and saw that its owner was nowhere about but the animal seemed to have a liking for me. I stepped out fairly briskly, but the horse still followed, and I became a little alarmed.

Eventually I slipped into a shop doorway but the horse, still with its cart behind, mounted the pavement and came towards me.

What would have happened next I do not know, but at that moment the milkman came running up and, grabbing the horse, backed it away.

Then the milkman looked at me with a

grin. 'It's all right,' he said, 'My horse wouldn't have hurt you. I reckon he must have seen that sack on your back and thought it was his nose-bag. You see, he hasn't had his breakfast yet and he's hungry.'

M. R. Longsight (1970)

FIDELITY

WITH REFERENCE to the letter of Mrs Jones and the quotation from the poem 'Fidelity', it is a well-known poem by William Wordsworth and was composed in 1805 to commemorate the faithfulness of a dog which remained for the space of three long months by the dead body of its master, who died on Helvellyn.

Many have met their deaths on the fells but none will be remembered as long as this young man, Charles Gough. It was the fidelity of his little dog which inspired Wordworth, and Sir Walter Scott who visited the scene later. Both were inspired to commemorate the event in verse. Wordworth's poem of eight verses gives an excellent description, while that of Scott, commencing 'I climbed the dark brow of the mighty Helvellyn', is written in his usual grand, romantic style.

The story may bear telling again. It was in the spring of the year 1805, that a young man, Charles Gough, came to spend a holiday in Patterdale, with the usual pursuits, angling and walking. He was always accompanied by his dog, Foxey, the heroine of the event, described as a small, yellow-haired terrier bitch. On the morning of 18 April the fells were sprinkled with snow, but Gough announced his intention of walking across the Helvellyn range to Wythburn where he had friends. He seems to have been an experienced walker and knew his route. He left, as usual, with Foxey.

No concern was felt at his lodging when he did not return, since he had said he might be away for a few days. Then it was ascertained that he had failed to arrive on the other side.

Those were the days before organised mountain rescue teams. Doubtless some search and enquiry was made but it was actually three months before the scanty remains of Gough were found on Helvellyn, near Striding Edge, the finder being the shepherd as described in the poem.

Gough had evidently fallen and, if not killed outright, had subsequently succumbed to his injuries and exposure.

What of Foxey? During all those three long months, haunted by who knows what canine terrors, in extremities of hunger and exposure, this faithful friend of man scorned to leave her dead master and remained near him until he was found. Doubtless she subsisted on carrion for, as every fell walker knows, dead sheep are by no means scarce on the fells.

The happier side of the story is that the somewhat emaciated Foxey was taken care of by Gough's friends and recovered. The remains of Gough who came of Quaker stock, were interred in the graveyard of the Quaker Meeting House at Tirril, near Penrith.

The late Canon Rawnsley of Keswick

was instrumental in having a memorial stone placed on Helvellyn above the scene of the tragedy, suitably inscribed, and including the pathetically haunting closing lines of the poem which will cause little Foxey to be ever remembered.

Samuel Thompson (May 1975)

A HECTIC NESTING TIME

FROM COCKERMOUTH comes what is surely the nesting time story to end them all. A thrush nested in Main Street. Her three young ones, now flown, must have had a uncomfortable time.

First, roadmen, using flame to remove the surface before relaying, scorched the tree's leaves almost up to the nest. Mother thrush sat tight. Then a fun fair, with all its bands, banners, and noise came to town. Mother thrush was literally unmoved. There followed the annual carnival, and the grand parade passing under the tree. The bird stayed put, even while decorations were strung from tree to tree.

Then came a real crisis. A local cat, Lulu by name, was spotted poised and watching on the next tree. Her intentions were all too clear. Mother thrush, thereupon, retaliated in an entirely unexpected way. She attacked the cat on the branch, swooping down, pecking her on her face and beating her with her wings. The cat, a notorious stalker of birds in the locality and fit to scale any tree, was transfixed with astonishment and fright. She howled, for there is no greater funk than a cat when turned on. And her howls and the screams of the throstle attracted Lulu's owner, who is a local policeman, Constable Hewitt.

He rescued Lulu. But only using a ladder, and in face of repeated assaults by the intrepid mother thrush who, a few days later, had the satisfaction of seeing her fledglings fly away to fend for themselves. She remained on the nest several days, preening herself somewhat complacently. She had a right to. Now Lulu the cat stays in the yards and gardens behind the police station. She no longer climbs the trees of Cockermouth's Main Street.

(August 1955)

ENCOUNTER WITH A ROEBUCK

APRIL IS a good month to seek out and identify the roebuck which are relatively common in the Lakeland woods. In April, new buds on the trees create a slight haze of green and visibility is good for both the quarry and he who stalks it. On balance, therefore, I prefer to sit in a well placed high-seat, little more than a plank set among branches, waiting for an unsuspecting buck or doe to wander by.

OPPOSITE
Drawing by E. Jeffrey.

HAYESWATER AND
HIGH STREET

Last April, on a cold, dry sunny afternoon, I exchanged the comfort of my car for a favourite high-seat.

My perch in the tree overlooked a meadow at the corner of a wood, and also offered a view up a steep ride, where dead bracken was criss-crossed by roe tracks.

It was just after five in the afternoon. I had plenty of time to merge into the landscape. A cock pheasant confidently made his way out into the meadow and began to feed. I was startled by the chatter of a squirrel – a red squirrel, using the branches as a high level foot-path.

During the first hour, the wind slackened. The sun was bright but the air cooled. The prospect of seeing a roe, smallest and most graceful of Lakeland's native deer, kept me warm.

Some 60 yards along the edge of the wood, near a clump of young rhodod-endrons, something moved. Could the wind be playing tricks? I trained my binoculars on the spot and searched feverishly. A roebuck emerged.

Cautiously, the slender animal appraised the surroundings before taking another step or two out of the woods.

I imagined I could hear him thinking: 'Nice quiet meadow, sheltered from the wind, final warmth of the declining sun, tasty new grass shoots – even a pheasant for company.'

The buck gracefully cleared a drainage ditch between the wood and the meadow and began to graze. His grey coat glistened, reflecting good health. A touch of white on his nose, the white patch on his throat and the pure white rump combined to confirm that he was a young buck.

The prongs of his antlers were covered in soft grey velvet, and looked like a small crown, rising some 3 inches above the tips of his ears. This velvet would soon be rubbed away on some young sapling. The head was carrying six points. He was a good roebuck for the future.

The roebuck continued to graze, stopping frequently to study any sound or movement that caught his attention. From time to time he shook his head up and down, and then gently, with his hoof, he scratched the coronet at the base of the right antler.

Unaware of my intrusion, the roebuck came to within 30 yards of my high-seat. He would surely pass me within a few feet. However, glancing round, he started grazing back to the edge of the wood, before bedding down at the edge of the meadow, with his back to the woods. The buck started to chew his cud.

The cold had begun to penetrate my bones. I had visions of spending the night in the high-seat. Then the pheasant called. The deer, also alarmed, headed for the safety of the wood.

The next time we meet, the April velvet will have gone.

Norman Dewhurst (April 1977)

CUMBRIAN MEMORIES

'OWD JOE O' Wasdale 'Ead' took a dim view of folk who climb the fells without looking for sheep, but with Penrith as my gate to George Basterfield's wild Cumberland, I sought out spring flowers refreshed by the rolling morning mists. There were purple mountain-saxifrages among the damp mountain rocks, and early purple orchids in the woods; blue moor-grass flowered in abundance on the dry, limestone rocks and foetid hellebore, relative of the garden 'Christmas rose', grew green at Severgham. Bitter vetch in the mountains and purple bush-vetch in the hedgerows, water-avens, sweet woodruff and red lungwort all went to make a Lakeland spring.

As I reached the lonely sheep-pens of John Peel's Troutbeck on my way to Derwentwater, the world took on an alluring form, diversified by the stiff, frowning rocks in huge profile high against the sky and the soothing green of lovely St. John's Vale, warm beneath slanting beams of sunshine. The utter loveliness of England here is kept green by its incessant rains: Keswick has more than Manchester or Liverpool.

A wreath of wet mist, as white as cotton wool, rolled off Blencathra, washing the bare, grey rock of Sharp Edge and bejewelling the grassy slopes, and then it all streamed back again. From the mountains the scene was tremendous; great lakes lay at their feet and dark cloud shadows crawled across miles of greenery where stood the artists' little stone cottages, with blue aubretia gardens, rose trees around the door – and often no sanitation.

Spending a night at Derwent Bank, where a biscuit-tin was nailed up for the postman because blue tits were nesting in the letter-box, I went to sleep with the sedge-warbler storming in the reed-bed below my window and a corncrake creaking like a wicket-gate to outcry another I could hear a mile away on the opposite shore of Derwentwater.

A woodcock roding where it nested in the mossy shades at Lingholme appeared every 5 or 10 minutes, with a grunt and his long bill held downwards, to fly along the same aerial path or 'road' that marked his woodland territory.

In the morning I was watching the heron, which came snigging at the bottom of the garden, now feeding its young in the same green palace of trees, trees full of the quiet, spluttering songs of wood-warblers, the gabbling exuberance of blackcaps and the goldcrest's sibilant trill. Sandpipers whistled where they scraped a nest by the lake and a pair of pied flycatchers began house-hunting in an old tree.

Next day I passed by Bassenthwaite and the brown shoulder of Grisedale Pike, to make the long climb of the Whinlatter Pass where the dark and lonely pinewoods have increased the chaffinches from when I knew it as an open fellside. At 1,600 feet high on the Lorton Fells I reached the lonely old stone sheep-farm of Darling How, where I slept snug and warm in the hay loft for a week years ago, shaving at daybreak in the cold horse-trough in the farmyard.

Then I followed the rushing waters of Whit Beck, streaming on their way down to Cockermouth. That devil on wings, the carrion-crow, was feeding young in almost every wood – it completely overran the birds' sanctuary of Lord's Island in Derwentwater. All the big sycamore trees hung with green flowers in the dales, humming loud with the music of almost every insect that could fly to its feast of nectar.

The honeyflow was turned on by the sunshine, but as bees don't like the company of so many flies at the flowers, they garnered little of the riches. Though mayfly didn't hatch until well into June, wading late in the evening into the cold strong current of the river with 'partridge and orange' I lured rising trout for supper.

Elizabeth Bennett, invited in *Pride and Prejudice* to accompany her uncle and aunt to the Lakes exclaimed: 'Adieu to disappointment and spleen! What are men to rocks and mountains? Oh, what hours of transport we shall spend.' The northbound trains disembark hikers and holidaymakers who share her thoughts and hurry to the bare rocks.

In the quiet woods of black pines that cast long shadows, splashed here and there with patches of sunlight, one might think the silent forest empty of life unless one read the bare patch on a young fir's bark and the faint trail through the ferns in the birch stand. Here live the little roe on which I have set my heart.

I spent three days visiting the woods around Carlisle, where years before I used to watch roe deer. Certain places remain firmly implanted in one's mind over the years. I returned to recognise and welcome individual trees in these woods, like meeting old friends again. No sound of the outer world penetrates the hushed and dim interior.

The rides where the wood-warbler twittered its first song in May lay rough with ling, little golden brown tufts of wood-rush and spear-like bog-rushes. Deep, peaty dykes were full of rusty brown water and banked with fishbone shapes of northern hard-fern.

Wild and wary, a single roe family occupied the expansive birch copse at the warm and sunny southern end of the forest, sheltered from the cold helm winds that blow over the Cheviots. They had no fear of the busy traffic along the A6, and at night they stole past Floriston village or down the fertile valley of the border Esk.

I stopped suddenly, almost breathlessly, upon hearing a queer gruff bark ahead. Standing in the distant shadows with its grey face and white nose-patch surmounted by short, sharply-pointed antlers, a single roe buck, a delicate creature by red deer standards, interrogated me with its inquisitive eyes and pricked ears. He cocked his ears more erect than a red deer, as I looked through my binoculars.

Then he bolted, leaping as nimbly as I've seen desert gazelle, until the shadows of the wood swallowed him up, with my last glimpse the bobbing white of his stern.

Eric Hardy (June 1966)

RETURN OF THE EAGLE

John W. Best tells of sighting the lordly eagle in Lakeland.

IN THE VALE OF Borrowdale lies the hamlet of Rosthwaite. Here, more than 200 years ago, was kept a long rope by which a man could be lowered over the imposing precipices of the sur-rounding crags to destroy the eyrie of the golden eagle and the eagle's offspring. The rope was borrowed by the neighbouring dales.

Old parish records reveal the names of

local tenants at that period. They were given a shilling for every eagle they killed or for those shot on the wing. As the records have it, this they did annually to protect their stock during the lambing season, and to discourage marauding eagles from swooping down to carry off the lambs. One eyrie, it was reckoned, cost the average of a lamb a day.

In the Crosthwaite Parish Registers dated 1713, the entries read:

To John Jackson for killing
    an old Eagle   1s. 0d.
Widow Harris's son for 3
    young Ravens   1s. 0d.
Edward Berket for a
    young Eagle   6d.

It has always been a debatable question among naturalists as to whether the lamb losses were heavy enough to justify such drastic action. This policy of extermination was pursued with such vigour that today only the place names are left, where once the eagles had been.

You find Eagle's Crag, Eagle's Nest Ridge on Great Gable. The birds' last stronghold was on the cliffs of Birkness Combe, over the Honister Pass at Buttermere.

Today the majestic eagles are protected by law. Under the auspices of The Royal Society for the Protection of Birds a reward scheme has been inaugurated, whereby any farmer or gamekeeper who has eagles nesting on his land and can show that he has been responsible in helping them to breed successfully, can claim up to £10. The eagle is in any case a specially protected bird. Anybody killing it, or attempting to kill it, is liable to a fine of £25, or one month's imprisonment.

Over recent years reports have gradu-

ally increased from observers of eagles being seen once again in Lakeland. At first the birds were thought to be buzzards that nest in this area, and are frequently mistaken for the eagle by their soaring flight. However, these large hawks of the same family of birds of prey as the eagle, are smaller, the silhouette of their wings in flight being much rounder at the extremeties, and they are easily identified by their mewing call. Eagles also have proportionately longer wings.

Having studied the various observations, and taken note of the localities in which the bird had been seen, I was able to pin-point a possible viewing place on the map. One mid-summer's morning I left my Lakeland hotel with a packed lunch, map, compass, binoculars, and a climbing rope.

The sun had emerged from behind cloud. I admired the view of a valley below and gaunt mountains beyond. A winding river had become a shimmering ribbon of silver. A mass of grey crags was my goal. A beck cascaded in a series of waterfalls, to disappear in the stunted foliage beyond the edge of a gully. Although the floor of a corrie was lush with vegetation the going was good, and I scrambled up and over a ridge. Here I was forced to make a traverse under the cliffs to the left to avoid an active bog that filled the basin below.

The silence was suddenly shattered by the sharp cry of 'kek-kek-kek'. It was the call of the peregrine falcon, vibrating from cliff to cliff as the grey bird flew along the rock face screaming its defiance for an intrusion of its domain. It made for a ledge beneath the overhang of a sheer precipice just ahead. So perfect was the camouflage of the predator's grey speckled plumage that after scanning the rock face with my glasses I was just able to pin-point its position. The bird glided off, to disappear over the top of the crags.

I reached a vantage point overlooking the ghyll and observed a huge solitary bird with an enormous wing span soaring above. It was circling low over a small area of the crag opposite. I instinctively concealed myself behind a convenient boulder. By resting my powerful bino-culars on top of the rock, and lying inclined against it, I could study the bird for a long period if necessary without hand shake.

As it wheeled, taking advantage of the wind currents, the breeze ruffled the dark brown feathers on its back, and the broadly spread up-curved primaries with the pinions divided like fingers. As I watched, the bird brought its wings up in the form of a V, spreading the broad tail feathers. Then, with head down and talons extended, it dropped behind a rocky outcrop.

As the bird had inclined its head, the gold tinge of its plumage, extending down the neck, reflected in the rays of the sun. This was an adult golden eagle.

When next it rose into view I expected to see, transfixed in those powerful talons, some lifeless crushed mammal, but this was not so. The legs, feathered to the toes, were drawn up, and the eagle continued the circling manoeuvre, re-peatedly attacking again and again, some form of prey behind the outcrop.

The magnificent bird soared and banked, with an occasional flap of its huge wings. Across the ghyll was a solitary tree, windswept and denuded of most of its foliage. It was on the topmost branch that the eagle eventually perched. A time check revealed that I had been stationary for three-quarters of an hour. I moved slightly and the eagle launched itself gracefully, with motionless out-stretched wings, and soared spirally into the blue sky.

Since that day I have seen many eagles, and even heard their 'yelping' call. There has been no eagle occasion to beat that long, hard first look at our largest wild bird.

(*May 1966*)

No Crowding, Please

The reference to the story of the fighting cockatoo recalls a similar one, which I first heard some seventy years ago. It was a favourite of my father's. I don't know where he got it, or whether it had any foundation in fact.

The bird in this case was a parrot, and it belonged to the man who admitted the public to a travelling circus. It used to sit on its perch close to the entrance, and had picked up its master's patter as he issued the tickets:

'One at a time, please – don't crowd – *plenty* more left!'

One day the bird escaped. Search was made for it, and at last they found it – in a field, surrounded by a mob of rooks which were pecking out its feathers. And above the hubbub could be heard the shrill voice, repeating again and again: 'One at a time, please – don't crowd – *plenty* more left!'

H. Lang Jones (January 1956)

16

GOOD OLD DAYS

HOLIDAYS IN AMBLESIDE – 70 YEARS AGO

OLIDAYS! WHAT memories that word conjures up! I can still recall the excitement of the preparations for our annual family holidays in Ambleside. We lived on the outskirts of Barrow-in-Furness so travelled by train which in itself seemed quite an adventure. The coaches had no corridors, each carriage seating six a side if necessary. Just below the luggage rack there were pictures of various holiday resorts and sometimes a mirror. After a change at Ulverston the train stopped at the attractive stations of Greenodd and Haverthwaite, now closed to passenger traffic, before pulling into Lakeside where the steamer was moored across the platform ready to take us up the Lake. These steamers were simply designed, graceful boats with one funnel, named after water birds and we looked out eagerly to see if ours would be the *Teal*, *Tern* or *Swan*.

In Ambleside we had what was known as 'apartments', the use of two bedrooms and a sitting room with 'service' which meant that we bought our own food each day but our hostess cooked and served it. The houses all had little cards bearing the word 'apartments' in the windows and this system lasted right up to the 1930s.

The period of our Ambleside holiday coincided with the years of the First World War but the hostilities did not affect the civilian population and life and holidays seemed to go on quite normally.

Our holiday home was situated on the main road and we could sit on the wide sill of our bedroom window looking out on to the Stock Beck, Mill House and the Old Bridge House, then used as a Cobbler's Workshop. Our hostess was a Mrs Beetham and it would be hard to find a more kindly and welcoming one. She was an excellent cook and on the days, quite frequent, when we arrived back soaking wet she had hot water ready in no time, for washing, and dried our shoes and macs again for the next day's outing.

Most of our days were spent walking. There was very little traffic and one could walk quite peacefully on the main roads to Skelwith Falls, to Rydal and Grasmere and even up Kirkstone Pass. But we preferred the fells and the hills. We climbed Wansfell, and up past Sour Milk Ghyll to Easedale Tarn where there was a little hut selling cups of rather smokey tea much appreciated on hot days. Some of our happiest times were spent on Loughrigg climbing to various vantage points or doing the Terrace Walk skirting Rydal and Grasmere Lakes.

I often marvel how we did all this walking and climbing as the youngest member of the family was only 6 years old on our first visit to Ambleside! There was much to delight our childish eyes; a tarn on Loughrigg was full of water lilies which would have done credit to the pool of a stately home.

The hills, especially towards the top of Wansfell, were carpeted with heather much more widespread I think than it is today. We used to search for a piece of pure white but it was more difficult than looking for four-leaved clover. Miniature cotton grass growing in damp places intrigued us and we gathered sphagnum moss to line our hanging baskets.

One day we went on an excursion to Keswick by charabanc. These were organised by the various hotels and we patronised one from the *Salutation*. There were four rows of rather hard seats perched high up, open to the weather and drawn by horses. Our coachman, very smart in his uniform, was a merry type called Bill Ellery, who established friendly relations with his passengers, joking with us and passing on useful bits of information. The road from Grasmere to Thirlmere up Dunmail Raise was very steep for the horses and at one specially difficult part we all had to get down and walk. On the return journey a metal 'slipper' was attached to one of the wheels to slow it down and prevent the vehicle careering away too fast.

Our parents tried to make the holidays educational as well as enjoyable. We studied the Roman camp at Waterhead and looked for glacier marks on the rocks in the park. We were steeped in the literary associations, learning about Harriet Martineau and Dr Arnold as we passed the houses where they had lived. We knew that Coleridge's son, Hartley, had spent some time at Nab Cottage which we saw to such advantage across Rydal Water, but it was the Wordsworth connection which was most important to us. We gazed in awe at the Lucy Gray Bridge, debated the site of the daffodils in the poem and clambered over the rocks known as Wordsworth's seat.

Now in my eighties I look back with nostalgia to those happy Ambleside holidays and am glad that I knew the district in more leisurely times before the advent of the motor car and so many tourists. Although exiled to southern England I still devote part of my garden to heathers with a special place for the one called 'Loughrigg'.

Gladys Rollinson (August 1989)

OPPOSITE
'Holidays on the farm.' Oakbank Farm, Loweswater. (*Colin Denwood*)

OUR POSTMAN – JIMMY

A postal strike brought back memories of an occasion when the same thing was threatened many years ago. It would have been a major catastrophe to our little isolated village in Cumbria. Not so much because there would be no letters, but because Jimmy our postman wouldn't be popping in to brighten our day.

NOWADAYS, OUR letters are delivered by four different postmen in a Post Office van and the only indication that you have received a letter is the faint 'plonk' as the envelope hits the floor.

It wasn't like this forty years ago when Jimmy, our one and only postman, had to put all the letters and parcels in a big wire carrier on the front of his bike with the overflow stuffed in a bag carried on his back, and he would start off – hail, rain or snow – at 8 a.m. to deliver the mail to all the scattered farms and cottages in this very hilly district.

Jimmy earned approximately 55s. per week for his services and if there was a particularly heavy snowfall in winter, making the country lanes impassable on a bike, he would carry his sack of mail on his back across the fields. I cannot recall one single day when he failed to deliver his letters to this village.

Everybody had a soft spot for Jimmy – he was a personal friend to us all and his sharp country wit gave us many a laugh. I remember in the war years when fruit was rationed, my father used to send from down South 10 lb. parcels of Cox's Orange Pippins up to me – and you could always tell what was in the parcel because the lovely aroma used to seep through the cardboard box. Jimmy must have viewed these large consignments with dread and fury as he thought of the long hills he had to push them up before reaching our farm and one hot day he came in the kitchen door, dumped the parcel of apples on the table and said wearily, as he wiped the sweat off his brow, 'I wish to goodness he'd send the damned TREE'. . .

Our postman was also our local grapevine, besides bringing us all the tit-bits of news and messages from neighbours, cough medicine and pills from the doctor and giving us his opinion and advice into the bargain.

I remember one tale he was fond of telling, the only time he said he was at a complete loss for a suitable answer. He was walking up the path of an old couple's cottage to deliver their mail and could hear them shouting at each other and arguing, long before they were aware of his approach. 'Now, what's all this row about?' he demanded as he got to the door. 'There's no sense going on to each other like that – just look at that cat and dog lying peacefully side by side in front of the fire, you want to take a lesson from them'. Grandad gave Granny a baleful look and said bitterly, 'Aye, but you tie 'em together and then see what 'appens.'

CHRISTMAS. Every Christmas we were terrified Jimmy would get the sack; everyone realised what a strain it was for him with all the extra mail to deliver and every farm and cottage he visited on Christmas Eve would try to show their appreciation by tempting him with their potent brew of homemade damson wine, elderberry wine and mince pies.

By the time he got to us he would be well and truly plastered, totter up the path practically incapable and fold up on the kitchen sofa. We let him sleep it off while the menfolk sorted out the letters and went off to deliver them, until he sobered up. One Christmas he was found in the roadside with His Majesty's Mail bag substituted for a pillow, and although this episode was repeated with much mirth round the countryside, not one word of it ever reached the postmaster's ears.

After all these years of faithful service we gave dear old Jimmy a party and presented him with a cheque on his retirement. For once he was absolutely speechless, tears running down his cheeks as we all fervently sang 'For He's a Jolly Good Fellow'!

Mona Atkinson (December 1988)

LET'S PLODGE!

IN THESE parts you are never a country child until you have answered this summer call: 'Let's plodge.' Once again the old dialect word is streets ahead of the correct 'paddle'. 'Plodge' expresses perfectly the exciting plop of your bare foot as you plunge it into our cold hill water.

I can still thrill to a plodge across the river where the larches grow below the bracken and ling, and to a barefoot walk among the dry riverside grass where thrift, heartsease, sandwort, scented thyme and the rare and beautiful Grass of Parnassus grow. Psychiatrists would go out of business if everybody could forget and plodge now and again.

It is a feat of skill to skip over the hot bleached stones when you come out of the water. All the time there's the continual gossip of the summer river to listen to, but this appealed most in the romantic teens, when Ethel M. Dell and her ridiculous, splendid lovers were so wonderful.

For a child, the thing is to plodge – to cross to the other side and explore the woods; to float on an empty drum, or just to conquer that dark, deep pool where an eel might lurk. The cuckoo calls and you give it a careless *cuckoo* back again, tuck your knickers a bit higher and venture deeper and deeper. When you reach your new world, you shed your humdrum identity and become an adventurer, for bairns are always somebody else.

A succession of water passes before me as I sit here looking beyond the river flats to the procession of hawthorn brides across the brackened fell; the endless rush of pebbles as the tide sucks back on the West Cumbrian coast; buttercups in the meadows bordering a crystal pool where willows bend and dip; lonely burns, ice-cold and blue, where the wind continually stirs the cotton grass, where the patient black-faced sheep crop the bent and ling, and grouse *beck-beck* over the limitless home of fox and corbie.

There is a sad dark tarn among the grey fells, tragic and gloomy even when the sun shines and, best of all, a wide, flat stone in the middle of the South Tyne under Williamstone Fell, with me, feet and hands in the cold running water, just lazing on a sunny June day, with the scent of larches carried on the warm wind.

In winter, when the dark nights came, the tune changed to: 'Let's go Guising.' Mother's cupboards were raided to find sequinned capes, weird 1890 hats, long skirts and bustled coats, for we were still somebody else, dressed in the fashion of a previous generation.

We would step out into the dark and go knocking on doors. When a good lady was kind enough to answer, we would sing or recite and, giggling in our furbelows, step inside to show off our finery.

So, river and attic gave us a good deal of fun, and the call still comes at the appropriate season to our children – 'Let's Plodge' or 'Let's go Guising.'

Elizabeth Birkett (July 1973)

Two Lakeland farmers met for the first time in twenty years. 'I've not forgotten thoo,' said one. 'I'm allus lewkin' in t'*Westmorland Gazette* to see if thoo's dead!'

T. W. (1965)

THE COLLIER

ON A RECENT visit to Keswick I saw, in a large craft shop, a beautiful prodded rug. As I ran my fingers over the 'proddy', memories of my childhood came flooding back.

Home was a tiny terraced house that was crammed with children, warmth and love. A coal fire blazed in the hearth, its heat keeping a big, black kettle boiling on the hob and firing the oven in which my mother baked her own bread and tea-cakes. Before they went into the oven they were set to rise on the brass fender which gleamed with the application of barrowloads of 'Brasso' and aeons of elbow grease.

'Proddy' rugs on the floor included a suit, too threadbare for Dad to wear any longer, garments that had gone beyond the hand-me-down stage and anything else that had outlived its original purpose. Necessity made craftsmen of us all. Everybody in the family, from the oldest to the youngest, prodded a bit of material in as they passed by. If you could wield a prodder at all you were a fully paid-up member of the Prodder's Union.

On winter nights when the wind, crying with cold, poked its icy fingers under the door we would all sit round the 'proddy' frame, pushing bits of material through the hessian. This was the time for catching up on the day's events, doing general knowledge quizzes, reciting poetry or just having a sing song.

When the frame was set up it divided the little living room into two. Those who sat nearest the fire, sat till their back-bones almost melted then crawled underneath to swop seats with somebody whose spine was a long column of ice in the draught from the front door.

At that point in time, the centre of my universe was not a knight in shining armour but a knight who came home covered in coal dust: my Dad. Tall he was, black-haired and his cornflower-blue eyes only became more vivid when the mascara of coal dust caked his long lashes. Trouser legs tied at the knee with string, clog corkers snapping sharply on the road, he would swing his bait tin as he strode along.

Every day I would wait, in a frenzy of anticipation, until I saw him stride out of the lonning end. Like a whippet I would hurtle off to meet him as soon as he came into view. I can still feel that dizzying rush of air as he scooped me from the ground and swung me high into his arms.

Home together we would go, to share his tea. This was a ritual, reserved for the youngest child in the family – and this was my time. A huge mug of hot, sweet tea, a soft-boiled egg and a thick slice of toast, made on a toasting fork served to stave off his hunger until we all ate a cooked meal later. Cutting the toast into 'soldiers', hot and dripping with farm butter, he would plunge one into the soft, golden yolk and give it to me. Pouring some of his tea into a saucer he would blow on it until it was cool and I would slurp it like a greedy puppy.

He would always tell me the story, the same story, every time. He was going to find a house, just a little house, with a little garden and he and I were going off to live in it. Just the two of us.

We never did, of course. Long before machines took the place of men my father leased his life and wore out his lungs wresting the coal from a drift mine in the mean, solitary glow of his carbide lamp . . .

E. M. Branthwaite (November 1989)

[162]

17

HAUNTING MEMORIES

FERRY HO!

THERE IS the grim story of a demon ferryman who stole men's souls, The Crier of Claife. On wild nights he gave the call of 'Ferry ho!' One night it was answered by the ferryman and next morning he was found speechless and almost insane from shock, but before his death soon after he made it understood that his passenger had been an evil spirit.

On one of the islets of the lake, St. Mary Holme, there was in those days a chantry chapel served by a monk, and this good Father, with bell, book, candle and holy water, went forth and called up the demon, banishing him to the heights of Claife above Ferry Nab, there to be imprisoned within the crags for ever. But 60 years ago, before the dawn of speed boats and two world wars, there were still stories of dreadful cries and echoing shouts of 'Ferry ho!' from the heights of Claife.

One night in early June as we paddled idly on the quiet lake, homeward bound after a long day's mayfly fishing, the peace of the night was shattered by dreadful cries, echoing over the dark trees and the faintly shimmering mirror of the still lake. 'Gosh,' breathed somebody, rather shakily, 'The Crier,' and we listened, resting on our oars, awed, and somewhat scared, waiting for what (or who?) might come next. Then it came, loud and clear in the twilight silence, *Whoo-Whoo-Whoo*, pealing out from the dark heights and over the lake, answered this time from a little wooded point not far away from us. *Whoo-Whoo-Whoo* it mocked derisively.

The tension snapped abruptly. 'Owls,' said our coxwain, 'Just owls calling. Give way, my hearties.' We at the oars gave way with vigour, owls or no owls, glad to be away from a spot so haunted by sinister memories of the past, and the dark height of Claife and their demon prisoner. But in these prosaic days The Crier and his legend are forgotten, and the peace of the lake is only broken by the speed boats and the summer steamers.

M. C. Fair (June 1952)

Some years ago two of us were staying at a very uncomfortable Lakeland inn. I woke up suddenly in the night and said to my pal: 'We'd better get up, Jim. The gas is escaping!'

'I don't blame it,' replied my pal with a groan.

T. Smith (March 1972)

WHAT IS A BOGGLE?

WHAT IS a boggle? In the Cumbrian parlance it means bogey or phantom, being a corruption of the term, *bogle*, a boglin and spectre.

I have chuckled at the names of some West Cumbrian Irish boggles – Peddy Cass, Pencil Ned, Mary Bloody-bones, Nanny Knockabout, Cabbage Dan, Old Ned, Jackson's Ghost, Boggle Harry, Tom Rawhead, Ghost Jack, Devil Dandy and Old Clapperton.

Many boggles are said to haunt the scenes of murders or suicides, while others are reputedly visible premonitions of death or accidents. I heard of a poltergeist boggle that threw things about in an old cottage near the Border. Just before the war, some lads reported seeing a trio of boggles that were already known to haunt Burgh Marsh.

West Cumberland has long been noted for its boggles, and as recently as 1968 three families were driven from a large house at Church Road, Harrington, by the spectre of a hideous hag in grey.

Also in West Cumberland was the Derwent Chain Boggle, clanking its fetters on the river bank below Great Broughton. A similar bogey, the 'Petteril Prowler,' scared the tenants of the lonely Kitchen Hill Cottages, near Catterlen. Another riverside horror drove two sturdy Penrith anglers from one of their favourite fishing spots one night in 1967.

Back in West Cumberland, the 'Knocker' lived up to its name in an old cottage at Frizington. That boggle terrified family after family with its loud rappings and great thuds.

My native town of Wigton had its share of manifestations, the most feared being a headless horror known as the Clinic Ghost. The late T. W. Carrick, in his *History of Wigton*, referred to the town's oldest haunted house at Burnfoot.

When the town's Conservative Club (now the *Kildare Hotel*) was being built in the 1880s, the Kildare Court Boggle was said to have been seen at the site. It had always been regarded as an omen of disaster and so it proved to be in that instance.

My father (a boy then) was one of a group of people watching hunks of dressed sandstone being pulled up by block, chain and tackle to the top of the great building.

A Mr Johnston took the quickest way up by standing on a block of stone that was being hoisted upwards. The chain broke near the top! Down came the sandstone, and with it the unfortunate Johnston! He landed upon his feet – after a drop of somewhere between 50 and 80 feet – and died from severe internal injuries.

Just past the spot stands the now derelict *Crown and Mitre*, which has a sinister sealed-up 'suicide room'. Weird noises are heard at night. The landlord's eldest daughter tried to sleep in the room next to the sealed one. In the early hours of one day she reached out of bed for the candle and matches but touched a cold, clammy human face!

An aged Wigtonian showed me an old, ivy-grown building near South End wherein, many years ago, a madman killed his wife and family with an axe. The ghosts of the maniac's victims are said to haunt the place.

My informant also mentioned the Phantom Hag of Church Street, the

White Lady of Low Moor, the Quarry Hill Boggle and the Greenhill Ghost. The last named spectre was alleged to have extinguished the lamps on horse-drawn vehicles and cycles in the days before electric lighting became general for road traffic.

The Dancing Boggle of Westnexton was said to have whirled people around in a merry reel, while the Great Orton Spectre chased the unwary across an airfield. The Janet Tree Ghost scared late travellers by hobbling in front of their conveyances and abruptly vanishing into a roadside tree near Shap.

A solitary phantom that several times appeared to me and other persons simul-

'Half the ingredients are protected species.'

taneously was the headless Langrigg Boggle. The presence of that ghost was the main reason why I was able to rent the Langrigg cottage (with a good garden) for a mere 6s. per week!

Many years ago my father visited the famous Biddle's Ghost Show when it came to Wigton. After the performance, a sceptic in the audience jeered at the supernatural but changed his attitude when confronted by a shimmering blue phantom on the banks of the river Wiza some months later.

The shimmering boggle was last seen in the tower of a nearby factory about fifteen years ago.

A ruined bungalow at the southern edge of Kirkbride airfield was reputed to be haunted by the spirit of a dipsomaniac woman whose husband, a doctor, had confined her there for her own good.

At Boltongate, legend decreed that fairies mischievously turned the church around one night, but a more sinister story is associated with the place. The local squire differed with the rector and had him unfrocked.

In his agony of mind, the clergyman shot himself, but before doing so he left a note cursing the squire, his family and his beautiful manor of Kilhowe, also prophesying that Kilhowe would crumble stone by stone, while the squire and his kin would die in misery.

The curse was fulfilled. The squire and his family died miserably, and Kilhowe crumbled to dust.

My cousin Joe and I cycled to Boltongate to investigate rumours of the rector's ghost having been seen beside his grave. We saw no manifestation. Another phantom had been reported at Kilhowe ruins, so we sallied forth. Joe disappeared into a shrubbery and came back in a hurry, gasping, 'C'mon, Tom! Let's git oot! There *is* a boggle here! Ah've just seen it!'

Today, nothing remains of what was once one of the loveliest mansions in the whole of the John Peel Country.

Tom Jackson (June 1972)

CUMBRIAN HAUNTINGS

A competition held in the magazine in 1972 invited readers to give their own accounts of Cumbrian hauntings. Here are some of the entries . . .

A 'Yeti' on Silver How

IT WAS A wet November, about five years back. I was on a walking tour, and my next stop was Grasmere. I had planned great things for that day but a low black blanket of cloud and a chilling downpour had seen me seek the shelter of the Grasmere bus.

Gazing out of the rain-spattered window it struck me that the landscape lacked substance on that day. The mountains were card-thin, the houses sodden paper cut-outs. The scene was ghost-grey to the point of invisibility. Grasmere village appeared like a series of mournful candles, the electric lights a lament for the brief grey day.

I bought a book in the corner bookshop – a paperback collection of all things fantastic and macabre – and retired to my guest house to read the evening away until supper.

The next morning offered no better prospects for walking. A dense mist lay silent and damp. Disappointed, but not prepared to tolerate another day of inactivity, I started out for Silver How. Just below the summit the air shivered as a breeze shook its dampness, producing a corresponding shiver on my part.

My thoughts flew involuntarily to the vividly remembered tales of last evening. Suddenly my eyes saw massive shapes swelling before me in the mist. Substance they had but they were not defined. They pulsed in the clammy air, sent fingers of ghostly being clutching through the mist.

My heart grew hot, my skin cold, and my damp hair stiffened with an electric shock of apprehension. The forms shuffled nearer.

An explosion rocked the fell! Before I was capable of suffering further, the apparitions scampered away with a blood-curdling bleating which shook comprehension into me and slowly brought a smile to my face.

Stuart Dickinson

'It' Visits Eden Hall

MY GRANDMOTHER, Ellen Whiteside (nee Bewley) was employed when she was a young girl by the Musgraves at Eden Hall. She told us that shortly before she was married she went to visit the housekeeper there and stayed the night.

She slept with the housekeeper's niece in a room that had been the night nursery. During the night they were wakened by someone coming into the room. This person adjusted the window blind, opened and closed some drawers and appeared to poke the fire, although it was summer and there was no fire. Finally 'it' paused at the bedside and went out.

The girls told the housekeeper the next morning; she laughed at them and said they had been dreaming. Some time later, my grandmother heard that a woman who had been a nurserymaid at Eden Hall, and had married a railway employee at Clifton, had regained consciousness shortly before she died and said she had had a lovely dream.

She said she had been back to Eden Hall, had gone into the nursery, straightened the curtains, put away some things in the chest of drawers, poked the fire and glanced at the bed to see that the children were all right. The date of her death coincided with my grandmother's visit to Eden Hall.

Mrs N. O. Martin

A Bed-mate

I GOT INTO bed and was soon asleep. Suddenly I awoke and felt a creepy sensation. A cold shiver ran through my body, my limbs became incapable of movement, and my eyes focused themselves on a point to the left of my bed, though I could see nothing in the dark.

The bed sagged. Who was getting into bed? My wife? But I wasn't at home now. Where was I? Then I remembered. I was in a strange farmhouse to which I had been directed for bed and breakfast.

Then who? My colleague, who occupied the next room? Perhaps he couldn't sleep. He always was a cold mortal. I held my breath. Surely he would say something – a word of explanation. But no! How thoughtless could one be.

I too was cold, but I would not have dreamt of intruding upon *him*. Ah well! These Southerners! I'd better get back to sleep, and let him know what I thought of him in the morning.

I turned over, then froze with horror. There was no doubt at all about it – *before getting into bed I had locked my bedroom door on the inside!*

M. Higginbottom

In Good Voice

A FEW years ago I lived in an old house on the shores of Windermere. Not feeling too well, on a hot day, I decided to lie down. The bedroom was stuffy and hot, like an oven.

Soon I fell asleep. In my dream I heard

laughing and singing from what sounded like coach and horses coming nearer. I could see lots of people gaily dressed and singing *Oh dem golden slippers!* at the top of their voices.

Then the voices and coach passed into the distance. I woke up feeling cold and shivery; the room was no longer stuffy and from every part of it seemed to come the sound of a choir singing and music too beautiful to describe; it reached a crescendo and then there was silence.

I told an old resident of Far Sawrey about my dream. He asked if I had not heard about the wedding party who passed the water gardens to Belle Grange, from where the old ferry used to operate. They had boarded the ferry and half-way across it had sunk. They were all drowned.

My dream had been 'real', for I had not known about the wedding party.

Joyce Bunting

A Lowther Haunting

IN THE past, the Lowther Estate used to hold a Rent Dinner each half year. A large marquee was erected near the castle and the farm tenants were summoned to pay their rents and spend a convivial afternoon (which sometimes extended well into the night).

On one occasion the chief agent said to the tenant of Boggle Hall Farm, Plumpton: 'Well now, Willie, your farm is called Boggle Hall. Tell me, have you ever really seen a boggle on the farm?'

'Ah hev that, Mr Little. Ah hev that! It shows up as regular as clockwork.'

'Tell me about it; what is it like; when do you see it?'

'Why,' said Willie, 'yeh knaw aw aboot it. Posty fetches it up t'path twice a year fra' Lowther Office!'

John Peel

[168]

18

SEASONS IN LAKELAND

FROM A LAKELAND COTTAGE IN SPRING

THIS IS the season when in Lakeland something new comes out of every day. I cannot go out of my gate and along the stream-side without making at least half a dozen 'discoveries'. On some days lately there has been so much to find and examine that it seems as though some fast-working magician has been busy overnight dropping treasure here, there and everywhere.

In the next few weeks this usually deserted dale will be busy once more with holiday traffic, and many hikers and wayfarers will pass this way. I wonder if they, too, will make discoveries.

Let me set down here what I have found so that those who journey forth this Easter may also find them in this or some other Lakeland dale.

Just now it is natural to seek for and find 'palm' or 'pussy willows' near streams and ditches. There is a good deal of it to be found in some areas of Lakeland with the soft silvery catkins that are so decorative a feature. Actually this particular species of the willow family is known as the sallow and produces male and female catkins on different trees. The rich golden variety we all seek for is the male.

It was while searching near the sallows that I found the first flowers of self-heal. This is a short stumpy plant of the deadnettle family, bearing purple flowers. Others of the family to look for are bugle, with blue or white flowers; hedge wound-wort, with red flowers; and wood sage, with creamy pink flowers. They all bear a resemblance in leaf to the common nettle – but they don't sting. Hence their family name.

You may find buttercups, too, although it is too early in this part of Lakeland. That other flower which looks so like it and shows its golden petals early is the celandine. Dog's mercury should be out in the woods, and it is possible to find the arum lily ('cuckoo pint' 'wake robin' and 'lords and ladies' are other names for the same plant). It is a remarkable flower with its purple spathe protected by a green sheath, but cattle and birds leave it alone because of the poison it hides.

Daffodils and primroses are out in sheltered places. There is a bank near here which in another week will be a mass of primroses, and the top of it is surmounted by a row of nodding daffodils standing among the green shoots of the bluebells that will follow. Then there are violets and butterbur and the tiny white blossom of the wild strawberry, and perhaps – in the meadows – the first cowslips to be found.

This, of course, is the month of the cuckoo. I shall listen for it very carefully round about 15 April, which is the date – within a few days either way – on which I have heard it in this valley for many years past. Incidentally, this answers a question from a correspondent who

Summer tranquillity at Eden Bridge, Lazonby.
(*Colin Denwood*)

writes to me to ask when he should listen for the bird.

For what it is worth I will pass him on some further information – that the direction in which he is facing when he first hears the cuckoo's call will be that in which he will reside during the coming year; while if he will run to the next stile and look under his left foot he will find there a hair that will be the colour of the hair of the person he is to wed (provided of course, that my correspondent is not married!).

There are parts of the world where the cuckoo is looked upon as a bird of ill omen. Russia is one; there it is regarded as the companion of witches, as black cats and broom-sticks are here. In the Highlands of Scotland, I believe, it is always thought of as an unlucky bird, and it is the height of ill fortune to hear the cuckoo before breakfast.

As the cuckoo flies around our countryside, looking for nests of the right kind in which to deposit its eggs, other birds mob it ceaselessly, not because they are aware of its parasitic habits – they seem to accept the lodgers without fuss – but, so a naturalist friend tells me, because the beautiful bird resembles a hawk.

Anne Utting (April 1957)

SUMMER IN A LAKELAND POST OFFICE

I T IS 'ALL hands to the counter' in the village post office as the summer tourists flood in. In the heat of June last year they came in all states of undress. Some were in danger of over-flowing their scanty clothing. Although we are not anywhere near the sea or a suitable swimming lake, bikinis and bathing trunks were fashionable wear.

However it is the conversation at the post office counter that is often extra-ordinary.

'Have you any stamps?' I am asked.

'Yes. What did you want?'

'What have you got?' comes the reply.

'Everything from ½p to a £1.'

'Oh,' is exclaimed in amazement.

'Is it for a postcard?' I ask, watching the queue get longer. 'This country or abroad?'

'Oh, it's a postcard to Bingley.'

'Do you want a 6½p or an 8½p then?' My patience is fast wearing out.

'Does the 8½p get there quicker?'

'Yes.' I feel it difficult to be polite.

'Well, I'll have a 6½p then.'

The next customer, although licking an ice cream which is dripping on to the counter, is thankfully more precise. I am recovering my patience when I am assailed by another innocently vague holidaymaker.

'Can I have six stamps, please?'

'Yes, what value?'

'What?' comes the reply, looking as though I had asked a very stupid question.

I try again: 'First or second-class, letter or card, this country or abroad?' I say, perhaps a little brusquely. It is a hot afternoon and I am wearing more than a bikini.

'I'll have eight at 6½p and six at 8½p.' I tear them off thankfully. I might even get a sit down in a minute.

'No. I mean six at 6½p and eight at 8½p.' There is a waft of hot breeze through the open door and the odd stamps blow away. I wonder whether the Tourist Board know what they are doing to me.

Mostly it's the sort of innocent thick-ness which irritates me but sometimes there is the awkward customer who treats me as if I'm thick, which by the way I don't think I am. There is the hoity-toity lady who refuses an 8½p stamp because two bits of the perforation are missing at the bottom left-hand corner.

'I want a complete stamp,' she snaps through the grill looking at me as though I am something unpleasant in the zoo.

There are the people who can't find their money, people who produce a £10 note for one stamp and those who insist on sticking on their stamps at the counter in spite of the queue behind them. And the children with tin whistles.

Life in a holiday village post office is not always sweetness and light. Some-times I have to go to the back door to make sure the mountains are still there.

S.P.M. (May 1977)

LAKELAND IN OCTOBER

ON THESE rich October days, Lakeland looks like the palette of an artist at the end of a day of painting. The fells blaze with the colours of dying bracken fronds and red-berried rowans, terminating with the whiteness of bents and grasses. There is double beauty in the valleys when, on still days, deciduous trees have their umbrellas of multicoloured leaves reflected in the lakes.

The uplands are colourful, but strangely quiet after the summer visitors, both humans and birds, have left. Ring-ousel – white-bibbed mountain blackbird – is now wintering by the Mediterranean. Hosts of smaller birds have drifted to lower ground, followed by the small but fiery merlin hawk, which turns to them at mealtimes.

Swallows and martins no longer hawk winged insects over water or round the farm buildings, and the streamlined swift has gone tearing southwards to warmer lands. Cuckoo, warbler, flycatcher, having felt the first chill of autumn, have left the country.

There are compensations, provided by the native birds and those which, in turn, fly to Britain from their ice-locked nesting areas. Robins sing winsomely in the evening. Blackbirds go clattering down the hedgerows. Rooks caw between spells of gobbling down acorns. Finches and titmice fuss round the bird tables.

In late October, families of whooper swans settle on many of the lakes and dip their slim necks to feed in the reed beds. They are particularly fond of Elterwater, which the old Norsemen named after them – 'swan lake'. Frosty-voiced field-fares settle on the berried hedgerows with their cousins, the redwings. Wild geese take the fell route across Lakeland from Solway to Morecambe Bay.

Many of the lively little Herdwick sheep are having a winter holiday by the sea, and in the more gentle country men trim the hedges ready for another busy farming year.

(Editorial, October 1957)

During the First World War a well known Westmorland farmer (then a small boy) and his mother, spent a holiday at a village on the shores of Morecambe Bay.

They arrived one evening after dark. Next morning the lad walked across the road, and saw the tide which was full in and up to the shore. 'Eee,' said he, – 'what a gurt beck.'

G. N. Emmott (April 1965)

THOUGHTS AT A LAKELAND FIRESIDE

GATEWAYS HAVE been bogs most of the summer and where there has been much traffic of beast and man the mud remains. Now it is worse with autumn rain. And although it may often appear that Lakeland farm folk take mud for granted it is without doubt a great weariness of the flesh. The outward evidence can be seen at any farmhouse or farm cottage around this Westmorland valley. Boots, little and big, 'rubbers' and hob-nailed, lie scattered around the back door just where the tired, complaining hands have dragged them off the weary feet.

How glad the folk were to throw them there after squelching round the yards and fields for yet another wet day, and make for the lamp-light and fireside within. Not because it was cold but because it would be cheerful.

The last man home, as he sat on the step outside to struggle with the slippery knots of leather laces, could hear the children arguing over the games, strewed about the kitchen floor. Soon, it would be their bed-time. It was his roof they were under. Evidently they were happy. Most men brood a little whilst unlacing heavy boots after a day's toil round in them.

The babble of young voices, one quarrelsome, another triumphant, rising above the general murmur now and then, settles a good many problems of today. The dumb ache of weariness gives way to a whimsical inspiriting view of things.

Fortunately we have fuel for our firesides. We can call for 'a bit more wood on the fire' without feeling any qualms of conscience, and the farm kitchen or cottage hearth can still be a cheerful, friendly place. We have 'kindling' in

plenty, too, for wild weather shakes a lot of dead stuff out of the big trees.

Yet even by firesides work goes on, and I do not think only of the vast quantities of knitting which every winter produces from every farm.

There is much good talk, too, and the swapping of old Lakeland stories and newer anecdotes gathered at market and elsewhere. Prospects are talked over for the coming season, prices are compared and plans made. There can be satisfaction on a Lakeland farm even in winter,

Bowness in winter. (*T. Proctor*)

OPPOSITE
An ice-house near Cockermouth, 1895.

As you have had many accounts in *Cumbria* of Lakeland farms, I thought you might like to have these thoughts from

despite the mud and the weather, and the minor ills of life.

A Farmer's Wife (January 1955)

19

CHRISTMAS IN CUMBRIA

LAKELAND CHRISTMAS

Beef with bread, cheese and ale, Mummers' plays and bee-watching – these were some of the features of Chrismas past.

ON CHRISTMAS DAY 170 years ago Dorothy Wordsworth wrote in her *Journal:*
'Friday, Christmas Day. A very bad day. We drank tea at John Fisher's but were unable to walk – the roads very slippery. We received a letter from Coleridge while we were at John Fisher's – a terrible night.'

The next day they walked to Rydal:
'It was very pleasant – Grasmere Lake a beautiful image of stillness, clear as glass, reflecting all things; the wind was up, and the waters sounding. The lake of a rich purple, the fields a soft yellow, the Island yellowish-green, the copses red brown, the mountains purple. The church and buildings, how quiet they were!'

There is no mention of any celebrations or Christmas fare such as Charles Dickens knew as a boy (only a dozen years or so later) and which he pictured in the Cratchitt household. That family was as poor as the Wordsworths, for Mr Scrooge's clerk had to keep himself, his wife and six children in a four-roomed house on a weekly salary of 15s.

Yet they had a goose – and such a goose; ate it up at one sitting and got 'up to the eyes in sage and onions.'

Lakeland folk generally must have fared better than the Wordsworths, for an old Cumbrian ballad described a 'Kermas' celebration in which:

*They feast on roast beef and on raised
    goose pyes*
And giblet and mince pie and sweet,
*And many good things – Lamplugh, puddin',
    forbye,*
Smooks on a brood teable that neet.

*They woken next mornin' and find thersels
    queer*
And o'out o'soarts for hard wark;
But Kersmas comes nobbet yance in a year
And measst on't is bent after dark.

Perhaps not all the ingredients of such feastings were lawfully obtained; it is on record that when a Whitehaven ship was wrecked near Drigg the owners went to collect some of the contents. Much of it had vanished but footprints in the snow led them to neighbouring houses where they found the plundered goods.

It was a custom on some of the larger estates for the 'big house' to distribute Christmas cheer to their tenants, sometimes on the day itself but often a few days after. This might consist of presents of tea, sugar, flour or meat – or of the 'left overs' after a house party, usually handed out on Boxing Day.

That was probably the only occasion when many Lakeland folk tasted tarts, custards, jellies or unpoached game, when normal fare was beef or bacon with bread and cheese and ale. For this they sang 'for he's a jolly good fellow' by way of thank you.

'Frumity', known in the Yorkshire dales where wheat was more easily available, does not appear to have been as regular a dish in the fell country except where there was arable land. 'Frumity' was a sort of wheat porridge made with milk and spices.

There were 'Mummers' in Lakeland who used to go round the villages singing and dancing. They decorated themselves with ribbons and greenery and carried sticks and clubs. One is on record as wearing a fox's mask fixed to his head with a fox's brush hanging from his coat tails. They played a variety of musical instruments from fiddles to tambourines. And, of course, they rattled a Christmas box.

Many of them were accomplished jesters, like the famous Archie Armstrong who began as a Border sheep stealer and ended up as a landed gentleman of Cumberland. On one occasion, when constables were searching moorland cottages near Arthuret in Cumberland for a sheep stealer, they came upon an apparently half-witted boy rocking a cradle.

By chance one of them kicked the cradle and revealed that it contained not a baby but one of the stolen sheep.

The boy, who was Archie Armstrong, was taken to Jedburgh, tried, and sentenced to death. But he made the court laugh so much by his wit that the judge, who was King James I (then James VI of Scotland) made him Court Jester instead. Hence the local rhyme:

Archie, by Kings and Princes graced,
Of late, jested himself into a fair estate.

One of a series of drawings by E. Jeffrey for 'Notebook'.

[177]

One Yuletide custom which has vanished and, indeed, is something of a mystery, is that of the 'auld wife hakes', particularly at Keswick, where they were termed 'auld wife Saturdays.' Other than an occasion for sports and feasts their significance has been lost. Similarly little is known about the rival revelries at the two hostelries, now no more, of the *Nag's Head* and the *Cherry Tree* at Wythburn. Yet Wordsworth's *Waggoner* knew their fiddling and jigging and jollity.

> *Blithe souls and lightsome hearts have we,*
> *Feasting at the Cherry Tree.*

The poet notes that at the end of each jig the man had the pleasant task of kissing his partner . . .

This recalls the story of the young Cumberland farmer who one Christmas was sitting with his prospective young woman, one on either side of the fire. At intervals he would walk across and kiss her, always saying, 'Now Betsy, I must trouble you again.' To which she replied: 'Oh, no trouble at all, Peter.'

In the larger Lakeland towns, apprentices and errand boys pushed highly decorated boxes in front of customers expectantly, and when regular postal services came into being the postman always lingered hopefully on his Christmas Day round – for letters and parcels were always delivered on the great day then.

A Christmas remembrance of his boyhood always made one old Lakeland dalesman chuckle. He was attending the village school when there was a startling innovation. The one lady teacher, who usually taught the girls, thought the boys, too, should know something about cookery.

So to everyone's astonishment she brought to school all the ingredients for a Christmas pudding. They had a glorious morning preparing, mixing and stirring, and then put a giant pudding to boil on the ancient coal range in the schoolroom. At dinner time she told all the children to each bring a penny and a basin for a portion and the pudding would be divided between them.

They all obeyed and paid up, except one small boy; he said his mother had told him not to pay his penny unless he knew that there were plenty of three-penny bits hidden in the pudding – and he had to make sure he got one.

He also had a story of Wythburn church where, one Christmas morning, the vicar saw his clerk sitting on the roof. Asked why he was there he replied that one of the local farmers had broken a rope during the week and had used the bell-rope. So the clerk was ringing the bell by hand. He'd rung it twice and this was the third time, 'and then I'sll be wi' ye.'

This 'carefulness' among Lakeland folk is proverbial, as evidenced by the story of a cleric who was asked what he would charge for preaching a funeral sermon. His reply was: 'My regular charge is 30s. I *could* preach one for £1, but it wouldn't be worth listening to.'

Even at Christmas this virtue is not forgotten, as was shown at a West Cumberland dinner table when the farmer said to his farm man:

'Have some more Christmas pudden', lad?'

'Yes, please.'

'What's te say, lad?'

'No thanks.'

'That's reet. Allus speak up, lad.'

Many old dalesfolk remember when their parents always 'watched the bees' at Christmas, which really meant listening to the hive, for it was believed that the bees 'sang' the Old Hundredth psalm on the morning of Christmas Day. From this you could tell the exact time of Christ's birth by their loud humming. That must have been a solemn ceremony, even more than 'telling the bees' when one of the household died, as was done in many parts of Lakeland until comparatively recent times.

If, hopefully, you look up the origin of St. Bees Head in case this commemorates the custom, you will find the name comes from St. Bega, an early Irish saint.

Doubtless the old Lakeland dalesfolk would find our Christmas a puzzling occasion. They would ask what it was – a religious festival or a secular feast. But that may be true of much of our national life. Perhaps they would find our modern Christmas too much for them, as Dorothy Wordsworth found her simpler Christmas too much for her. She wrote in her Journal rather sadly:

'My head ached and I lay long in bed and took my breakfast there.'

H. J. S. (December 1971)

JONTY WILSON'S CHRISTMAS

Mummers' Plays, parties at the 'big' houses, sledging at Hollow Basin, goose for dinner and family parties were some of the elements of Christmas past in Westmorland.

GO TO KIRKBY LONSDALE and ask for 'Mr Wilson,' and there will be blank stares. Visit the Lunesdale market town and ask for 'Jonty', and there is instant recognition of the local blacksmith and raconteur who has been an active and useful member of local life for over seventy years. The fame of Jonty Wilson extended far beyond the town through his many talks to live and radio audiences.

Jonty lives at a house in Fairbank that has been used by blacksmiths for 200 years; it is only 100 yards from the smithy. Blacksmiths seem to have discovered the secret of longevity, for Harry Jackson – a former resident of the house – was 'turned 90 when he died.' The present blacksmith is still hale and hearty at the age of 77.

We talked our way back down the years, with particular reference to how Christmas was celebrated in the days of Jonty's youth – a time when some folk lived well in big houses but most of the families existed frugally, like Bob Cratchitt in the Dickens' Christmas story.

Before Christmas arrived, the spirit of the festival was already evident in the tours made by the mummers. In their play St. George fought the Saracen, which suggests that the tradition, in the form practised by the youth of Westmorland, goes back to the Crusades. Jonty had been 'the valiant knight' in the cast of eight, and 'we went for miles around' chanting:

Ladies and children, as you sit round the fire,
Put your hands in your pockets, that's all we
desire.
Put your hands in your pockets and pull out
your purse,
And give us a trifle, you won't be much worse.

Then there were the parties at the big houses for which the servants were privileged to send out invitations. A young man who wanted an invitation to a party had to catch the eye of one of the servant girls well before Christmas. It was not an easy matter. The girls were only allowed out for about two hours a week or on occasions for which special permission had been obtained.

One of the last families to carry on the tradition in the Kirkby Lonsdale area were the Wilsons of Rigmaden Park. There would be a meal, friendly games

Jonty Wilson of Kirkby Lonsdale. (*G. H. Hesketh*)

and a dance. 'A lot of people in those days could play a concertina or a fiddle; we had plenty of music.'

Before Christmas, too, farming families visited each other in a round of parties, which usually included 'carding' and a bumper meal. The local brass band was active in the ten days before Christmas, as well as during the festival itself. A popular 'pitch' in the town was outside Fountain House, then the home of Johnny Pickard, who was known to be a liberal subscriber to everything.

If it was possible, families were re-united at Christmas. It is Jonty's opinion – based on hard fact – that it was easier to travel when he was young than it is today.

John Wilman, of the *Royal Hotel*, ran a coach service to Kendal (return fare, 1s.!) and, following a change of horses, people could also travel to Windermere. The train service was excellent, and each train arriving at Kirkby Lonsdale station was met by horse-drawn coaches. Trains were also met at Arkholme.

On Christmas Day, years ago, people found it impossible to lie on in bed, for at 6 a.m. the church bells were being rung. And Kirkby Lonsdale's bell-ringing tradition continues lustily to this day. Children were soon astir and running about.

Get up, old wives, and bake your pies,
'Tis Christmas Day this morning.
The cock shall crow and let you know,
'Tis Christmas Day this morning.

Father Christmas did not leave much for the children. Families collected hazel nuts, or even walnuts, and put them away for the Christmas season. 'Kids didn't eat things haphazardly, like they

[180]

The Twelve Days of Yule

The first day of Yule, I gave my dearest
  dear
Sprigs of berried hollins from a bush at
  Buttermere.
The second day of Yule, from Borrow-
  dale's lone fells
We heard adown the valley the chimes of
  far-off bells.
The third day of Yule, where children's
  voices rang
Beside the banks of Rydal, a robin
  bravely sang.
The fourth day of Yule, my dearest dear
  gave me
A shepherd's crook from Caldbeck, made
  from a hazel tree.
The fifth night of Yule, we saw the
  Northern Lights
Playing over Pavey Ark – greens and
  pearly whites.
The sixth day of Yule, below the
  Langdale Pikes
A bright-eyed fox was drinking in one of
  Stickle's sikes.

The seventh day of Yule, we came down
  Striding Edge,
Then watched the falling waters under
  Aira bridge.
The eighth day of Yule, a watchful heron
  flew
Along the Pass of Honister to a sanctuary
  he knew.
The ninth day of Yule, on the way to
  Dunmail Raise
We heard folk in the little kirk, singing
  psalms of praise.
The tenth day of Yule, up on Hard Knott
  Pass
A flock of Herdwicks nibbled among the
  short sweet grass.
The eleventh day of Yule, just below Blea
  Tarn
We sheltered from a dark-blue storm,
  inside a weathered barn.
The twelfth day of Yule, on Glaramara
  side
My dearest dear learned that I would love
  her till I died.

DOROTHY UNA RATCLIFFE

do today.' A Christmas stocking might include nuts, an apple, sometimes an orange and, usually, for some inexplicable reason, a cheap whistle.

For the families who found it hard to live because of small wages, breakfast – as always – consisted of basins full of porridge, and in the morning, if there had been a snowfall, the children would be out and about with their home-made sledges visiting Sellet Banks, half a mile from the town, or going to Hollow Basin, whose sides are so steep a sledge travelled down one side and halfway up the other side without the owner having to dismount.

Christmases were invariably white. It was said (without truth) at snowtime that the blacksmith would repair the booleys (hoops) of the local lads if they slid and sledded down the road outside the smithy; this made the surface so treacherous the farmers had to patronise the blacksmith to have the horseshoes 'sharped'!

Christmas dinner included a fat goose. There was an abundant supply of geese from the local farmers. Brawn, pork, black pudding and giblet pies were other reasonably cheap delicacies of the time, and the meal was washed down by rum punch (for adults) and ginger wine (the children).

Food cost little by modern standards. Butter was about 10d. a pound and quite often the families who made it had to sell to augment their income. You could go to the big house and obtain dripping, which the cook was allowed to dispose of, and twopennyworth of dripping might last a family for a week.

On the afternoon of Christmas Day everyone took it quietly, especially the old folk. No one bothered too much about afternoon tea, though delicacies like homemade scones were available. The average working family could not afford to allocate much more than twopence a day per person on food and drink.

Evening was a time for entertainment, family style, with ghost stories being related by firelight or music created by melodian. The musical talent available was surprisingly varied, and there were some good singers to help sustain the Christmas spirit in the home.

Youngsters were packed off to bed before 10 p.m. The old folk might linger on with their revelry until early morning.

When Jonty Wilson was young, the ordinary workman at an estate like Underley was paid 18s. a week. There was a slightly higher wage, 22s., for the more skilled men. For this a man was expected to work from 6 a.m. until 6 p.m.

No pay was given for absence from work on Christmas Day or Boxing Day. Many people resumed work on Boxing Day because they could not afford to devote it to unremunerative enjoyment.

Peter Jackson (December 1970)

AULD YEAR'S NICHT

AFTER THE cooking and dining on Christmas Day, Boxing Day is the one I enjoy most. The Hunt meets at a local pub and there is always plenty of food left over from the day before. The Christmas Tree (annual Christmas party) takes place in the afternoon in the village hall, followed by a dance in the evening which everyone attends.

When Christmas is over we look forward to New Year. Living so near the Scottish border, 'Auld Year's Nicht' is an excuse for 'a good let oot.'

Friends drop in for supper, the pubs are packed full and everyone manages to get to 'the do' in the village hall in time for *Auld Lang Syne.* The poor harassed doorkeepers manage to cope and are given a drink from the first footers' bottles.

New Year wishes and kisses are exchanged and the dancing at one end is stopped while a space is cleared for a

St Andrew's Churchyard, Penrith. (*Colin Denwood*)

young man doing a step dance. He produces a hunting-horn from his pocket which he promptly blows.

The dancing continues in its gloriously uncivilised way, mellowed by a mixture of alcohol and good will. Everyone enjoys themselves as only members of a long established fellside community can.

People come and go on their way 'first footing,' toasts are drunk and a mouth organ is played as granny and grandad dance a jig. The menfolk are reluctantly dragged off home to let folk get to bed.

Next morning 'I just want a cup of tea' is the cry at breakfast as everyone tries to drag along doing the morning's work, while the aspirin bottle gets good trade. A few people continue to come and go, but the celebrations draw to a close.

'We're awe stoke-fed,' folk say, glad to get back to plainer fare – bacon and tatties, scones and cheese.

Barbara Smith (December 1973)

Scene: Dale Head Farmhouse, Victorian era, when the usual time for all workers to retire was 9 p.m. Son of the household returned home at the later hour of 10 p.m., and was greeted by the angry voice of his father upstairs:

FATHER: 'Is that you, Jacob?'
JACOB: 'Yes, fadder. I'm drunk.'
FATHER: 'I'll drunk tha'.'
JACOB: 'It's cost me nowt, fadder.'
FATHER: 'Fine lad, Jacob. Come to bed.'

J. Thompson. (1954)

'I can't hear any heavy rain, so why is the postman late . . .?'